How Finance Works

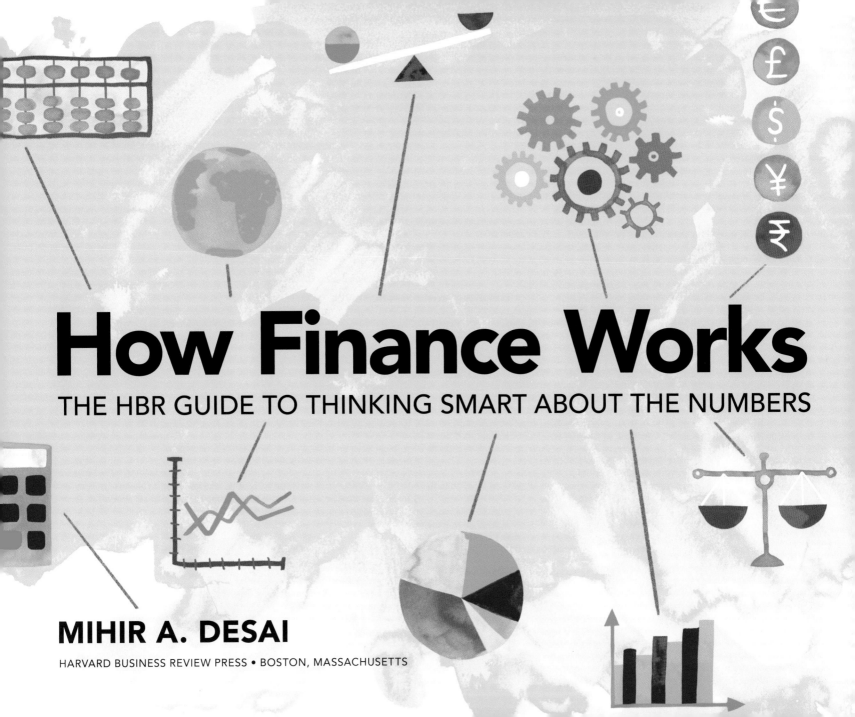

How Finance Works

THE HBR GUIDE TO THINKING SMART ABOUT THE NUMBERS

MIHIR A. DESAI

HARVARD BUSINESS REVIEW PRESS • BOSTON, MASSACHUSETTS

Library of Congress Cataloging-in-Publication Data

Names: Desai, Mihir A. (Mihir Arvind), 1968- author.
Title: How finance works : the HBR guide to thinking smart about the numbers / Mihir A. Desai.
Description: [Boston] : [Harvard Business Review Press], [2019]
Identifiers: LCCN 2019003300 | ISBN 9781633696709 (pbk.)
Subjects: LCSH: Finance. | Business enterprises—Finance.
Classification: LCC HG173 .D433 2019 | DDC 658.15—dc23 LC record available at https://lccn.loc.gov/2019003300

The paper used in this publication meets the requirements of the American National Standard for Permanence of Paper for Publications and Documents in Libraries and Archives Z39.48-1992.

To Parvati, Ila, Mia, and Teena

Contents

How Finance Works

Introduction

For many, finance is cloaked in mystery and quite intimidating. This unfortunate outcome is no coincidence. Many in finance like to shroud what they do in order to intimidate outsiders. But if you want to progress in your career, you'll need to engage deeply in finance—it is the language of business, the lifeblood of the economy, and increasingly a dominant force in capitalism. So neglecting finance and hoping to survive meetings by thoughtfully nodding your head is an increasingly untenable choice.

Fortunately, you can learn the central intuitions of finance without mastering the intricacies of spreadsheet modeling or the pricing of derivatives. This book aims to provide you with the most central intuitions of finance so that you will never find finance intimidating again. Mastering the intuitions won't make you a financial engineer—there are likely more than enough of those. Instead, internalizing these intuitions will provide the foundation for addressing financial issues with confidence and curiosity for the rest of your life.

The book emerged from my efforts to teach finance to MBA students, law students, executives, and undergraduates with a wide variety of backgrounds. During the last two decades of teaching, I've emphasized diagrams, graphs, and real-world examples over equations and Mickey Mouse numerical examples in an effort to preserve relevance while also shearing off unneeded complexity. In the process, I've found that it's possible to maintain rigor without being overly precise. I'll try to do the same in the pages that follow.

Prerequisites

My father spent his career in marketing for pharmaceutical companies in Asia and the United States. At age fifty-eight, he turned to finance for a rewarding second career that lasted more than a decade. He combined a deep understanding of the industry with newfound financial expertise to become an equity research analyst. But it was a difficult journey.

During that decade, I was learning finance as an analyst on Wall Street, as a graduate student, and as a young professor. We had long conversations in which he would ask me about the many things that he would encounter in this foreign world of finance that he didn't understand. As I tried to communicate the intuitions for price-earnings multiples and discounted cash flows, he showed me the power of curiosity and perseverance as he made that difficult transition.

The only prerequisites for this book are those same two qualities: curiosity and perseverance. With sufficient curiosity about finance, you'll have the questions that will guide your learning through these chapters. And with sufficient perseverance, you can work your way through the harder material and know that you will arrive at the other side with a deeper appreciation for finance and a toolkit for your professional life. I hope you'll find it both demanding and worthwhile.

Intended Audience

This book is for everyone who wants to deepen their understanding of finance. Those new to finance will find material that is accessible and provides core intuitive building blocks and the foundations to start speaking about finance. Those immersed in finance know that it is easier to "talk the talk" of finance than it is to "walk the walk." The central intuitions of finance are slippery, and the book will provide an opportunity for them to deepen their understanding beyond the rote application of ideas or terms. Ambitious executives will be able to reflect on their many interactions with financial experts and investors and engage with them more meaningfully.

A Road Map

You can dip in and out of this book as you desire or as questions in your workplace arise, almost like a reference book. But the book has been architected consciously and is meant to be read through from front to back. The chapters build on each other.

Chapter 1: Financial Analysis

We will begin by creating a foundation in financial analysis that provides much of the language of finance. How do you interpret economic performance using historical financial accounts? What do all those ratios and numbers mean? A challenging but fun game will allow you to see the real-world relevance of the many ratios that finance focuses on. By design, this chapter stands apart from the rest of the book. Hands-on and interactive, it's an expansive introduction and warm-up before moving into other parts of the book.

Chapter 2: The Finance Perspective

Many think that financial analysis and ratios are what finance is all about. In fact, it's just the beginning—to see that, we'll establish two foundations of the finance perspective: cash matters more than profits; and the future matters more than the past and the present. What are the true sources of economic returns? Why might accounting be problematic? If the future matters so much, how do we arrive at values *today* based on those future cash flows?

Chapter 3: The Financial Ecosystem

The world of finance—of hedge funds, activist investors, investment banks, and analysts—can seem baffling and somewhat opaque. But it is critical to understand that world as you progress in finance and as a manager. We'll try to answer two questions: Why is the financial system so complex? Could there be an easier way?

Chapter 4: Sources of Value Creation

The most critical questions in finance relate to the origins of value creation and how to measure it. We'll dig deeper into some of the tools developed in chapter 2 to answer many questions: Where does value come from? What does it mean to create value? What is a cost of capital? How do you measure risk?

Chapter 5: The Art and Science of Valuation

Valuation is a critical step in all investment decisions. In this chapter, we'll explore how valuation is an art informed by science and outline what the art is and what the science is. How do you know how much a company is worth? What investments are worth making? And how can we avoid the most common pitfalls in valuation?

Chapter 6: Capital Allocation

Finally, we'll examine a fundamental problem that preoccupies financial managers at every company—what to do with excess cash flows. This chapter integrates much of what we've learned along the way. Should you invest in new projects? Should you return cash to shareholders? If so, how?

Guides to the World of Finance

Throughout, we'll rely on five individuals who bring their insights and experiences from the real world to accompany the book's conceptual framework. I have chosen them to provide multiple perspectives on the financial ecosystem developed in chapter 3.

Two chief financial officers (CFOs) represent corporations, two investors represent both private and public perspectives, and an equity research analyst (like my father) stands in the middle of the financial ecosystem.

The first CFO, Laurence Debroux, is the CFO of Heineken, a global beverage company with operations in more than a hundred countries. Debroux went to business school in France, joined an investment bank, and then de-cided to move to the corporate side. Having served as the CFO of a number of companies, she's a great guide to thinking about how corporations around the world invest and how they interact with capital markets.

The second CFO is Paul Clancy, former CFO of Biogen, a global biotechnology company. Clancy spent a number of years at PepsiCo before becoming CFO at Biogen. He provides a particularly valuable perspective on how to think about funding innovation and R&D activities.

The first investor is Alan Jones of Morgan Stanley, the global head of private equity for the investment bank. Jones and his team find undervalued companies and try to buy them on behalf of clients.

The second investor protagonist is Jeremy Mindich, a cofounder of Scopia Capital. Mindich began as a journalist but realized that his ability to dig deep into companies would help him succeed in finance as well. After working for various hedge funds, he cofounded Scopia Capital, now a multibillion-dollar hedge fund in New York. As a hedge fund manager, Mindich is constantly evaluating companies, determining whether they're under- or overvalued.

The two investors will explain how they assess companies, value them, and subsequently try to create value with their investments.

The fifth expert is Alberto Moel, formerly of Bernstein, an equity research analysis firm. Moel interacts regularly with companies by talking to CFOs and CEOs and providing recommendations to investors. He'll show how analysts examine companies, figure out what's going on inside them, and determine their value, in effect serving as a bridge between the corporations represented by Debroux and Clancy and the investors represented by Jones and Mindich.

Together, they'll ground our insights in the real world and help you understand how to use these lessons in practice. The implications for practice will also be featured in brief Real-World Perspectives throughout the book and extended case studies, called Ideas in Action, that conclude the chapters. Reflections are occasional questions that relate to the ideas in the chapter, and every chapter ends with questions that cover all the relevant material.

So let's start with a little game.

1

Financial Analysis

Using ratios to analyze performance—all while playing a game

To help you develop financial intuitions, we're going to play a little game. This game will introduce the world of finance by creating an understanding of how to use numbers to evaluate performance—the critical process of financial analysis. Financial analysis answers some of the most fundamental questions that financial professionals—from CFOs and managers to investors and bankers—need to answer, questions that go to the root of a company's performance, viability, and potential.

Financial analysis is much more than accounting. In this chapter, we won't go through the mechanics of accounting (e.g., debits and credits) but rather develop intuition around financial ratios that use accounting. In using ratios during this game, you'll understand that by comparing numbers in a common way, you can develop intuition for the sources of performance.

How safe is it to lend to a company? How financially rewarding is it to be a shareholder of a company? How much value does this company provide? Each of these questions cannot be answered by looking at any one number in isolation. Ratios provide a comparison of relevant numbers in a common way, which makes sense of otherwise meaningless numbers. In the context of this game, you will identify fourteen leading companies just on the basis of a series of ratios. After seeing how industries can be identified by ratios, you'll use your newfound knowledge to analyze one company's performance across time—and see how numbers can be used to create a narrative of the company's fortunes and failures.

Let the games begin!

Making Sense of the Numbers

Take a look at table 1-1, which is the backbone of this chapter. It provides a variety of ratios for fourteen real companies in 2013 that span different industries, organized by column. Notice that the companies have been anonymized by design. That constitutes the game: as you progress through this chapter, exploring the ratios, you'll develop your financial intuition by matching each column of numbers to the corresponding company.

Table 1-1 is roughly organized into three horizontal sections. The first section represents the distribution of assets owned by a company, which includes its cash holdings, equipment, and inventory. The second section shows how these companies finance those assets, by either borrowing money and/or raising money from their owners or shareholders. The final section is a series of financial ratios that assess performance, which requires going beyond what a company owns and how they finance those purchases. Sometimes finance people seem to divide everything by everything, just to confuse us. But this

isn't the case. Ratios make interpretation possible because single numbers in isolation are meaningless (i.e., Is $100 million of income good or bad? You can only know by comparing that figure to revenue or something else).

The industries and associated companies represented are shown in table 1-2. As you can see, these are leading companies from varied industries.

There are 406 different numbers in table 1-1, which can be quite intimidating. Many may not make a lot of sense right now. Don't panic. I'll quickly explain what twenty-eight of the numbers mean—the "100s" across the rows for total assets and total liabilities and shareholders' equity represent various totals for the first two sections. The companies aren't the exact same size, but rather, the figures are percentages that represent the *distribution* of assets and financing sources. Accordingly, the numbers in those two sections add up to 100 when rounded.

To help in your analysis, table 1-3 provides a general representation of a balance sheet with the specific data for Starbucks—a global retail chain—in 2017. The "assets" side (or the left side) of the balance sheet seen in table 1-3(b) enumerates what Starbucks owns, and the "liabilities and shareholders' equity" side (or the right side) outlines how those assets are financed. On your personal balance sheet, your clothes, washing machine, television, automobile, or home are your

TABLE 1-1

The unidentified industries game

Balance sheet percentages	A	B	C	D	E	F	G	H	I	J	K	L	M	N
Assets														
Cash and marketable securities	35	4	27	25	20	54	64	9	5	16	4	2	16	7
Accounts receivable	10	4	21	7	16	12	5	3	4	26	6	2	2	83
Inventories	19	38	3	4	0	1	0	3	21	17	21	3	0	0
Other current assets	1	9	8	5	4	4	6	6	2	4	1	2	5	0
Plant and equipment (net)	22	16	4	8	46	7	16	47	60	32	36	60	69	0
Other assets	13	29	37	52	14	22	10	32	7	5	32	31	9	10
Total assets*	**100**	**100**	**100**	**100**	**100**	**100**	**100**	**100**	**100**	**100**	**100**	**100**	**100**	**100**
Liabilities and shareholders' equity														
Notes payable	0	0	8	3	5	2	0	0	11	0	4	4	1	50
Accounts payable	41	22	24	2	6	3	2	8	18	12	13	2	6	21
Accrued items	17	15	8	1	5	3	3	9	4	5	5	1	6	0
Other current liabilities	0	9	9	9	6	18	2	7	11	10	4	2	12	3
Long-term debt	9	2	11	17	29	9	10	33	25	39	12	32	16	13
Other liabilities	7	17	17	24	38	9	5	18	13	10	7	23	22	4
Preferred stock	0	15	0	0	0	0	0	0	0	0	0	0	0	0
Shareholders' equity	25	19	23	44	12	55	78	25	17	24	54	36	38	10
Total liabilities and shareholders' equity*	**100**	**100**	**100**	**100**	**100**	**100**	**100**	**100**	**100**	**100**	**100**	**100**	**100**	**100**
Financial ratios														
Current assets/current liabilities	1.12	1.19	1.19	2.64	1.86	2.71	10.71	0.87	0.72	2.28	1.23	1.01	0.91	1.36
Cash, marketable securities, and accounts receivable/current liabilities	0.78	0.18	0.97	2.07	1.67	2.53	9.83	0.49	0.20	1.53	0.40	0.45	0.71	1.23
Inventory turnover	7.6	3.7	32.4	1.6	NA	10.4	NA	31.5	14.9	5.5	7.3	2.3	NA	NA
Receivables collection period (days)	20	8	63	77	41	82	52	8	4	64	11	51	7	8,047
Total debt/total assets	0.09	0.02	0.19	0.20	0.33	0.11	0.10	0.33	0.36	0.39	0.16	0.36	0.17	0.63
Long-term debt/capitalization	0.27	0.06	0.33	0.28	0.70	0.14	0.11	0.57	0.59	0.62	0.18	0.47	0.29	0.56
Revenue/total assets	1.877	1.832	1.198	0.317	1.393	0.547	0.337	1.513	3.925	1.502	2.141	0.172	0.919	0.038
Net profit/revenue	−0.001	−0.023	0.042	0.247	0.015	0.281	0.010	0.117	0.015	0.061	0.030	0.090	0.025	0.107
Net profit/total assets	−0.001	−0.042	0.050	0.078	0.021	0.153	0.004	0.177	0.061	0.091	0.064	0.016	0.023	0.004
Total assets/shareholders' equity	3.97	2.90	4.44	2.27	8.21	1.80	1.28	4.00	5.85	4.23	1.83	2.77	2.66	9.76
Net profit/shareholders' equity	−0.005	−0.122	0.222	0.178	0.171	0.277	0.005	0.709	0.355	0.384	0.117	0.043	0.060	0.039
EBIT/interest expense	7.35	−6.21	11.16	12.26	3.42	63.06	10.55	13.57	5.98	8.05	35.71	2.52	4.24	NA
EBITDA/revenue	0.05	0.00	0.07	0.45	0.06	0.40	0.23	0.22	0.05	0.15	0.06	0.28	0.09	0.15

*Column totals have been rounded to equal 100.

Source: Mihir A. Desai, William E. Fruhan, and Elizabeth A. Meyer, "The Case of the Unidentified Industries, 2013," Case 214–028 (Boston: Harvard Business School, 2013).

TABLE 1-2

Industries and companies to identify in the game

Industry	Company
Airline	Southwest
Bookstore chain	Barnes & Noble
Commercial bank	Citigroup
Computer software developer	Microsoft
Department store chain, with its "own brand" charge card	Nordstrom
Electric and gas utility, with 80 percent of its revenue from electricity sales and 20 percent of its revenue from natural gas sales	Duke Energy
Online direct factory-to-customer personal computer vendor, with more than half of its sales to business customers and most its manufacturing outsourced	Dell
Online retailer	Amazon
Parcel delivery service	UPS
Pharmaceutical company	Pfizer
Restaurant chain	Yum!
Retail drug chain	Walgreens
Retail grocery chain	Kroger
Social networking service	Facebook

assets. Any debt you might have is a liability, and the rest is your shareholders' equity. Shareholders' equity and net worth are interchangeable terms—we'll use shareholders' equity in what follows.

To assess performance from the ratios in the third section, we'll draw on income statements, which reflect the ongoing operations of a firm. Table 1-4 provides a general representation of an income statement with the specific data for Starbucks in 2017. Income statements show how a company

TABLE 1-3

Representative balance sheets

Assets: What a company owns	Liabilities and shareholders' equity: how assets are financed
Current assets	Current liabilities
Cash	Accounts payable
Accounts receivable	Other current liabilities
Inventories	Noncurrent liabilities
Other current assets	Long-term debt
Noncurrent assets	Other liabilities
Property, plant, and equipment	
Intangibles and other assets	**Shareholders' equity**
	Retained earnings
	Other equity accounts
Total assets	**Total liabilities and shareholders' equity**

(a) Balance sheet

Assets		Liabilities and shareholders' equity	
Cash	19%	Accounts payable	5%
Accounts receivable	6	Other current liabilities	15
Inventories	9	Long-term debt	36
Other current assets	2	Other liabilities	5
Property, plant, and equipment	34		
Intangibles and other assets	29	Total shareholders' equity	38
Total assets*	**100**	**Total liabilities and shareholders' equity***	**100**

*Totals have been rounded to equal 100.

(b) Balance sheet from Starbucks' 2017 annual report

TABLE 1-4

Representative income statement from Starbucks' 2017 annual report

Income

Revenue	100%
Cost of goods sold	−40
Gross profit	60
Selling, general, and administrative expenses	−42
Operating profit (or earnings before interest and taxes, EBIT)	18
Interest	−1
Pretax income	17
Taxes	−6
Net profit	**11%**

realizes net profit after taking into account all its revenues and costs, much as you might consider your salary as revenue and your costs (e.g., food, housing, and so on) before you can figure out what you might be able to save.

Much of finance involves looking at a bunch of numbers and coming up with interesting things to say about them. Knowing a little about the ratios in table 1-1, what do you think about these numbers? You may be curious why some are so different from others. If so, excellent! The beginning of much financial analysis consists of looking at a series of numbers and thinking they are interesting. The best first step when looking at a sea of numbers is to look for extreme numbers and then create a story about these numbers. Before

we figure out which company is which, let's go through each section and identify some of the more extreme numbers. We will then explain what the numbers represent.

Assets

Because companies invest in assets in order to fulfill their mission, it is critical to develop an intuitive understanding of assets. In some sense, assets are the company itself. Häagen-Dazs, for example, owns the ice cream it's going to sell, the factories to make that ice cream, and the trucks to deliver it. Assets are no more complicated than that. As seen in table 1-5, assets are ordered by the degree to which they can be changed into cash; assets that can easily be changed into cash are called current assets, and they appear at the top. What numbers strike you as particularly interesting in each row of table 1-5?

Cash and marketable securities

Starting with the first row of table 1-5, notice that companies F and G have more than half of their assets in cash and marketable securities. That should strike you as strange. Why would any company hold so much cash? This is a deep question in finance today as companies hold more cash than ever before—in aggregate, $2 to $3 trillion for US companies

TABLE 1-5

Assets for the unidentified industries game

Balance sheet percentages	A	B	C	D	E	F	G	H	I	J	K	L	M	N
Assets														
Cash and marketable securities	35	4	27	25	20	54	64	9	5	16	4	2	16	7
Accounts receivable	10	4	21	7	16	12	5	3	4	26	6	2	2	83
Inventories	19	38	3	4	0	1	0	3	21	17	21	3	0	0
Other current assets	1	9	8	5	4	4	6	6	2	4	1	2	5	0
Plant and equipment (net)	22	16	4	8	46	7	16	47	60	32	36	60	69	0
Other assets	13	29	37	52	14	22	10	32	7	5	32	31	9	10
Total assets*	**100**	**100**	**100**	**100**	**100**	**100**	**100**	**100**	**100**	**100**	**100**	**100**	**100**	**100**

*Column totals have been rounded to equal 100.

alone. As one example, Apple holds more than $250 billion in cash. We'll return to this question in more detail later, but large cash holdings can generally be understood as (a) an insurance policy during uncertain times, (b) a war chest for making future acquisitions, or (c) a manifestation of the absence of investment opportunities.

Given the forgone interest, it is unwise for companies to hold cash alone, so they invest much of their cash in government securities that can quickly be turned into cash—so-called marketable securities. Since marketable securities can be quickly converted into cash, they are often combined with cash in balance sheets.

Accounts receivable

Accounts receivable are amounts that a company expects to receive from its customers in the future. As trust grows in a relationship between a company and its customers, the company might be willing to allow customers to pay later. Many companies extend credit, allowing their customers, usually other businesses, to pay after thirty, sixty, or even ninety days. One company (N) has the majority of its assets in receivables. Why do you think that is? Why would companies B, H, and I have such few receivables?

Reflections

Consider three companies: Walmart (a multinational retail corporation), Staples (an office supplies chain), and Intel (a semiconductor chip manufacturer). Which one will have the highest amount of accounts receivable relative to its sales?

In 2016, Walmart had accounts receivable on its balance sheet of $5.6 billion, or 1.1 percent of sales. Staples had $1.4 billion in accounts receivable, or 6.7 percent of sales. And Intel had $4.8 billion, or 8.9 percent of sales. Companies like Intel that sell to other companies will have a higher amount of their sales reflected as receivables. Walmart has limited receivables because it largely deals with consumers. Staples represents an interesting middle case as it has both business-to-business and business-to-consumer businesses.

Inventories

Inventories are the goods (or the inputs that become those goods) that a company intends to sell. Inventories include raw materials, products that are being finished, and final goods. Häagen-Dazs's inventories include all the ice cream it produces and the associated chocolate, dulce de leche, and coffee beans needed to make its ice cream.

Notice that some companies (E, G, M, and N) don't have inventories. How could a company have nothing to sell? The answer is—and this is going to be the first clue for the overall exercise—that those companies likely provide services. Think of a law firm, an advertising company, or a medical practice—they don't have physical goods they sell, so they are service providers.

Property, plant, and equipment

"Property, plant, and equipment" (PP&E) is the term for the tangible, long-term assets that a company uses to produce or distribute its product. This can include its headquarters, factories, machines in those factories, and stores. For example, a utility might have large hydroelectric dams and retail stores may have many outlets as part of their PP&E. Notice that companies I, L, and M have large shares in this category, higher than 60 percent. Which industries would those be?

Other assets

In addition to the large amounts of cash for some companies, there are some companies, like company D, with large amounts in "other assets." Indeed, the rising importance of both cash and other assets are two dominant trends in finance. But what does "other" mean? Other assets can mean many things, but are likely to be intangible assets—things you can't put your hands on but are valuable nonetheless—things like patents and brands.

The one twist to this is that accountants don't assign value to intangible assets unless they know those values precisely. So, for example, Coca-Cola has a very valuable brand, maybe the most valuable thing it owns, but it really doesn't know exactly how valuable its brand is. So accountants ignore it. That's the accounting principle of conservatism. The idea that we should ignore something just because we don't know its precise value is also something that makes many people in finance distrust accounting.

When a company buys another company, many intangible assets that couldn't previously be valued precisely now have a value according to accounting, because someone actually paid for it as part of an acquisition. This leads to one particularly important component of other assets: goodwill. When a company acquires another company for more than the value of its assets on their balance sheet, that difference is typically recorded on the acquiring company's balance sheets as goodwill. As a consequence, companies with lots of other assets and goodwill are likely those that have bought other companies with many intangible assets that were previously unrecorded because of conservatism.

Reflections

Microsoft spent $26.2 billion in 2016 to acquire LinkedIn, which had assets with a book value of $7.0 billion. The $19.2 billion Microsoft paid above the book value will show up on Microsoft's balance sheet as "other assets," including goodwill. What did Microsoft pay for that was worth that additional $19.2 billion?

As one example, Microsoft could benefit from LinkedIn's information on its 433 million users to optimize its marketing of enterprise solutions and productivity products. The value of the data on LinkedIn's users never showed up on its balance sheet because of the difficulty in valuing it, but by purchasing LinkedIn, Microsoft made that value manifest.

Liabilities and Shareholders' Equity

The second section, liabilities and shareholders' equity, provides information on how companies finance themselves (see table 1-6). Essentially, there are only two sources of finance for purchasing assets—lenders and owners. Liabilities represent those amounts financed by lenders to whom the company owes amounts; shareholders' equity, or net worth, corresponds to the funds that shareholders provide.

TABLE 1-6

Liabilities and shareholders' equity for the unidentified industries game

Balance sheet percentages	A	B	C	D	E	F	G	H	I	J	K	L	M	N
Liabilities and shareholders' equity														
Notes payable	0	0	8	3	5	2	0	0	11	0	4	4	1	50
Accounts payable	41	22	24	2	6	3	2	8	18	12	13	2	6	21
Accrued items	17	15	8	1	5	3	3	9	4	5	5	1	6	0
Other current liabilities	0	9	9	9	6	18	2	7	11	10	4	2	12	3
Long-term debt	9	2	11	17	29	9	10	33	25	39	12	32	16	13
Other liabilities	7	17	17	24	38	9	5	18	13	10	7	23	22	4
Preferred stock	0	15	0	0	0	0	0	0	0	0	0	0	0	0
Shareholders' equity	25	19	23	44	12	55	78	25	17	24	54	36	38	10
Total liabilities and shareholders' equity*	**100**	**100**	**100**	**100**	**100**	**100**	**100**	**100**	**100**	**100**	**100**	**100**	**100**	**100**

*Column totals have been rounded to equal 100.

You might notice parallels in your own life. Your debts (credit cards, mortgages, car loans, and student loans) have helped you finance your assets (a house, a car, and most important, your very valuable human capital). The difference between your assets and liabilities is your shareholders' equity (or net worth).

As you'll see in table 1-6, the patterns of financing are different across all the companies and industries. Company G, for example, uses a lot of shareholder equity as a source of financing. Others, like company N, use very little. That mix of financing is referred to as capital structure—a topic we'll return to in chapter 4. Liabilities are ordered by the length of time companies have to repay them; and liabilities that need to be paid back soon are labeled "current."

Accounts payable and notes payable

Accounts payable represent amounts due to others, often over a short time, and typically to the company's suppliers. One company's accounts payable frequently correspond to another company's accounts receivable. Company A owes a large amount of money to its suppliers. Why would that be?

One possibility is that company A is in financial trouble and can't pay its suppliers. Another possibility is that it willfully takes a long time to pay its suppliers. Which explanation is more plausible?

Sometimes firms may have notes payable, a short-term financial obligation. You'll notice that company N is the only one that heavily uses notes payable. Company N also has far more receivables than the other companies, making it look altogether strange. Which company do you think would look so distinctive?

Reflections

Previously, we considered the accounts receivables positions of Walmart, Staples, and Intel. For each company, think about which customer might owe them money. In other words, which companies have accounts payable that correspond to the accounts receivables for these three companies?

Intel is the simplest example. It sells its chips to manufacturers of electronics with computing ability, so Lenovo or Dell would be its customers. So Intel's accounts receivable correspond to the accounts payable of Lenovo or Dell.

Accrued items

Accrued items broadly represent amounts due to others for activities already delivered. One example is salaries: a balance sheet may be produced in the middle of a pay period, and the company may owe salaries that have not been paid yet.

Long-term debt

As we move from short-term liabilities to long-term liabilities in table 1-6, we encounter debt for the first time. Unlike the other liabilities, debt is distinctive because it has an explicit interest rate. You've likely encountered debt in your life. For example, students borrow money and, in doing so, take on debt to pay for college, just as homeowners borrow to buy homes. In table 1-6, you'll see that some of the companies borrow a fair amount—30 percent to 40 percent of their assets have been financed with debt.

Preferred and common stock

Shareholders' equity represents an ownership claim with variable returns—in effect, the owners get all residual cash from the business after costs and liabilities. Debt has a fixed

Reflections

Take a look at the percentage of assets associated with long-term debt for company E (29 percent) and company I (25 percent). Which company's debt do you think is riskier?

To answer this question, you should also consider the cash levels of the two companies—company E has 20 percent of its assets in cash while company I has only 5 percent of its assets in cash. Financial analysts sometimes think of cash as "negative debt" because it could be used to pay off debt immediately. In this case, company E can be considered to have net debt of 9 percent while company I has net debt of 20 percent. In this sense, company I would be riskier to lend additional amounts to relative to company E.

those profits can be paid out as dividends or reinvested in the company. These retained earnings are a component of shareholders' equity because it is as if the owners received a dividend and reinvested it in the company—just as they did when they originally invested in the company.

Only one company, company B, has preferred stock. Why is that? For that matter, what is that? How could one type of owner be preferred? Preferred stock is often called a hybrid instrument because it combines elements of both debt and equity claims. Like debt, a preferred dividend can be fixed and paid before common stock dividends, but like equity, preferred stock is associated with ownership and is paid after debt in the event of a bankruptcy. Preferred stock is, unsurprisingly, preferred: when the world goes bad, preferred stockholders get paid before common stockholders, and when things go well, they get to benefit from the upside, unlike debt holders, as shareholders.

Why would a company issue such a security? Imagine a company that has hit hard times and faces a risky future. Would you want to invest in their common stock if failure was a real possibility? And would you want to lend to it and only get a fixed return that might not correspond to the riskiness of the business? The unique attributes of preferred stock can allow a company to finance itself during precarious times.

return (i.e., interest rate) and no ownership claim, but it gets paid first before equity holders in the event of a bankruptcy. Equity holders have a variable return and an ownership claim but can be left with nothing if a company goes bankrupt. Typically, shareholders' equity, net worth, owner's equity, and common stock are all effectively synonyms. Shareholders' equity is not only the amount originally invested in a company by the owners. As a company earns net profits,

Reflections

Venture capital firms, which provide funding for entrepreneurial ventures, almost always receive preferred stock in exchange for their funding. Why do they prefer this form of financing?

Preferred stock allows them to protect their investment in the event that the company does poorly, while still participating in the upside if the company does well. They do this by converting their preferred stock into regular common stock when things go well.

Understanding Ratios

Now that we've had a chance to think about how companies are represented by their balance sheets, let's get to something even more meaningful in terms of analyzing a company—financial ratios. Ratios are the language of business, and finance people love to create them, talk about them, flip them upside down, break them apart, and so on.

Ratios make numbers meaningful by providing comparability across companies and through time. For example, Coca-Cola's net profit for 2016 was $7.3 billion. Is that a lot of money for the company? It's hard to tell without con-

text. Alternatively, knowing that Coca-Cola's net profit was 16 percent of its revenue (net profit divided by revenue) is much more helpful. Likewise, knowing that Coca-Cola has $64 billion in liabilities may not mean very much; knowing that 71 percent of its assets are financed with liabilities (liabilities divided by assets) tells us a lot more about that company. You can also compare those ratios to other companies' ratios and to previous performance.

Broadly speaking, the ratios in table 1-7 deal with four questions. First, how is the company doing in terms of generating profits? Second, how efficient or productive is the company? Third, how does it finance itself? The final question revolves around liquidity, which refers to the ability of a company to generate cash quickly. If all your assets are in real estate, you are illiquid. And if all your wealth is in your checking account, you're highly liquid.

Liquidity

Most companies go bankrupt because they run out of cash. Liquidity ratios measure this risk by emphasizing the company's ability to meet short-term obligations with assets that can quickly be converted into cash. Suppliers like to see high liquidity ratios because they want to ensure that their customers can pay them. For shareholders, greater liquidity cre-

TABLE 1-7

Ratios for the unidentified industries game

Financial ratios	A	B	C	D	E	F	G	H	I	J	K	L	M	N
Current assets/current liabilities	1.12	1.19	1.19	2.64	1.86	2.71	10.71	0.87	0.72	2.28	1.23	1.01	0.91	1.36
Cash, marketable securities, and accounts receivable/current liabilities	0.78	0.18	0.97	2.07	1.67	2.53	9.83	0.49	0.20	1.53	0.40	0.45	0.71	1.23
Inventory turnover	7.6	3.7	32.4	1.6	NA	10.4	NA	31.5	14.9	5.5	7.3	2.3	NA	NA
Receivables collection period (days)	20	8	63	77	41	82	52	8	4	64	11	51	7	8,047
Total debt/total assets	0.09	0.02	0.19	0.20	0.33	0.11	0.10	0.33	0.36	0.39	0.16	0.36	0.17	0.63
Long-term debt/capitalization	0.27	0.06	0.33	0.28	0.70	0.14	0.11	0.57	0.59	0.62	0.18	0.47	0.29	0.56
Revenue/total assets	1.877	1.832	1.198	0.317	1.393	0.547	0.337	1.513	3.925	1.502	2.141	0.172	0.919	0.038
Net profit/revenue	−0.001	−0.023	0.042	0.247	0.015	0.281	0.010	0.117	0.015	0.061	0.030	0.090	0.025	0.107
Net profit/total assets	−0.001	−0.042	0.050	0.078	0.021	0.153	0.004	0.177	0.061	0.091	0.064	0.016	0.023	0.004
Total assets/shareholders' equity	3.97	2.90	4.44	2.27	8.21	1.80	1.28	4.00	5.85	4.23	1.83	2.77	2.66	9.76
Net profit/shareholders' equity	−0.005	−0.122	0.222	0.178	0.171	0.277	0.005	0.709	0.355	0.384	0.117	0.043	0.060	0.039
EBIT/interest expense	7.35	−6.21	11.16	12.26	3.42	63.06	10.55	13.57	5.98	8.05	35.71	2.52	4.24	NA
EBITDA/revenue	0.05	0.00	0.07	0.45	0.06	0.40	0.23	0.22	0.05	0.15	0.06	0.28	0.09	0.15

ates a trade-off. Yes, they want to ensure that the company doesn't go bankrupt. But highly liquid assets, like cash and marketable securities, may not provide much of a return.

Current Ratio

$$\frac{\text{Current assets}}{\text{current liabilities}}$$

The current ratio asks a question on behalf of a company's suppliers: Will this company be able to pay its suppliers if it needs to close? Will its current assets be sufficient to pay off its current liabilities (including those owed to suppliers)? This ratio is a key way to think about if a supplier should extend credit to a company and if a company will be able to survive the next six or twelve months.

Quick Ratio

$$\frac{(\text{Current assets} - \text{inventory})}{\text{current liabilities}}$$

Reflections

Let's think about three different companies: Rio Tinto Group, a global mining and metals corporation; NuCor Corporation, a mini-mill steel producer; and Burberry, a luxury fashion house. For each, which ratio would you prefer to see— the quick ratio or the current ratio?

This question hinges on which company you think has the riskiest inventory. In many ways, Burberry is likely to have the riskiest inventory because there is no spot market available for it to liquidate its inventory. If it makes a stylistic mistake on a new product, it may find it impossible to sell that inventory, even at a discount. By contrast, Rio Tinto—and NuCor, to a lesser degree—may be more able to dispose of their inventory quickly because they deal in materials that have a spot market.

The quick ratio resembles the current ratio, but excludes inventories from the numerator. Why make a big deal out of inventories? You might think inventories are about operations, but to finance people, inventories represent risk that needs to be financed. And inventory can be very risky. Think about BlackBerry, which competed in the smartphone market where products quickly grow obsolete. In 2013, the company released the Z10 late and was forced to declare that $1 billion of inventory was, in fact, worth zero. For companies with high-risk inventory, the quick ratio provides a more skeptical view of their liquidity.

Profitability

Profitability can be assessed in a number of different ways because the appropriate measure depends on the specific question being asked. And profitability can also be assessed without traditional accounting-based profit measures.

As always, it's important to compare profits to something. For example, you could look at net profit, or the income after all costs and expenses, and compare it to sales (to represent the margin) or to shareholders' equity (to represent the return to a shareholder). Both are key measures of profitability. One measure asks: For every dollar of revenue, how much money does a firm get to keep after all relevant costs? The other, when you divide profits by shareholders' equity, asks: For every dollar a shareholder puts into a company, how much do they get back every year? That's the notion of a return, specifically a return on equity.

Profit Margin

$$\frac{\text{Net profit}}{\text{revenue}}$$

As seen in table 1-1, there are several different measures of profits that consider different sets of costs. Gross profit only subtracts the expenses related to the production of goods from revenue, while operating profit also subtracts other operating costs, such as selling and administrative costs. Finally, net profit also subtracts interest and tax expenses from operating profit. Interestingly, companies A and B have negative profit margins, while companies D and F have profit margins of approximately 25 percent.

Return on Equity (ROE)

$$\frac{\text{Net profit}}{\text{shareholders' equity}}$$

This ratio, often called return on equity (ROE), measures the annual return that shareholders earn. In particular, for every dollar of equity that shareholders invest in a business, what is their annual flow of income? As two examples, company C has an ROE of 22 percent, while company M has an ROE of only 6 percent.

Return on Assets

$$\frac{\text{Net profit}}{\text{total assets}}$$

Often called return on assets, this ratio asks: How much profit does a company generate for every dollar of assets? This corresponds to asking how effectively a company's assets are generating profits.

EBITDA Margin

$$\frac{\text{EBITDA}}{\text{revenue}}$$

EBITDA is one of the all-time great finance acronyms and is best said quickly—"E-BIT-DA." It's also an indication that we're moving away from the accounting idea of profits and toward the emphasis on cash in finance. What is EBITDA? Let's begin by breaking it into two parts—EBIT and DA.

EBIT is just a fancy finance term for something you already know as operating profit. If you work up from the bottom of the profit statement, you can recharacterize operating profit as "earnings before interest and taxes," or EBIT. Since some companies have different tax burdens and capital structures, EBIT provides a way to compare their performances more directly. For example, an American publisher and a German publisher might face different tax rates. Net profit, which factors in taxes, would provide a distorted view; EBIT, which excludes tax charges, would not.

What about DA? DA stands for "depreciation and amortization." Depreciation refers to how physical assets, such as vehicles and equipment, lose value over time, and amortization refers to that same phenomenon but for intangible assets. The reason to emphasize DA is because they are expenses that are not associated with the outlay of cash; it is just an approximation of the loss of value of an asset. Suppose you build a factory. In accounting, you have to depreciate it and charge yourself an expense for that depreciation. But in finance, we emphasize cash and there was no cash outlay, so EBITDA—or earnings before interest, taxes, depreciation, and amortization—is a measure of the cash generated by operations. Because DA was subtracted to arrive at EBIT, DA needs to be added back to get to EBITDA.

As we'll see in chapter 2, the emphasis on cash is a lynchpin of the finance perspective. One example I'll develop more fully later, Amazon, has little profitability but significant EBITDA. Among the companies in table 1-7, it's notable that company D generates a remarkable amount of cash—45 percent, or 45 cents for every dollar of revenue! Similarly, company L has a reasonable profit margin of 9 percent, but a whopping EBITDA margin of 28 percent. Why would that be?

Financing and Leverage

Leverage is one of the most powerful concepts in finance, and it corresponds roughly to our previous discussions of financing choices and capital structure. You may have friends in finance who get weepy-eyed when they talk about leverage. Empires have been built and destroyed because of leverage, and you'll see why.

Why is it called "leverage"? The easiest way to understand the power of leverage is to recall the power of a lever in an engineering context. Imagine a big rock that you can't possibly move by yourself. A lever will allow you to move that rock, seemingly magically, by multiplying the force you apply to the task. And that's a precise analogue for what happens with leverage in finance. Just as a lever lets you move a rock you couldn't otherwise move, leverage in finance allows owners to control assets they couldn't control otherwise.

Let's consider your own personal balance sheet after you buy a home. What if no mortgages were available for you to buy a home? If you had $100, you could only buy a home that was worth $100. With a mortgage market, you can borrow money to buy a home that is worth, say, $500. Let's see what your balance sheet looks like under those two circumstances. (See table 1-8.)

TABLE 1-8

Balance sheets for home purchases

Case A		Case B	
Assets	**Liabilities and shareholders' equity**	**Assets**	**Liabilities and shareholders' equity**
$100 home	$100 net worth	$500 home	$400 mortgage $100 equity

In effect, leverage allows you to live in a house you have no right to live in. It almost as magical as the lever helping you move a rock.

Here's the big question: Are you richer in case A or case B? Some think you're richer in case A because you don't owe anything. Some think you're richer in case B because you live in a larger home. In fact, your wealth is no different; in both cases, you have $100 of shareholders' equity.

Leverage not only allows you to control assets you have no right to control, but it also increases your returns. Imagine that the house increases in value by 10 percent in the two cases. In case A, the return to your shareholders' equity is 10 percent. In case B, your return is 50 percent if the house value increases to $550, but the mortgage remains at $400.

Unfortunately, it's not all milk and honey. If the house declines in value by 20 percent, the return to your shareholders' equity is −20 percent in case A, but in case B, your return is −100 percent! So managing leverage is critical because

Real-World Perspectives

Alan Jones, global head of private equity for Morgan Stanley, commented on private equity's use of leverage:

The home mortgage analogy is really quite apt. Say we are buying a company that is worth $100. We can buy that company outright with either $100 of equity or with $70 of debt that we borrow from someone else and $30 of our own capital. If the value of that asset doubles during our ownership, in the first instance, our return is that incremental $100, or about a 100 percent return over whatever time we've held it. But if we bought that same asset using $70 of other people's money (i.e., debt), we've got equity that's now worth $130 versus the $30 that we originally invested. So instead of just doubling our money, we've gotten a return of more than four times on our money. As a result, people are attracted to get as much of "other people's money" as they can.

it enables you to do things you couldn't otherwise do and because it magnifies your returns—in both directions.

Debt to Assets

$$\frac{\text{Total debt}}{\text{total assets}}$$

The ratio of total debt to total assets measures the proportion of all assets financed by debt. It provides a balance sheet perspective on leverage.

Debt to Capitalization

$$\frac{\text{Debt}}{\text{debt} + \text{shareholders' equity}}$$

The ratio of long-term debt to capitalization provides a somewhat more subtle measure of leverage by emphasizing the mix of debt and equity. The denominator in this ratio is capitalization—the combination of a company's debt and equity. As we saw, there are two primary types of financing for a company, and we think about them differently. Debt has a fixed interest cost associated with it, while equity holds a variable rate of return—which means it fluctuates—along with ownership rights. This ratio tracks what proportion of a company's financing comes from debt and therefore diverts attention from liabilities that are part of operations.

Assets to Shareholders' Equity

$$\frac{\text{Assets}}{\text{shareholders' equity}}$$

Leverage provides the ability to control more assets than an owner would otherwise have the right to control. This ratio tells us precisely how many more assets an owner can control relative to their own equity capital. As a consequence, it also measures how returns are magnified through the use of leverage.

Interest Coverage Ratio

$$\frac{\text{EBIT}}{\text{interest expense}}$$

The three previous measures were constructed from balance sheets, but the critical question is often the degree to which a company can make its interest payments. The ratio of EBIT to interest expense measures a company's ability to fund interest payments from its operations and uses only data from the income statement.

Reflections

Over the past two decades, pharmaceutical companies have been slowly increasing their leverage. For example, in 2001, Merck had a debt-to-equity ratio of 0.53; Pfizer's was 1.14. In 2016, Merck's debt-to-equity ratio was 1.28; Pfizer's was 1.58. What was going on in this industry to cause this shift?

One possible explanation for this change is that pharmaceutical companies are generating more stable cash flows that can service larger debt amounts. Large pharmaceutical companies increasingly purchase promising technologies from bio-technology companies rather than undertaking the risky process of developing new treatments and medicines themselves. As a result, large pharmaceutical companies' overall risk has decreased, and lenders have been more willing to extend credit to them.

Private equity companies sometimes use debt in transactions known as LBOs—leveraged buyouts—to purchase companies. In these transactions, the company borrows to buy out many shareholders, leaving it much more highly levered than previously.

What sorts of industries would you expect to be the targets of LBOs?

In short, companies with stable business models and committed customers are good candidates for LBOs. If the business has stable cash flows, it is able to sustain higher leverage in a more secure way than companies with very risky technologies. Classic LBO targets include tobacco companies, gaming companies, and utilities because of their committed customers and predictable demand with little threat of substitution.

As one example, a ratio of 1 indicates that a company is just able to make its interest payments with its current operations. In your own life, consider the comparison between your monthly income and any mortgage payments as an analogous measure.

A hybrid measure using elements from both the income statement and the balance sheet—debt/EBITDA—is a way to combine information from the balance sheet and the income statement.

Productivity or Efficiency

Productivity is a popular buzzword, but what does it mean from a finance perspective? In short, increases in productivity

Reflections

The effect of information technology over the past several decades is an important example of productivity increases. For example, retailers and wholesalers, and Walmart in particular, contributed significantly to the aggregate productivity gains of the 1990s in the United States. According to the McKinsey Global Institute, "Wal-Mart directly and indirectly caused the bulk of the productivity acceleration through ongoing managerial innovation that increased competitive intensity and drove the diffusion of best practice"[1] in retail. How were these gains manifest in the economy?

These gains could be manifest in rising wages, returns to capital providers, and lower prices for consumers. While many commentators have bemoaned the absence of wage gains from rising productivity, these productivity gains have reduced consumer prices significantly, and lower-income individuals have benefited from those reduced prices. So productivity gains may not have reduced income inequality, but they did reduce consumption inequality.

mean you can squeeze more from less. More narrowly, productivity ratios measure how well a company utilizes its assets to produce output. Over the long run, increases in productivity are the most important contributor to economic growth.

Asset Turnover

$$\frac{\text{Revenue}}{\text{total assets}}$$

This ratio measures how effectively a company is using its assets to generate revenue. This is a critical measure of a company's productivity.

Inventory Turnover

$$\frac{\text{Cost of goods sold}}{\text{inventory}}$$

Inventory turnover measures how many times a company turns over or sells all its inventory in a given year. The higher the number, the more effectively the company is managing its inventory as it sells products. Because inventory is essentially a risky asset that needs to be financed, a higher inventory turnover is financially valuable.

We can use this turnover number to get another measure of inventory management: days of inventory.

Days Inventory

$$365 \div \text{inventory turnover}$$

Dividing the number of days in a year (365) by the inventory turnover provides the average number of days a piece of inventory is kept inside a company before it is sold. Take a look at company C in table 1-1. It turns over its inventory more than thirty times a year, which corresponds to keeping inventory around for slightly more than ten days. In contrast, company B has an inventory turnover of only four times a year, which means that inventory is sticking around for almost a hundred days!

Receivables Collection Period

$$365 \div \frac{\text{sales}}{\text{receivables}}$$

After a company sells its inventory, it needs to get paid for it. The lower this figure, the faster a company is getting cash from its sales. As you can see, company N looks pretty strange—it collects cash from its customers after more than twenty years! What could give rise to such a situation?

Do you notice anything about the numbers for the other companies? The remaining companies can be roughly divided into one group that collects very quickly (fewer than thirty days) and another group that collects more slowly. That difference will be a significant clue for what types of companies they are.

Let the Games Begin

Now that you have a better understanding of all the numbers, try to puzzle your way through which numbers correspond to which company. You'll learn more by trying to arrive at the solution yourself than simply reading ahead.

To get started, see table 1-9, where some of the more notable numbers from our previous discussion are highlighted. Rather than trying to identify all fourteen companies at once, let's focus on two subsets—service companies and retailers—that we can clearly identify, and then we'll look at the rest.

Service Companies

Looking at the ratios, service companies are relatively easy to spot. Since they provide services rather than tangible goods, they don't hold inventories—which points to companies E, G, M, and N. So which four companies can we match to E, G, M, and N? Two of the companies have "service" in their name: the parcel delivery service, which is UPS, and the social networking service, which is Facebook. What

TABLE 1-9

The unidentified industries game

Balance sheet percentages	A	B	C	D	E	F	G	H	I	J	K	L	M	N
Assets														
Cash and marketable securities	35	4	27	25	20	54	64	9	5	16	4	2	16	7
Accounts receivable	10	4	21	7	16	12	5	3	4	26	6	2	2	83
Inventories	19	38	3	4	0	1	0	3	21	17	21	3	0	0
Other current assets	1	9	8	5	4	4	6	6	2	4	1	2	5	0
Plant and equipment (net)	22	16	4	8	46	7	16	47	60	32	36	60	69	0
Other assets	13	29	37	52	14	22	10	32	7	5	32	31	9	10
Total assets*	**100**	**100**	**100**	**100**	**100**	**100**	**100**	**100**	**100**	**100**	**100**	**100**	**100**	**100**
Liabilities and shareholders' equity														
Notes payable	0	0	8	3	5	2	0	0	11	0	4	4	1	50
Accounts payable	41	22	24	2	6	3	2	8	18	12	13	2	6	21
Accrued items	17	15	8	1	5	3	3	9	4	5	5	1	6	0
Other current liabilities	0	9	9	9	6	18	2	7	11	10	4	2	12	3
Long-term debt	9	2	11	17	29	9	10	33	25	39	12	32	16	13
Other liabilities	7	17	17	24	38	9	5	18	13	10	7	23	22	4
Preferred stock	0	15	0	0	0	0	0	0	0	0	0	0	0	0
Shareholders' equity	25	19	23	44	12	55	78	25	17	24	54	36	38	10
Total liabilities and shareholders' equity*	**100**	**100**	**100**	**100**	**100**	**100**	**100**	**100**	**100**	**100**	**100**	**100**	**100**	**100**
Financial ratios														
Current assets/current liabilities	1.12	1.19	1.19	2.64	1.86	2.71	10.71	0.87	0.72	2.28	1.23	1.01	0.91	1.36
Cash, marketable securities and accounts receivable/current liabilities	0.78	0.18	0.97	2.07	1.67	2.53	9.83	0.49	0.20	1.53	0.40	0.45	0.71	1.23
Inventory turnover	7.6	3.7	32.4	1.6	NA	10.4	NA	31.5	14.9	5.5	7.3	2.3	NA	NA
Receivables collection period (days)	20	8	63	77	41	82	52	8	4	64	11	51	7	8,047
Total debt/total assets	0.09	0.02	0.19	0.20	0.33	0.11	0.10	0.33	0.36	0.39	0.16	0.36	0.17	0.63
Long-term debt/capitalization	0.27	0.06	0.33	0.28	0.70	0.14	0.11	0.57	0.59	0.62	0.18	0.47	0.29	0.56
Revenue/total assets	1.877	1.832	1.198	0.317	1.393	0.547	0.337	1.513	3.925	1.502	2.141	0.172	0.919	0.038
Net profit/revenue	−0.001	−0.023	0.042	0.247	0.015	0.281	0.010	0.117	0.015	0.061	0.030	0.090	0.025	0.107
Net profit/total assets	−0.001	−0.042	0.050	0.078	0.021	0.153	0.004	0.177	0.061	0.091	0.064	0.016	0.023	0.004
Total assets/shareholders' equity	3.97	2.90	4.44	2.27	8.21	1.80	1.28	4.00	5.85	4.23	1.83	2.77	2.66	9.76
Net profit/shareholders' equity	−0.005	−0.122	0.222	0.178	0.171	0.277	0.005	0.709	0.355	0.384	0.117	0.043	0.060	0.039
EBIT/interest expense	7.35	−6.21	11.16	12.26	3.42	63.06	10.55	13.57	5.98	8.05	35.71	2.52	4.24	NA
EBITDA/revenue	0.05	0.00	0.07	0.45	0.06	0.40	0.23	0.22	0.05	0.15	0.06	0.28	0.09	0.15

*Column totals have been rounded to equal 100.

Source: Mihir A. Desai, William E. Fruhan, and Elizabeth A. Meyer, "The Case of the Unidentified Industries, 2013," Case 214–028 (Boston: Harvard Business School, 2013).

about the other two? Banks are service providers and so are airlines, so the other two companies are Southwest Airlines and Citigroup. The airline is somewhat tricky because you might have thought that those planes and spare parts are inventory. But the airlines' primary line of business does not involve selling planes or spare parts—they transport people, and that's clearly a service with no notion of inventory.

Let's try to figure out which column in table 1-10 corresponds to which company by beginning with some low-hanging fruit.

Company N: The outlier

Which company owns receivables that take a long time to collect, and a large fraction of their financing comes from notes payable? Who could expect to collect from customers in twenty years on average?

The answer is a bank. Banks are difficult to relate to because their balance sheets are mirrors of our own. The loans that you consider your liabilities are a bank's assets. So the mortgage from the housing example is an asset for a bank. And the deposits that you consider your assets are the bank's liabilities—its notes payable. Citigroup has the highest amount of leverage in the group, a characteristic that is true of the banking industry in general.

TABLE 1-10

Identifying the service companies

Balance sheet percentages	E	G	M	N
Assets				
Cash and marketable securities	20	64	16	7
Accounts receivable	16	5	2	83
Inventories	0	0	0	0
Other current assets	4	6	5	0
Plant and equipment (net)	46	16	69	0
Other assets	14	10	9	10
Total assets*	**100**	**100**	**100**	**100**
Liabilities and shareholders' equity				
Notes payable	5	0	1	50
Accounts payable	6	2	6	21
Accrued items	5	3	6	0
Other current liabilities	6	2	12	3
Long-term debt	29	10	16	13
Other liabilities	38	5	22	4
Preferred stock	0	0	0	0
Shareholders' equity	12	78	38	10
Total liabilities and shareholders' equity*	**100**	**100**	**100**	**100**
Financial ratios				
Current assets/current liabilities	1.86	10.71	0.91	1.36
Cash, marketable securities, and accounts receivable/current liabilities	1.67	9.83	0.71	1.23
Inventory turnover	NA	NA	NA	NA
Receivables collection period (days)	41	52	7	8,047
Total debt/total assets	0.33	0.10	0.17	0.63
Long-term debt/capitalization	0.70	0.11	0.29	0.56
Revenue/total assets	1.393	0.337	0.919	0.038
Net profit/revenue	0.015	0.010	0.025	0.107
Net profit/total assets	0.021	0.004	0.023	0.004
Total assets/shareholders' equity	8.21	1.28	2.66	9.76
Net profit/shareholders' equity	0.171	0.005	0.060	0.039
EBIT/interest expense	3.42	10.55	4.24	NA
EBITDA/revenue	0.06	0.23	0.09	0.15

*Column totals have been rounded to equal 100.

What's it like to run a bank? Banks run a "spread" business where they charge you more for loans than they give you on their deposits. In the process, they take your short-term capital (deposits) and transform it into long-term capital (loans) for the economy. That transformation of short-term capital into long-term capital is why we value banks so greatly and why they sometimes fail. The mismatch between a bank's assets and liabilities combines with high leverage to create little margin for error. Nearly every financial crisis begins with questions about asset quality, which lead to outflows of deposits, which must be funded with rapid sales of loans by the banks, which lead to declining loan prices, which lead to an uncontrollable cycle that can result in their destruction.

Capital-intensive service providers

How can we distinguish between the remaining three companies? Companies E and M have much more property, plant, and equipment than the other companies, including company G. Southwest Airlines and UPS are fundamentally transportation companies, and they both own planes and a lot of equipment. Take a look at the numbers to see how they differ in other respects. (See companies E and M in table 1-10.)

One of the most significant differences between these two companies is that company M gets paid in seven days, on average, which likely means it sells mostly to individuals. In contrast, company E takes considerably longer to collect, which would suggest that it's much more likely to be selling to other businesses. Southwest Airlines sells to people like you and me, and we pay immediately. UPS, in contrast, does business with other companies as a logistics provider. So company E is likely to be UPS, and company M is Southwest Airlines. Can you find another data point that backs up this hypothesis?

Company E has a lot of other liabilities. What are those long-dated liabilities that UPS owes? These liabilities are pensions and obligations to retirees. It takes some knowledge of these companies to know this, but UPS has one of the largest defined benefit pension plans in the world. Defined benefit pension plans are something that budget airlines avoid, but UPS, an older company that was once owned by employees, has maintained their traditional pensions.

The cash-rich, equity-dependent service company

By the process of elimination, Facebook is company G. But does it conform to what you expect? Company G has a large amount of equity and lots of cash—is that consistent with G being Facebook? Facebook is the youngest company on the list, and it had recently gone public in 2013. Because values on balance sheets are recorded at the time of the issuance or acquisition (remember that conservatism principle?), high equity numbers can coincide with younger companies. What did it do with all the money that it raised? At the time, it held the money it raised in cash.

As Facebook has matured, its balance sheet has changed. Facebook has since completed a number of large acquisitions, including WhatsApp and Instagram. How would those acquisitions be manifest in their balance sheets? Facebook's cash levels have come down, and those "other assets" we discussed have risen. Because Facebook bought other companies for much more than their book value (because Facebook valued all those intangible assets that accounting ignores), Facebook's goodwill accounts would have increased. It paid $19 billion for WhatsApp in 2014, and the book value of WhatsApp was only $51 million. That excess of the purchase price over the book value showed up as goodwill for Facebook.

Retailers

When reviewing the receivables collection period, we saw that the companies were divided between those that collect quickly and those that take considerably longer. What kinds of companies would collect from customers so quickly? Since retailers sell goods directly to consumers, their receivables collection period is going to be short because customers pay immediately via cash or credit. In contrast, businesses that do business with other businesses give credit of a minimum of thirty days.

So the retailers are A, B, H, I, and K. Which companies on the list are retailers that sell directly to consumers? Amazon, Barnes & Noble, Kroger, Walgreens, and Yum! are all retailers. We can exclude Nordstrom here because the chain has its own brand charge card, so its customers, unlike those of the other companies, can take a long time to pay for their purchases. Through its charge card, Nordstrom behaves more like a bank than a retailer.

How can we sort through these five retailers? If you've ever worked at a retail store, you know that it's all about moving inventory. These five companies differ dramatically in the way that they turn over their inventory. Some turn over inventory really quickly (company H). Others take a long time (for example, company B). (See table 1-11.)

Companies with distinctive inventory turnover

So which company in this group would move inventory really quickly? Company H turns their inventory thirty-two times a year, so they have only eleven days of inventory at any one time. You should hope that this is Yum! and, in fact, it

TABLE 1-11

Identifying the retailers

Balance sheet percentages	A	B	H	I	K
Assets					
Cash and marketable securities	35	4	9	5	4
Accounts receivable	10	4	3	4	6
Inventories	19	38	3	21	21
Other current assets	1	9	6	2	1
Plant and equipment (net)	22	16	47	60	36
Other assets	13	29	32	7	32
Total assets*	**100**	**100**	**100**	**100**	**100**
Liabilities and shareholders' equity					
Notes payable	0	0	0	11	4
Accounts payable	41	22	8	18	13
Accrued items	17	15	9	4	5
Other current liabilities	0	9	7	11	4
Long-term debt	9	2	33	25	12
Other liabilities	7	17	18	13	7
Preferred stock	0	15	0	0	0
Shareholders' equity	25	19	25	17	54
Total liabilities and shareholders' equity*	**100**	**100**	**100**	**100**	**100**
Financial ratios					
Current assets/current liabilities	1.12	1.19	0.87	0.72	1.23
Cash, marketable securities, and accounts receivable/current liabilities	0.78	0.18	0.49	0.20	0.40
Inventory turnover	7.6	3.7	31.5	14.9	7.3
Receivables collection period (days)	20	8	8	4	11
Total debt/total assets	0.09	0.02	0.33	0.36	0.16
Long-term debt/capitalization	0.27	0.06	0.57	0.59	0.18
Revenue/total assets	1.877	1.832	1.513	3.925	2.141
Net profit/revenue	−0.001	−0.023	0.117	0.015	0.030
Net profit/total assets	−0.001	−0.042	0.177	0.061	0.064
Total assets/shareholders' equity	3.97	2.90	4.00	5.85	1.83
Net profit/shareholders' equity	−0.005	−0.122	0.709	0.355	0.117
EBIT/interest expense	7.35	−6.21	13.57	5.98	35.71
EBITDA/revenue	0.05	0.00	0.22	0.05	0.06

*Column totals have been rounded to equal 100.

is. The grocery chain also has perishable goods, but given its selection of dry food and canned goods, its turnover will be considerably slower than that of a restaurant chain.

At the other extreme, company B turns over inventory really slowly—almost 100 days. Which company has inventory that ages relatively well and takes a long time to move? If you've ever been in a bookstore, that should sound familiar. But is there anything else about company B that feels like a bookstore?

Company B is also notable because it's losing money. Bookstores worldwide are disappearing. Bookselling is a very tough business, given the rise of Amazon, and this shows up as a negative profit margin. And company B is also the only one that had to issue preferred stock, further indicating its troubled financial position.

The final three retailers

The remaining three companies—A, I, and K—differ sharply when it comes to property, plant, and equipment, with company A having the least of that item. We know that two of these companies are brick-and-mortar operations (Walgreens and Kroger), so Amazon, an online marketplace, would have lower property, plant, and equipment, and might be A.

But given Amazon's position in today's economy, let's find the confirming evidence. What else is distinctive about company A that might coincide with what we think about Amazon? First, company A was not making any money. If you've followed Amazon, you know that it's notorious for not making any profits. We'll explore Amazon further in chapter 2.

The second piece of confirmatory evidence is that company A has a large amount of payables, which could mean that it is in trouble or that it is granted credit easily by suppliers because of its size. Given the amount of cash that company A has, we know they are not in financial trouble. So, company A looks like Amazon, with its strong position in the marketplace and power over its suppliers.

That leaves us with two more: the retail drug chain and grocer for I and K.

One big difference is that company I has considerably more property, plant, and equipment than company K. Think about the last time you were in a grocery store or a drugstore. Which had a lot more equipment? In the grocery business, managing the cold chain is really expensive, so the one with more equipment, I, is probably the grocery store. But let's look for more clues.

Company I also collects more quickly than company K, further evidence that it's the grocer because grocery stores are more likely to get immediate payments. A significant fraction of drugstore revenues may come from insurance companies, which would mean drugstores would become a bit like a B2B firm. And company I is turning inventory faster as well, as we

would expect for a grocer. So we can conclude that company K is the drugstore Walgreens and company I is Kroger.

The Stragglers

After the retailers and service companies, we're left with a motley crew—Microsoft, Nordstrom, Duke Energy, Pfizer, and Dell—that are presented in table 1-12.

Three of the companies, C, D, and F, have barely any PP&E, while the remaining two companies have very significant PP&E. One is likely Duke Energy, which has power plants, and the other is likely Nordstrom, a brick-and-mortar retailer. But which is which?

To double-check, look at the three remaining companies and gauge their property, plant, and equipment. Dell, Pfizer, and Microsoft don't really do any heavy manufacturing so their low levels of PP&E make sense.

Which of the two companies with significant property, plant, and equipment is Duke Energy and which is Nordstrom? The key differentiating factor here is inventory. Nordstrom would have a large amount of inventory, while Duke Energy has very little (electricity can't be stored). So company L turns out to be Duke Energy, and company J is retailer Nordstrom. Also, the big EBITDA margin for company L means that it is generating a large amount of depreciation and amortization. That's what utilities do. And often

TABLE 1-12

Identifying the stragglers

Balance sheet percentages	C	D	F	J	L
Assets					
Cash and marketable securities	27	25	54	16	2
Accounts receivable	21	7	12	26	2
Inventories	3	4	1	17	3
Other current assets	8	5	4	4	2
Plant and equipment (net)	4	8	7	32	60
Other assets	37	52	22	5	31
Total assets*	**100**	**100**	**100**	**100**	**100**
Liabilities and shareholders' equity					
Notes payable	8	3	2	0	4
Accounts payable	24	2	3	12	2
Accrued items	8	1	3	5	1
Other current liabilities	9	9	18	10	2
Long-term debt	11	17	9	39	32
Other liabilities	17	24	9	10	23
Preferred stock	0	0	0	0	0
Shareholders' equity	23	44	55	24	36
Total liabilities and shareholders' equity*	**100**	**100**	**100**	**100**	**100**
Financial ratios					
Current assets/current liabilities	1.19	2.64	2.71	2.28	1.01
Cash, marketable securities, and accounts receivable/current liabilities	0.97	2.07	2.53	1.53	0.45
Inventory turnover	32.4	1.6	10.4	5.5	2.3
Receivables collection period (days)	63	77	82	64	51
Total debt/total assets	0.19	0.20	0.11	0.39	0.36
Long-term debt/capitalization	0.33	0.28	0.14	0.62	0.47
Revenue/total assets	1.198	0.317	0.547	1.502	0.172
Net profit/revenue	0.042	0.247	0.281	0.061	0.090
Net profit/total assets	0.050	0.078	0.153	0.091	0.016
Total assets/shareholders' equity	4.44	2.27	1.80	4.23	2.77
Net profit/shareholders' equity	0.222	0.178	0.277	0.384	0.043
EBIT/interest expense	11.16	12.26	63.06	8.05	2.52
EBITDA/revenue	0.07	0.45	0.40	0.15	0.28

*Column totals have been rounded to equal 100.

in the utility industry, people talk about EBITDA as opposed to profitability because they know how distorting all that depreciation and amortization can be.

Of the last three—Dell, Microsoft, and Pfizer—notice that company C has a really low profit margin and companies D and F have really astounding profit margins (greater than 20 percent) and EBITDA margins (greater than 40 percent). Which of the remaining three companies is in the commodifying industry? Over the past ten to fifteen years, the laptop industry has become very commodified, which shows up as depressed profitability. That kind of commodification hasn't happened in software or in pharmaceuticals.

Also, company C holds on to inventory for only slightly more than ten days, which matches Dell's just-in-time business model. Dell begins manufacturing only after it takes orders. As a consequence, it keeps inventory as low as possible.

Identifying the Last Two Companies

The two companies left look very much alike, which makes this last step the hardest. One important difference is that company D has a lot of other assets, which means it is probably in an intangible capital–intensive industry that has been consolidating.

If you follow the pharmaceutical industry, you probably suspect that company D is Pfizer. Pfizer has had a long string of acquisitions, from Pharmacia to Wyeth to Hospira, as the entire industry has consolidated. So company D is Pfizer, and company F is Microsoft. Another piece of confirmatory evidence can help us nail this down. You'll see that company D has considerably more other liabilities than company F. That, too, is consistent with D being Pfizer as it has an old-style pension plan, while Microsoft, as a much younger company, has a defined contribution pension plan. Finally, you may know that Microsoft holds large cash balances, which corresponds to company F.

We did it! That was a really tough game, but if you review these ratios and the underlying logic, you'll have a great foundation for understanding the rest of the book.

The Most Important Ratio

After going through all those numbers, is it possible to think of any one number as the most important number of all? Which of those many ratios is the most important for managers to focus on?

This question is controversial, but many financial analysts focus on return on equity (ROE), since that number measures the returns to owners, who are arguably the ul-

FIGURE 1-1

The DuPont framework

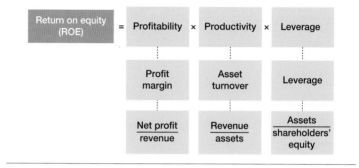

timate bosses within a company. Because ROE is a widely used measure, it's important to understand the factors that contribute to an ROE. The DuPont framework, a method of analyzing a company's financial health originated by the DuPont Corporation in the early part of the twentieth century, provides a useful way to understand the levers of ROE. (See figure 1-1.)

The DuPont framework breaks ROE algebraically into three ingredients: profitability, productivity, and leverage.

Profitability. The first important contributor to ROE is how profitable a company is. That goes back to the notion of profit margin. For every dollar of revenue, how much does it earn in net profit?

Productivity. Being profitable is important, but an ROE can be bolstered by productivity as well. To measure a company's productivity, we use the asset turnover ratio, which measures how efficiently a company can use its assets to generate sales.

Leverage. As we saw, leverage can magnify returns. It is also an important contributor to ROE. In this setting, we can measure leverage by dividing a company's assets by its shareholders' equity.

This simple formula allows you to discover the sources of a high ROE. Like all other measurements, ROE is imper-fect, and two problems stand out. First, because it includes the effects of leverage, it does not purely measure operational performance. That's why some people prefer a return on capital, which compares EBIT to a firm's capitalization (debt plus equity). Second, as we'll see later, it does not correspond to the cash-generating capability of a business.

The DuPont Framework in Action

Let's test our newfound financial intuition by looking at ten very different companies to see how their determinants of ROE differ. (See table 1-13.) As we look at the ten companies,

TABLE 1-13

DuPont analysis
ROEs and levers of performance for 10 diverse companies, 1998

	Return on equity (%)	=	Profit margin (%)	×	Asset turnover (times)	×	Financial leverage (times)
Bank of America Corporation		=		×		×	
Carolina Power and Light		=		×		×	
Exxon Corporation		=		×		×	
Food Lion, Inc.		=		×		×	
Harley-Davidson, Inc.		=		×		×	
Intel Corporation		=		×		×	
Nike, Inc.		=		×		×	
Southwest Airlines Co.		=		×		×	
Tiffany and Company		=		×		×	
The Timberland Company		=		×		×	

we'll try to answer two questions: First, which of the four pieces of the DuPont framework is going to be the most similar across these ten very different companies: ROE, profitability, productivity, or leverage? Second, for each portion of the formula, which companies will have the highest and lowest values?

For the first question, try to think about why these numbers might be different and what might drive them together. For the second question, try to think through what each piece of the Dupont framework represents conceptually.

The answer to the first question is ROE. The range of ROEs in table 1-14 is much narrower than the range of values in the remaining three columns (just compare the highest to the lowest). So why is ROE the most similar across all the companies?

While these companies don't compete in product markets, they all compete in capital markets. Consequently, the rewards to shareholders can't deviate too far from each other because capital will be driven away from low performers and toward better performers. That's why ROEs look most similar.

Should all the ROEs look the same? No, because of the relationship between return and risk (we'll do much more on this in chapter 4). If shareholders bear more risk, they're going to demand a higher return. So capital markets and the competition across companies drive returns to shareholders together and risk drives them apart.

Let's examine some of the highs and lows of the different columns, starting with profitability. Profitability for Food Lion is quite low, 2.7 percent. For Intel, it's remarkably high. Why?

While you might be tempted to attribute these gaps to different levels of competition, the reality is that all these companies operate in a competitive world. In fact, profitability measures a company's value addition and varies with the amount of that value addition. Food retailers just don't add much value, so even the very best food retailers get margins of only 4 percent. In contrast, think about Intel. It takes sand and makes it into computers. That's real value added. So profitability is going to reflect that underlying process of value addition.

Why is Food Lion the highest on asset turnover? What's it like to run a grocery store? It doesn't make money on every box of cereal sold. The whole game is turning over those inventories as quickly as possible. That's why asset turnover is the most important factor in achieving ROE for food retailers.

Finally, as discussed, leverage is a critical tool in finance. Which companies have high or low leverage? The bank is highest, but it is also exceptional in its business, so let's consider the remaining companies.

TABLE 1-14

DuPont analysis
ROEs and levers of performance for 10 diverse companies, 1998

	Return on equity (%)	=	Profit margin (%)	×	Asset turnover (times)	×	Financial leverage (times)
Bank of America Corporation	11.2	=	10.8	×	0.1	×	13.5
Carolina Power and Light	13.5	=	12.8	×	0.4	×	2.8
Exxon Corporation	14.6	=	6.3	×	1.1	×	2.1
Food Lion, Inc.	17.0	=	2.7	×	2.8	×	2.3
Harley-Davidson, Inc.	20.7	=	9.9	×	1.1	×	1.9
Intel Corporation	26.0	=	23.1	×	0.8	×	1.3
Nike, Inc.	12.3	=	4.2	×	1.8	×	1.7
Southwest Airlines Co.	18.1	=	10.4	×	0.9	×	2.0
Tiffany and Company	17.4	=	7.7	×	1.1	×	2.0
The Timberland Company	22.2	=	6.9	×	1.8	×	1.8

Of the remaining companies, which has the highest leverage and the lowest leverage? Carolina Power & Light has the highest leverage, and Intel has the lowest. Why? Varying levels of leverage reflect the amount of business risk because it is unwise to pile financial risk on top of business risk. Carolina Power and Light has stable demand, and its pricing is likely regulated, so its cash flows are steady. Accordingly, it can sustain higher amounts of leverage.

In contrast, a business that is very high risk, like Intel, should not carry large amounts of leverage. Think about what Intel does. It creates a new chip every two years that does twice as much in half as much space at half the cost. And it builds new plants around the world that cost billions of dollars to build the next generation of chips. If it gets one new version wrong, it can go out of business. With high business risk, there should be low financial risk. That's the pattern we see in leverage more generally.

So far, we've looked at how ratios differ across industries. But the best way to use financial analysis is to look at one company over time relative to its industry. We'll zoom in on one company from the DuPont analysis, Timberland, and try to tell a story with the numbers.

TABLE 1-15

DuPont analysis for Timberland Company, 1994
Ratio analysis of Timberland Company, 1994, and industry median

	1994	Industry average*
Profitability ratios (%)		
Return on equity (%)	*11.9*	*12.3*
Return on invested capital (%)	7.1	9.7
Profit margin (%)	*2.8*	*4.2*
Gross margin (%)	35.0	38.4
Turnover ratios		
Asset turnover	*1.3*	*1.8*
Inventory turnover	1.9	2.7
Collection period (days)	73.5	39.1
Payable period (days)	32.6	36.3
Leverage and liquidity ratios		
Assets to equity	*3.2*	*1.7*
Debt to assets (%)	68.5	39.6
Times interest earned	2.9	9.1
Current ratio	3.5	3.0

*Sample consists of five representative shoe companies: Brown Group, Kenneth Cole, Nike, Stride Rite, and Wolverine World Wide.

Profound Changes at Timberland

Timberland, a manufacturer and retailer of rugged outdoor wear, went through some profound financial and structural changes during the 1990s. Let's look at it in 1994, relative to its industry. (See table 1-15.)

The elements of the DuPont framework—ROE, profitability, productivity, and leverage measures—are in italics in the table. Look at these numbers and come up with as many conclusions as you can. Try to tell a story by comparing Timberland to its industry.

First, how is Timberland doing? If I were the CEO, I would emphasize that the ROE, 11.9 percent, is pretty much the industry average of 12.3 percent, so I would conclude that the company is doing great. Would you agree? When we do a DuPont analysis, however, a different story emerges. Where is all that ROE coming from? From profitability? No, Timberland is underperforming on profitability. From productivity? No, it's underperforming there as well.

Timberland's ROE is coming largely from leverage. Since its ROE comes from leverage, that means it's overcoming poor operational performance by making its owners bear more risk.

This is one of the major problems with ROE. As valuable as it is, leverage has a way of infecting the final calculation. That's why some people turn to slightly different measures, like return on assets and return on capital. These measures take out the confounding influences of leverage and show that managers at Timberland deploy capital less efficiently than their peers.

Return on capital (ROC), also known as return on invested capital or return on capital employed, is a particularly important measure, as it considers both capital providers and their combined return. What is their combined return? The return to capital providers is all operating income (or EBIT) after taxes, also known as EBIAT.

$$\text{Return on capital} = \frac{\text{EBIAT}}{\text{debt} + \text{equity}}$$

Other numbers also alert us to Timberland's underperformance. Look at its interest coverage or "times interest earned" number, which measures how many times it can cover its interest payments with its operating earnings. It is less than three, while for the rest of the industry, it's close to ten. What does that mean? The company is walking a financial tightrope that its competitors have chosen to avoid.

Let's look at Timberland's operations. Its inventory turnover is considerably lower than the rest of the industry. Second, its receivables collection period is really out of whack with the rest of the industry (73.5 versus 39.1). There could be a few causes of this long collection period. The first is bad management that is not being aggressive about collecting the cash owed to the company. Alternatively, it could be imprudently generous with credit to stimulate sales. More

dangerously, Timberland could have customers with outstanding debts that have been outstanding for more than two hundred days, with little likelihood of ever paying them. So it might be a sign of hidden bad debt. Its payables period, how long it takes to pay suppliers, is similar to the rest of the industry.

The Numbers, a Year Later

Let's look at Timberland's numbers in 1995. (See table 1-16.)

For the Du Pont analysis, the ROE is negative, which is driven by negative profitability. Productivity is up a little, and leverage is down a little.

Digging deeper, what do those leverage numbers tell us? The times interest earned number went from over three to under one. That means that Timberland didn't have enough operating profit to pay its interest. This was a near-death situation for Timberland. What should Timberland do in this dire situation? Timberland needed to raise more cash, and from the numbers, we can tell that's exactly what it did.

First, inventory turnover increased markedly, while gross margins dipped significantly. That pattern indicates a fire sale of sorts. It liquidated goods as fast as it could to raise cash to make its interest payments. Similarly, look at its re-

TABLE 1-16

DuPont analysis for Timberland Company, 1994–1995

*Ratio analysis of Timberland Company, 1994–1995,
and industry median, 1998*

	1994	1995	Industry median*
Profitability ratios (%)			
Return on equity (%)	11.9	–8.2	12.3
Return on invested capital (%)	7.1	0.7	9.7
Profit margin (%)	2.8	–1.8	4.2
Gross margin (%)	35.0	33.7	38.4
Turnover ratios			
Asset turnover	1.3	1.6	1.8
Inventory turnover	1.9	2.4	2.7
Collection period (days)	73.5	53.4	39.1
Payable period (days)	32.6	21.2	36.3
Leverage and liquidity ratios			
Assets to equity	3.2	3.0	1.7
Debt to assets (%)	68.5	66.2	39.6
Times interest earned	2.9	0.2	9.1
Current ratio	3.5	4.8	3.0

*Sample consists of five representative shoe companies: Brown Group, Kenneth Cole, Nike, Stride Rite, and Wolverine World Wide.

ceivables collection period—it dropped by twenty days. That didn't happen accidentally. Another way to raise cash is to contact the customers that owe money and ask them for, say, $0.80 on the dollar. In short, the company needed the cash and was willing to make deals because it needed to raise cash to make interest payments.

The final piece of working capital, in addition to inventory and receivables, is Timberland's payables, which were in good shape the previous year. Now, it's paying its suppliers more quickly, which may seem odd for a company that's strapped for cash. But the shrinking payables period was most likely directed by its suppliers, who, given Timberland's financial situation, were unlikely to extend credit. Instead, they may have demanded cash on delivery. The effects of working capital on cash will be a major theme in chapter 2.

The Numbers from 1994 to 1998

Now look at the numbers for the next few years. (See table 1-17.) It looks like things stabilized and turned around remarkably.

In 1996, Timberland's profitability was still slightly lower than the industry average, but its productivity was improving and its leverage was coming down. Timberland was moving more inventory, and not by cutting prices. If anything, its gross margin indicates that it was getting pricing power just as it was moving more goods.

In 1997, things were even better. The headline number is quite remarkable as its ROE was almost twice the average for the industry. And it was getting it from all the right

TABLE 1-17

DuPont analysis for Timberland Company, 1994–1998

*Ratio analysis of Timberland Company, 1994–1998,
and industry median, 1998*

	1994	1995	1996	1997	1998	Industry median*
Profitability ratios (%)						
Return on equity (%)	11.9	−8.2	12.3	22.1	22.2	12.3
Return on invested capital (%)	7.1	0.7	9.6	18.3	17.9	9.7
Profit margin (%)	2.8	−1.8	3.0	5.9	6.9	4.2
Gross margin (%)	35.0	33.7	39.4	41.7	41.9	38.4
Turnover ratios						
Asset turnover	1.3	1.6	1.5	1.9	1.8	1.8
Inventory turnover	1.9	2.4	2.6	3.3	3.8	2.7
Collection period (days)	73.5	53.4	53.2	34.7	33.4	39.1
Payable period (days)	32.6	21.2	18.6	16.0	18.9	36.3
Leverage and liquidity ratios						
Assets to equity	3.2	3.0	2.7	2.0	1.8	1.7
Debt to assets (%)	68.5	66.2	63.2	48.8	43.3	39.6
Times interest earned	2.9	0.2	2.5	5.6	10.2	9.1
Current ratio	3.5	4.8	3.7	3.5	4.0	3.0

*Sample consists of five representative shoe companies: Brown Group, Kenneth Cole, Nike, Stride Rite, and Wolverine World Wide.

places. It was turning over inventory almost twice as much as it was in 1994 and it was raising prices, as reflected by its gross margin.

The upward trend continued in 1998. Timberland was still achieving ROEs that were twice the industry average, but now the ROE was coming entirely from exactly the right places. ROE was not coming from leverage or productivity. It was coming from profitability. So what happened? That near-death experience prompted a move away from family management and toward professional management. That change accompanied Timberland becoming the chosen brand for hip-hop artists, which led to the remarkable turnaround in financial performance.

What did you learn from this exercise? You can use the financial ratios and numbers to tell a story about any company over time. You can play detective and create a narrative so these numbers make some sense. The numbers are available for all kinds of public companies and are readily accessible. I encourage you to use what we just learned to analyze any of your favorite companies.

Real-World Perspectives

Laurence Debroux, CFO of Heineken, commented on the most important thing students learning finance can do:

If you would have asked me twenty years ago about the most important trait for succeeding in finance, I would probably have told you to be hardworking and to be super-expert and driven. That actually leads you to a certain point, but after that it fails you. You can always be hardworking. But now, being persistent and curious are probably the two things I consider most important. Persistence is key, because you can't take the first answer as a final answer. Finance is about digging, trying to find what is behind the numbers, and what is going on with the assumptions. Is the number right, and if it's not, why not? Is it showing you reality or distorting it? Numbers are very dry if you just look at them like numbers, but if you want to know the reality behind them, that's where it starts being interesting. If you're interested and curious about what people do, then they become interested in what you want to bring.

Quiz

1. **Increased leverage allows companies to control more assets and increase their ROE. What's bad about leverage?**

   A. It reduces productivity, which can decrease overall ROE.

   B. Leverage-based profits are not cash-based and are ignored by finance.

   C. Leverage multiplies losses, too, as it increases a company's risk.

   D. There is nothing bad about leverage—using other people's money is a good way to increase the value of the company.

2. **What types of companies are more likely to have high leverage?**

   A. Companies with high growth opportunities in new industries

   B. Companies in stable, predictable industries with reliable cash flows

   C. Technology companies

   D. Companies with low profitability

3. In 2009, Warren Buffett invested $3 billion in Dow Chemical, via an issuance of preferred stock. Which of the following is *not* an advantage of preferred stock to the owner of the preferred stock?

    A. In the case of bankruptcy, preferred stockholders get paid before common stockholders.

    B. Even when common stockholders get no dividends, preferred stockholders may get dividends.

    C. Preferred stock is associated with ownership in the company, unlike debt.

    D. Preferred stock dividends must be in even-numbered percentages (2 percent, 4 percent, etc.).

4. Which of the following is least likely to be listed as an asset on a balance sheet?

    A. Gilead Sciences Inc.'s patent for the highly profitable hepatitis C treatment it developed in-house

    B. Google's corporate headquarters

    C. Payments owed to Ford Motor Company by dealerships for the purchase of cars

    D. The $42 billion in Facebook's bank accounts at year-end 2017

5. Which of the following companies is most likely to have the highest inventory turnover?

    A. Subway, a fast-food restaurant company

    B. Books-A-Million, a bookstore chain

    C. Whole Foods, a grocery store

    D. British Airways, an airline

6. Which ratio is a distinguishing feature of retail companies?

    A. High ROE

    B. Low receivables collection period

    C. High inventory turnover

    D. High total debt/total assets

7. BHP Billiton is one of the world's largest mining companies, and accounts receivable make up 21 percent of its total assets (in 2016). Which of the following companies is most likely to owe BHP Billiton money as part of BHP Billiton's accounts receivable?

    A. Bank of America, a global bank

    B. Mining Recruitment Agency, a recruiter for employees specialized in mining

    C. Sysco, a food distributor

    D. United States Steel Corporation, a steel manufacturer

8. Which of the following constituencies care most about a company's current ratio?

   A. Its stockholders

   B. Its suppliers

   C. Its competitors

   D. Its customers

9. True or false: a high ROE is always a good thing.

   A. True

   B. False

10. Home Depot, a home improvement supply store, issued $2 billion in debt in late 2016. What is the main difference between debt and other liabilities, like accounts payable?

   A. Debt carries an explicit interest rate.

   B. Debt represents ownership in the company.

   C. Debt is a residual claim.

   D. Debt is only owed to suppliers.

Chapter Summary

As I hope you've seen, financial analysis is about much more than just the numbers, which are simply tools to help us understand what drives performance across time, across companies, and across industries. Each number is helpful, but no one number tells the whole story. Indeed, each has limitations. Only by piecing together a story from these numbers can we truly understand a company. The process of financial analysis will become easier and more rewarding as you invest more time in it. Ideally, you should walk someone else through the unidentified industries exercise to test whether you understand the material.

I hope you feel that you've built a solid foundation of financial literacy. Much of it is very intuitive and involves telling a story with numbers. Next, we're going to think deeply about cash and why the future matters more than the past or present. If you can, try to use some of the tools from this chapter to look at your company's—or any company's—financials.

2

The Finance Perspective

Why finance is obsessed with cash and the future

Accounting statements are critically important for understanding corporate performance, but they have drawbacks. In reaction to those drawbacks, the field of finance has developed a distinctive approach to making decisions and analyzing performance.

That approach has two pillars. First, finance practitioners have questioned the best way to measure economic returns. While accounting emphasizes net profit, finance professionals consider net profit flawed, as it ignores several important issues. Finding solutions to these problems has caused finance professionals to turn toward cash as a better measure of economic returns. Indeed, they can sometimes be obsessed with cash.

Cash can mean many things, so we'll explore three alternative definitions of cash—earnings before interest, taxes, depreciation, and amortization (EBITDA); operating cash flow; and free cash flow. And we'll discover why free cash flow is so important for thinking about investment decisions and valuation decisions—and why it represents finance nirvana.

Second, the field of finance is preoccupied with the future and is fundamentally forward looking. This leads us away from the balance sheet in an attempt to answer some of the biggest questions in finance: How much are assets worth? Where does value come from? How do we measure value that arises from future cash flows? This focus on the future

Finance versus Accounting: Conservatism and Accrual Accounting

Finance takes issue with two of the foundations of accounting: conservatism and accrual accounting.

The Conservatism Principle

The conservatism principle implies that companies should record lower estimated values of their assets and, by extension, higher estimates of their liabilities—in short, they err on the side of being conservative. Thus, balance sheets typically record assets at their historical cost, not their current or replacement value, and many assets simply don't show up on their books. Apple's balance sheet in 2016, for instance, valued its brand at $0 even as *Forbes* valued the forty-year-old brand at $154.1 billion. Which do you think is closer to reality?

The Rules of Accrual Accounting

The rules of accrual accounting try to smooth out both revenues and costs in an effort to better reflect economic reality. They allow a company to capitalize an investment as an asset, and to expense it as depreciation charges every year over the asset's entire life, for instance. For example, Airbus Group, the European aerospace and defense manufacturer, built a new factory in Mobile, Alabama, that cost $600 million. Because of accrual accounting, Airbus would report more moderate profits over time rather than losses in 2015 and then profits after the plant started production. But this representation of profits is quite distinct from their true cash outflows, obscures the time value of money, and may reflect managerial discretion while cash flows would not.

Real-World Perspectives

Laurence Debroux, CFO of Heineken, commented on the importance of cash:

I always remember this sentence: revenue is vanity, result is sanity, and cash is king. Emphasizing only the growth of revenues can be ridiculous and dangerous. Measuring only on the growth of profit would also be dangerous. Cash is the most important. Your capacity to transform your business into cash that you can use to finance your activities, repay your debt, or distribute to your shareholders is the key.

leads us to consider the time value of money and methods for translating future cash flows into the present, which will be foundational in thinking about any investment or valuation decision.

What We Talk about When We Talk about Cash

In chapter 1, we used net profit to measure corporate performance. Although net profit has merits—it's a powerful measure for thinking about how shareholders have been doing—it has problems. First, it treats cash and noncash expenses symmetrically. Second, net profit also subtracts interest payments, which makes it hard to compare companies that finance themselves in different ways even though their operations could be quite similar.

Finally, and most importantly, many managerial decisions are involved in calculating profit. Accounting asks managers to make decisions in order to smooth returns, as accountants consider that to be more consistent with reality. For example, an up-front payment for a piece of equipment has to be capitalized, placed on the balance sheet, and then depreciated over time. Revenue similarly may need to be recognized over time. But this process of smoothing measures of performance is subjective, which allows managers to manipulate profits to their advantage. In contrast, cash is cash and, arguably, is not susceptible to similar levels of managerial discretion.

To build an alternative foundation for assessing economic returns, we need to identify cash flows as opposed to profits. But what do we mean when we say "cash"? Frustratingly, it turns out that the answer is "it depends." We'll begin where we left off in chapter 1—with EBIT and EBITDA—and then build up to operating cash flows and, finally, to finance nirvana: free cash flow.

EBIT Equation

Net profit
+ interest
+ taxes
_____
EBIT

As we saw, EBIT (or operating profit) gives a clearer view of how efficient and profitable a company is relative to net profit by not subtracting interest and taxes, which are not related to operational performance. EBIT still isn't quite a measure of cash, however, because it is calculated after subtracting noncash expenses such as depreciation and amortization. For a fuller picture, finance professionals turn to EBITDA: earnings before interest, taxes, depreciation, and amortization.

EBITDA Equation

Net profit
+ interest
+ taxes
+ depreciation
  and amortization
_____
EBITDA

Amazon's Net Profit, EBIT, and EBITDA

Amazon provides a compelling example of the distinction between these three different measures. (See table 2-1.)

In 2014, Amazon's net profit was −$241 million. Amazon's EBIT, however, was $178 million, and the difference of $419 million represents taxes, interest, and currency adjustments. What about EBITDA? Because of a whopping $4.746 billion in depreciation and amortization, the EBITDA here is $4.924 billion—a far cry from the net loss of $278 million. So Amazon generated lots of cash, as measured by EBITDA, but had losses according to profitability measures.

TABLE 2-1

Amazon.com Inc.'s income statement, 2014 ($ millions)

Sales	$88,988
Cost of sales (*including $4,746 in depreciation*)	−62,752
Gross margin	**$26,236**
Operating expenses	−26,058
Operating income (EBIT)	**$178**
Interest expense	−289
Tax expense	−167
Nonoperating income	37
Net profit (loss)	**−$241**

From EBITDA to Operating Cash Flows

Given the obsession with cash, it's not surprising that there is a separate financial statement dedicated to it: the statement of cash flows. Many finance professionals consider the statement of cash flows a company's most important financial statement. Rather than focusing on the income statement, which has the problems of noncash expenses and managerial discretion, or a balance sheet, which has the problems of historical cost accounting and conservatism, many people in finance focus on the statement of cash flows because it looks purely at cash.

Typically, a statement of cash flows has three parts: operating, investing, and financing sections. The first section, operating cash flows, provides both the next measure of cash

Reflections

EBITDA can be more relevant for some industries than others. Consider three companies: Electronic Arts (EA), the video games developer; The Michaels Companies, an arts and crafts retail chain; and Comcast, the internet, telephone, and cable television provider. Which of these companies is going to have the greatest amount of depreciation and amortization, and why?

One way to appreciate the difference that depreciation makes is to compare it to net profit. In 2015, the depreciation-to-net income ratios of EA, The Michaels Companies, and Comcast were 17 percent, 34 percent, and 106 percent, respectively. That's logical; unlike EA, a software company, Comcast has invested heavily to create a nationwide cable and internet

network. Because of those heavy investments, using net profit as a measure of performance can result in a distorted picture and flawed comparisons. The Michaels Companies is somewhere between EA and Comcast, given its brick-and-mortar footprint.

and brings together many of the elements that we've already discussed. In particular, recall from chapter 1 how Timber-land managed its inventory and receivables to generate cash. More generally, working capital—receivables, inventories, and payables—can have significant cash flow consequences.

Operating cash flow is distinct from EBITDA in several ways. First and foremost, it considers the costs of working capital, and, second, it accounts for tax and interest payments by beginning with net profit. And finally, it includes non-cash expenses other than depreciation and amortization, such as share-based compensation, in its final calculation.

What about the rest of the cash flow statement? Briefly, the investing section of the cash flow statement emphasizes the ongoing investments that bypass the income statement

Operating Cash Flow Equation

Net profit
+ depreciation and amortization
− increases in accounts receivable
− increases in inventory
+ increases in unearned revenue
+ increases in accounts payable
_____
Operating cash flow

FIGURE 2-1

Sample cash flow statement and Starbucks' cash flow statement, 2017

Operating activities

Net profit
  + depreciation and amortization
  (±) cash provided by changes in operating
  assets and liabilities
Net cash provided by operating activities

Investing activities

  – Additions to property, plant, and equipment
  (±) mergers/divestments
Net cash provided by investing activities

Financing activities

  – Cash dividend
  – repurchase of common stock
  + issuance of debt or equity
Net cash provided by financing activities

Net increase/(decrease) in cash and cash equivalents

(a) Cash flow statement

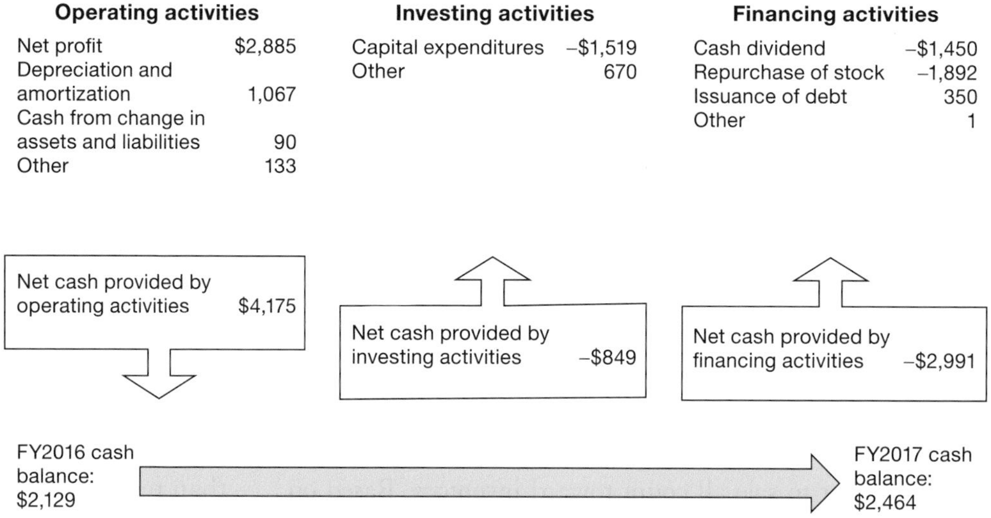

Operating activities	
Net profit	$2,885
Depreciation and amortization	1,067
Cash from change in assets and liabilities	90
Other	133

Investing activities	
Capital expenditures	–$1,519
Other	670

Financing activities	
Cash dividend	–$1,450
Repurchase of stock	–1,892
Issuance of debt	350
Other	1

Net cash provided by operating activities $4,175

Net cash provided by investing activities   –$849

Net cash provided by financing activities   –$2,991

FY2016 cash balance: $2,129

FY2017 cash balance: $2,464

(b) Cash flow statement based on Starbucks' 2017 annual report

and go straight into the balance sheet, such as capital expenditures and acquisitions. The financing section examines whether a company has offered debt or paid back debt or issued equity or bought back stock, and reveals the cash consequences of doing so. Figure 2-1 provides a generic statement of cash flows along with Starbucks' 2017 data. As the figure demonstrates, the statement maps how cash positions changed over the course of the year because of operating performance along with investing and financing decisions.

Working capital

Working capital, the capital that companies use to fund their day-to-day operations, is critical to understanding operating cash flows. While you might think of finance as associated only with debt and equity, finance is deeply embedded in the daily operations of a business.

$$\text{Working capital} = \text{current assets} - \text{current liabilities}$$

While working capital is a general term for the difference between current assets and current liabilities, it usually emphasizes three important components: accounts receivable, inventory, and accounts payable. Here's a quick recap of these accounting categorizations:

Accounts receivable. Accounts receivable are amounts that customers, typically other businesses, owe a company. The dollar amount can be reframed as a receivables collection period, which shows the average number of days it takes for customers to pay the company.

Inventory. The goods, and the associated inputs, held by a company prior to sale all count toward inventory. Based on inventory, you can generate a days inventory, which shows the average number of days that the company holds inputs and goods.

Accounts payable. The amounts a company owes to suppliers are accounts payable. Based on that, you can generate a days payable, which indicates the average number of days the company takes to pay suppliers.

A slightly more narrow way to define working capital is:

$$\text{Working capital} = \text{accounts receivable} \\ + \text{inventories} \\ - \text{accounts payable}$$

One simple way to think about the consequences of working capital is to note that the daily operations of a company result in an amount that needs to be financed, like any other asset. If the amount of working capital is lowered, that lowers the financing needs of a corporation. So the way you manage working capital has deep financial consequences.

The cash conversion cycle

A powerful way to frame the financing consequences of working capital is to frame working capital temporally rather than monetarily. This framing is called the cash conversion cycle.

To see the cash conversion cycle in action, imagine that you run a hardware store and all that you do is buy hammers from wholesalers and sell them to home improvement professionals. Several transactions are associated with a single hammer, and they don't happen at the same time. You have to buy the hammer, pay for it, sell it, and collect the cash for that sale. Let's say you sell the hammer seventy days after you bought it, and you don't get paid until forty days after the sale. Those figures correspond to a days inventory of seventy days and a receivables collection period of forty days. From a business perspective, this means that 110 days elapse from

Reflections

You have been tasked with managing the working capital for one of Home Depot's stores in Atlanta. Currently, its days inventory is fifty days, the receivables collection period is twenty days, and its payables period is twenty-five days, which leaves a financing gap of forty-five days. How would you use your knowledge of the cash conversion cycle to reduce the store's financing gap?

You could:

- Reduce the days inventory.

- Reduce the receivables collection period.

- Increase the payables period.

What are the trade-offs in reducing the store's days inventory? Why would you want to do it, and why would you consider not doing so?

One of the easiest ways of reducing the days inventory is to stock less inventory; you can be certain that the store will sell out faster and you will need less financing. However, the danger is that if customers can't find a certain brand of paint or kind of tool in your store, they will go to your rivals and may never come back.

What are the trade-offs in reducing your receivables collection period?

You can reduce your receivables collection period by extending less credit to customers. However, those customers may need, or be used to receiving, credit from their suppliers; without it, they may prefer to buy from Home Depot's rivals.

What are the trade-offs in increasing your payables period?

Paying suppliers late may erode relationships; they may become reluctant to supply products or be less willing to extend credit. If a hurricane were threatening to hit Atlanta, and everyone needed more supplies, your vendors might be more interested in working with your rivals than with you.

---

the time you buy a hammer to getting cash for it. In addition, you didn't pay cash for that hammer until thirty days after buying it.

From a cash perspective, you need to generate cash to pay for the hammer eighty days before receiving the cash.

If companies *pay* before getting *paid*, they must finance the shortfalls in their cash conversion cycles. None of this shows up in the measure of net profit or EBITDA. So just buying and selling hammers creates a financing need. (See figure 2-2.)

FIGURE 2-2

The cash conversion cycle

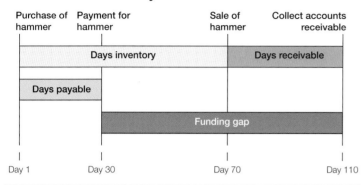

The gap in the cash conversion cycle raises several questions. How much is this gap going to cost to finance? How can the company change behaviors to reduce those costs? Will those changes cost more than the savings?

To better understand the underlying dynamics of a working capital cycle, imagine what happens in a recession. Companies hold on to their inventory longer, and even when they do sell a hammer, that contractor, who is getting squeezed by his customers will take longer to pay up. The whole cash conversion cycle expands, which is what occurred during the financial crisis in 2008. The recession increased days inventory and collection periods, and since banks were recoiling, there was no mechanism to finance those large gaps. That's why global trade collapsed by 50 percent in 2008.

Let's return to the hardware store. A supplier encourages you to pay within ten days by offering a 2 percent discount—a fairly typical offer. Is that a good deal?

While it's tempting to have a knee-jerk response to this offer, you don't have enough information to answer that question. This is a financing decision and requires consideration of alternative methods of financing. Since you'd be paying the supplier in ten days instead of thirty, you'd need to finance the twenty-day gap. Who is a cheaper source of financing for those twenty days—the bank or the supplier? Let's imagine that your bank charges an annual interest rate of 12 percent per year, which would be less than 1 percent for twenty days of financing. This means you would pay less than 1 percent to fund those twenty days if you took the deal from the supplier and used the bank to fund your cash conversion cycle.

The discount offered by the supplier can be reframed as a financing cost for those twenty days. If you refuse the discount, you give up 2 percent and you receive twenty days of financing. In effect, the supplier is charging 2 percent for a twenty-day loan. Would you rather pay 2 percent for a twenty-day loan or less than 1 percent for a twenty-day loan? The answer, of course, is less than 1 percent. The bank financing is cheaper; you should take the deal from the supplier and borrow from the bank for those twenty days.

Reflections

Salesforce.com is a software-as-a-service (SaaS) business, which typically sells subscriptions that work like magazine subscriptions. Business customers pay in advance and receive the use of software for the period they've paid for. What does that do to Salesforce's cash conversion cycle?

Salesforce.com will have a negative receivables collection period because it gets paid before it provides services. It has no inventory, so there's no days inventory, and it will not pay suppliers immediately, creating a payables period. By taking payments first and then providing services, Salesforce is getting customers, in addition to their suppliers, to finance its operations.

Many companies, such as Dell, use just-in-time manufacturing so they produce goods for sale only when needed. How does that affect Dell's cash conversion cycle?

Dell first takes the order from a customer and then starts manufacturing the product, thus decreasing its cash conversion cycle by lowering its days inventory and leading to a reduction in the financing costs of its working capital.

Tesla, the premium electric car manufacturer, has started taking deposits from customers for future models. How will that change its cash conversion cycle?

A deposit may not be the full price of a car, but it still represents customer financing of Tesla's operations. By giving Tesla a deposit in advance of delivery, customers reduce the amount that Tesla must rely on capital providers.

How Amazon Grows . . . and Grows

To see the power of working capital for the financial model of a company, let's return to the example of Amazon. Amazon actually manages its inventory, receivables, and payables in such a way that it ends up with what's called a negative working capital cycle, or negative cash conversion cycle. In the hardware store example, the store has a financing need created by its operations. Imagine if you lived in a world where buying and selling hammers wasn't a drain on cash, but buying and selling hammers actually *generated* cash. That's exactly the case with Amazon.

In 2014, Amazon averaged forty-six days of inventory, and it collected from its customers after twenty-one days on average (slightly long for a retailer because it reflects its cloud computing business). The icing on the cake is that Amazon,

Reflections

Say your company pays vendors in forty days and the prevailing interest rate is 20 percent. A supplier offers a 1 percent discount if you meet your obligations within ten days. Would you take the deal? Why?

On the one hand, the supplier is charging you an implicit interest rate of 1 percent for a thirty-day loan. On the other, the bank will charge an interest rate of well over 1 percent for thirty days (20 percent per twelve months). The supplier's financing is cheaper, so you should take the financing from the supplier, not the bank. In other words, don't take the deal.

due to its market dominance, can exert a large amount of power over its suppliers to make them wait before getting paid, and it averaged ninety-one days to pay its suppliers. That reflects a negative cash conversion cycle of twenty-four days.

The upshot for Amazon is that its operations become a source of cash. Amazon—and Apple, for that matter—have working capital cycles that allow them to grow rapidly without seeking external financing. That's another way of saying the cash they generate from their working capital becomes a powerful part of their business model.

In effect, suppliers are financing Amazon's and Apple's growth. Both companies are substituting cheaper sources of

Real-World Perspectives

Laurence Debroux, CFO of Heineken, commented on the importance of working capital:

Thinking about your working capital is good hygiene. You can always improve. At the same time, you should not become addicted, because it can lead to behaviors that you don't want to see. And that's true for sales and for purchasers: you have to be very careful.

At Heineken, we operate in eighty countries and want to operate with local procurement, so we really have to have a long-term, sustainable approach to our relationships with suppliers. If you insist on squeezing every last bit from every supplier in an effort to improve your working capital, then you're going to end up

killing those suppliers. This is not the ecosystem you really want to live in. So working capital is important; you need to look at it. At the same time, you need to be sure of the consequences that you're triggering when you actually push harder in working capital.

financing in the working capital cycle for external sources of financing. And that working capital consequence is a powerful dimension of their economic returns, which are not captured in EBITDA, or EBIT, or net profit.

Operating cash flows advance the journey toward cash nirvana by beginning with net profit, making adjustments for noncash expenses (most notably, depreciation and amortization and stock-based compensation), and finally adjusting for all the effects of working capital.

Finally, Free Cash Flows

The final cash measure is free cash flows, one of the most important measures of economic performance in finance. You'll see this number again and again when you look at how companies are valued or when companies discuss how they're doing.

The equation for calculating free cash flows provides a measure of the amount of cash flows truly unencumbered by the operations of a business. It's the purest measure of cash and

Reflections

Amazon.com adds stock-based compensation to its operating cash flows. Why is that?

Stock-based compensation is recorded as an expense in the income statement and lowers net profit, but like depreciation, it isn't a cash charge. That's why it is added back to operating cash flows. Over the last two decades, stock-based compensation has evolved into a major noncash expense for US companies.

If Amazon.com had issued stock to finance its growth—by building server farms that can host Amazon Web Services, for example—where would that show up in the statement of cash flows?

Issuing shares is a form of financing, so it would show up in the financing section of the statement of cash flows.

If you look at Amazon's working capital for 2014, it seems to be a drain on cash. But didn't

I say that Amazon's working capital is a source of cash for the company?

What seems to have happened is that between 2013 and 2014, Amazon's cash conversion cycle fell from minus twenty-seven days to minus twenty-three days. That's why Amazon's working capital required a cash investment during that period. A negative working capital cycle that becomes less negative is no different from a positive working capital cycle that gets longer.

FIGURE 2-3

Free cash flow

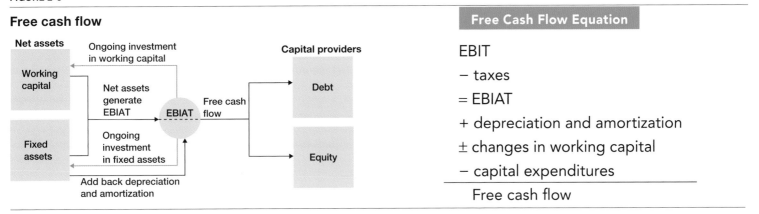

Free Cash Flow Equation

EBIT

− taxes

= EBIAT

+ depreciation and amortization

± changes in working capital

− capital expenditures

Free cash flow

---

forms the basis of valuation. It removes the distorting effects of noncash charges such as depreciation and amortization (like EBITDA), accounts for changes in working capital (like operating cash flow), and, finally, acknowledges that capital expenditures are required for growth and have been avoided so far. In short, free cash flow isolates the cash that is truly free to be distributed or used however the company sees fit.

To calculate free cash flow, let's start with EBIT to get a sense of operational performance. Since this has to be *free* cash flow, you need to account for taxes, which results in the next acronym, EBIAT, or earnings before interest after taxes. Then, add back those noncash expenses, such as depreciation and amortization. Second, penalize the company if its working capital needs are such that you must constantly invest capital into the working capital cycle. That's what we saw with operating cash flows. Third, make sure

you subtract any planned or required capital expenditures on an ongoing basis, because that is a cash charge not yet considered.

Figure 2-3 provides a diagram and equation for understanding free cash flow. You can visualize it by thinking about a simplified balance sheet. The net assets side of the balance sheet is divided between working capital (e.g., inventories and accounts receivables less accounts payable) and fixed assets (e.g., property, plant, and equipment), and the financing side of the balance sheet is divided between debt and equity. This modified balance sheet now distinguishes between the operations (the left-hand side) and the capital providers' (the right-hand side). The flows that operations generate that end up with the capital providers are the free cash flows, which are calculated as follows. The operations of a business generate EBIT, but the government takes its

Reflections

Amazon.com has been expanding from its core retail business into Web Services, a cloud computing service sold primarily to other businesses. What do you think that has done to Amazon's free cash flows?

First, cloud computing might have a different level of profitability than Amazon's retail operations, which would impact its EBIT. Prepayments by cloud computing subscribers would change its working capital cycle relative to a retail operation. Finally, Amazon may need to spend more on capital expenditures to build server farms, which will also result in different amounts of subsequent depreciation.

share to make it EBIAT. From there, you must consider the company's ongoing investments into working capital and fixed assets as it grows. Finally, noncash expenses such as depreciation and amortization should never have been expensed and must be added back. What's left is free cash flows.

Finance has slowly been moving toward free cash flow for evaluating returns over the last fifty years. Why? Because it captures all the cash consequences of a business, and it ensures that the underlying flows are free to the capital providers. Figure 2-4 provides a timeline that shows how, since the 1960s, attention has shifted from revenues to profits to EBITDA to operating cash flows to free cash flows, and what distinguishes these different measures.

FIGURE 2-4

The shift from revenues to free cash flows, 1960s–2020s

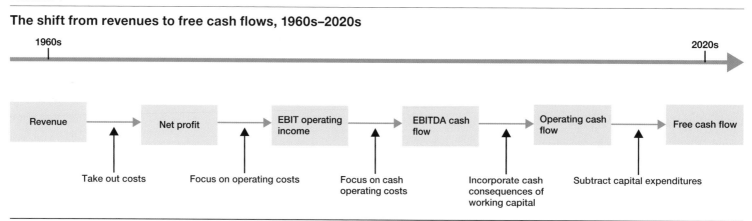

Real-World Perspectives

Alan Jones, global head of private equity at Morgan Stanley, commented:

We like to find a huge number of different changes that we can make when acquiring businesses. We do it methodically by working our way down the income statement, the cash flow statement, and the balance sheet. We start at the top of the income statement, where we can grow the top line better, improve our gross margins, make more of those gross margins fall to the bottom line where there are operating expenses that we can take out, and manage our tax position better.

Then we look at the cash flow statement. How are we doing on capital expenditures? Are we being rigorous in holding them to a high standard of expected return and then really policing the results when we see in two or three years how they've done? Working capital has been a huge opportunity for us. We continue to be amazed by the companies that pay little attention to working capital, and as a result, they have working capital ratios as a percent of sales that are completely out of control. As we look at the cash flow statement, we try to be very disciplined about managing our receivables and payables and inventory. Then we turn our attention to the balance sheet, where we look for noncore assets or where we can better manage the capital intensity of the assets that we own.

Amazon versus Netflix

Before moving on to the next big element of the finance perspective—looking to the future—let's see why taking a cash perspective can yield so much insight. Let's compare two leading companies—Amazon and Netflix—by looking at their revenue numbers. (See figures 2-5 and 2-6.)

The scales are different (Amazon is a much bigger company than Netflix), but it's clear that, between 2001 and 2017, both companies grew impressively. But that's just revenues.

Let's look at a few more financial indicators. (See figures 2-7 and 2-8.)

Amazon seems not to have made profits, at least until very recently. By the profits metric, Netflix appears to be more profitable than Amazon, with a profit margin of nearly 5 percent relative to Amazon's profit margin of less than 2 percent.

Now, look at their operating cash flows. Here things start to diverge, and we see the benefits of looking at these other measures. What's going on here? In Amazon's case, the

FIGURE 2-5

Amazon's total revenue, 2001–2017 ($ millions)

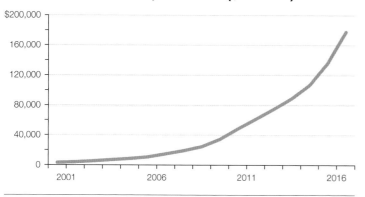

FIGURE 2-6

Netflix's total revenue, 2001–2017 ($ millions)

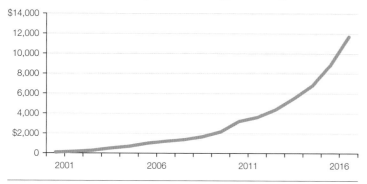

FIGURE 2-7

Amazon's profits and cash flows, 2003–2017 ($ millions)

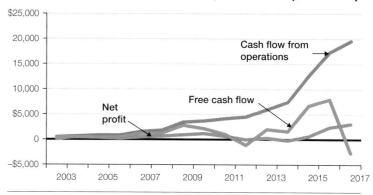

FIGURE 2-8

Netflix's profits and cash flows, 2003–2017 ($ millions)

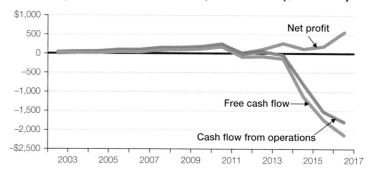

cash flow engine is being driven by all its noncash expenses and its management of working capital. On the other hand, what's happening to Netflix? Those profits are now translating into negative operating cash flows because of its heavy investments in content. In short, they are buying increasing amounts of content and quickly amortizing it, creating a cash drain. The story told by operating cash flow is totally different from that told by profits.

Finally, let's look at their free cash flows. Considering capital expenditures changes the view a bit more. Netflix doesn't have significant capital expenditures, so free cash flows aren't considerably worse than operating cash flows. Amazon has more significant capital expenditure (partly due to the Whole Foods acquisition), which in the most recent year makes its free cash flow negative.

All these measures tell a different story about what's going on in the two companies, stories we would have missed if we'd focused on revenue or net profit. Looking at all of the various measures, with a chief focus on free cash flow, makes it clear that the key question for both companies is one of asset intensity. If Netflix's content acquisition costs continue to soar, it may never generate positive cash flows. Amazon's acquisition of Whole Foods, an investment that expands its brick-and-mortar retail footprint, may significantly change its free cash flow profile.

Fixated on the Future

Accounting and financial analysis is preoccupied with characterizing the past and present. In contrast, finance professionals look to the future for the most important questions regarding the value implications of any decision. In short, the source of all value today is future performance as manifested in cash flows. That creates a problem for finance as not all future cash flows are created equal. Would you be indifferent to a dollar received today and a dollar received in ten years? Clearly, no. So finance prescribes thinking about the free cash flows an asset will generate in the future and figuring out what they are worth now.

That exercise is slightly more complicated than just adding up all those future cash flows. The reason is a fundamental idea in finance known as the time value of money. This core idea in finance is something really simple: $1 today is worth more than $1 a year from now.

Why? Well, if you have $1 today, you can do something with it and earn a return—which means that you'll end up with more than $1 a year from now. That simple insight also means that $1 received a year from now must be worth less than $1 received today. But how much less?

That differential depends on the opportunity cost of that money. What opportunity for earning a return are you giving up? What could you have done with the money if you didn't have to wait? Once you figure out the cost of waiting, you then "punish" that future cash flow by assessing a penalty that accounts for that opportunity cost. That's called a discount rate. The idea of punishing cash flows may seem odd, but that's literally what you're doing in discounting—you're punishing people who make you wait to receive your money because you don't like to wait and because you could have done something with that money if they hadn't made you wait.

In later chapters, we'll use these mechanics to do valuations of companies, but for now, let's consider the underlying idea behind discounting and some of the basic formulas.

Discounting

How can we operationalize the idea of the time value of money and the notion of opportunity cost? One simple way is by using the notion of an interest rate. Let's say that if you put money in the bank today, you'll earn 10 percent, and then one year from now, you'll end up with $1.10. Fundamentally, that makes you indifferent between $1 today and $1.10 a year from now. That's the first clue why $1 today is worth more than $1 a year from now.

As a consequence, now you know how to punish future cash flows for making you wait to receive them. Every time you have to wait a year, you "haircut" future cash flows by one plus the interest rate, because that's what you would have earned if you hadn't had to wait.

Discounting Formula

$$\frac{\text{Cash flow}}{(1 + r)}$$

where

$$r = \text{discount rate}$$

Here, r is the interest rate you could receive by making that relevant alternative investment—that's the opportunity cost you charge for being asked to wait. For example, say you want to figure out how much $1,000 received one year from now is worth today. Assume that a bank offers you an interest rate of 5 percent, and that is the relevant alternative investment you would have made if you had that money now. You can use the method described to calculate that a $1,000 payment received one year in the future has a present value of $952.38 using that 5 percent. If you give the bank $952.38 today, it will give you $1,000 next year.

Suppose that the interest rate suddenly rises to 10 percent. Would the $1,000 a year from now still be worth $952.38? Or would it be worth more or less? What if interest rates fall instead?

If interest rates rise to 10 percent, you would need to deposit $909.09 in the bank, instead of $952.38, to receive $1,000 in a year. And if interest rates fell—let's say to 2 percent—you would need to deposit only $980.39 to get $1,000 a year later. What does that imply? Well, you punish future cash flows much more in the 10 percent interest rate scenario (i.e., $1,000 a year from now is worth $909.09 today) because your opportunity cost is higher, and you punish future cash flows much less in the 2 percent scenario (i.e., $1,000 a year from now is worth $980.39 today).

Multiyear discounting

What if you have cash flows over multiple years into the future? Consider the logic of punishment described earlier. If you don't like to wait one year, you're really not going to like waiting five years. How do you account for that? If you have to wait more than one year, you'll have to discount those cash flows multiple times. Discounting over multiple years is similar to discounting over one year, except that the one-year discounting process has to be repeated. You can simply modify the original formula to handle more years:

Discounting Formula for Multiple Years

$$\frac{\text{Cash flow}_1}{(1 + r)} + \frac{\text{cash flow}_2}{(1 + r)^2} + \frac{\text{cash flow}_3}{(1 + r)^3} \ldots$$

Here, r is still the annual discount rate, or interest rate. To differentiate each year, I've introduced subscripts; the subscript next to the cash flow indicates the year that the cash will be received. For every additional year of waiting, you have to discount the flows more, because for each year of waiting, you have to charge more.

Suppose the bank is now offering a $1,000 payment for each of the next three years and the prevailing interest rate

is still 5 percent. How much is that worth to you? First, you need to figure out the current values of each of the payments. If you have cash flows from multiple years that you want to add, you have to first convert all of them, using the equation, to today's values. If you don't do that, you are effectively comparing apples to oranges. Once you've made all the flows into apples, you can add them up.

When you add the three values together, you arrive at how much the bank's offer is worth today:

$$\frac{1,000}{(1 + 0.05)} + \frac{1,000}{(1 + 0.05)^2} + \frac{1,000}{(1 + 0.05)^3}$$

or

$$\$952.38 + \$907.03 + \$863.84 = \$2,723.25$$

The impact of discount rates

Let's look at the impact of discount rates on the present value of cash payments. Assume you can receive $1,000 in cash flows every year for ten years. How does the value of that set of flows change with discount rates? As you can see in figure 2-9, it has a big effect.

Reflections

A friend needs to borrow some money from you. Would you prefer he pay you back in one year or in two years?

Most people would prefer to be repaid in one year because they could be doing something else with that money—this is the notion of opportunity cost. The cost of waiting is related to what you could have done with that money if you had it. A key idea in finance is thinking about the appropriate opportunity cost because that dictates how much you should charge for being asked to wait. The appropriate opportunity cost is not the same for all investments, because it has to reflect not just any alternative, but a relevant alternative.

If your friend insists that he can only pay you back in two years' time, what could he do to make you more willing to wait?

Asking the friend to pay you back additional amounts seems a pretty fair request for waiting the extra year. Thus, when forced to wait, people ask for additional returns.

What attributes would influence how much more of a return you would ask from your friend if you have to wait another year?

Many people would keep in mind the trustworthiness of the friend (how often he has paid you back in the past, how stable his job is, how much money he makes, etc.). The amount that you need to charge for waiting an extra year should reflect how risky you think your friend is. We'll return to the concept of charging for risk in chapter 4.

Sunk Costs and Net Present Value

One big lesson of the distinction between finance and accounting and the process of discounting is that sunk costs, which are costs that have already been incurred and can't be recovered, don't matter. While accounting carefully considers them in balance sheets and income statements, finance professionals view the amount paid for an asset as gone forever.

For example, say your company spent $100,000 on market research for a new product. Those amounts are gone, no matter what you find out about the product's future. Accordingly, any decision about the future of the product (i.e., should we launch it?) should incorporate the feedback of the market research, but the $100,000 you spent is irrelevant.

FIGURE 2-9

The effects of 2 percent versus 10 percent discount rates

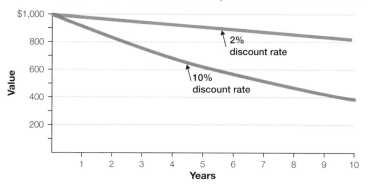

Total for 2% discount rate: $9,982
Total for 10% discount rate: $7,144

That's true not only of the cost of the research but also of the time spent on planning the creation and launch of the product. None of that will come back, no matter how much you want it to.

In short, assessing values requires you to: (1) look into the future, (2) think about what incremental cash flows will be generated over time, and (3) discount them back to the present using the notion of an opportunity cost of capital.

Working out the *present value* of a project involves adding up all the potential cash flows—positive and negative—after they've been discounted to today. (The cash you receive, or

inflows, are positive numbers; the cash you spend, or outflows, are negative numbers.) Determining the *net present value* entails the same calculations, but it includes the initial cost of the project.

For example, assume Nike is building a new shoe factory at a cost of $75 million. The plant will produce $25 million in cash every year from the shoes Nike will be able to make and sell, for the next five years. Let's use a 10 percent discount rate for this project.

Nike Factory Present Value

$$\frac{25}{(1.10)^1} + \frac{25}{(1.10)^2} + \frac{25}{(1.10)^3} + \frac{25}{(1.10)^4} + \frac{25}{(1.10)^5} = \$94.8M$$

The present value of the project is $94.8 million. By paying $75 million for a project that is worth $94.8 million, Nike will generate $19.8 million in additional value—that's the project's net present value. Because of the $19.8 million increase in value, Nike should go ahead and build the factory. This is one of the key decision-making rules in finance—companies should undertake only projects with positive net present values.

The next year, Nike takes another look at production. Unfortunately, sales have not been good. Instead of making

Reflections

Many people argue that because central banks have kept interest rates low since the 2008 financial crisis, stock markets have risen quickly. Why would that be?

One interpretation of the recent bull market is that the fall in interest rates has led to an increase in the value of stocks because each future cash flow, either dividends or capital gains, is discounted less—leading to higher values of stocks.

In countries that are considered risky, investors often ask for high rates of return to compensate for those risks. What kind of investments might companies make in those environments, given the high discount rate they are forced to use?

Investors may look for opportunities that provide returns over the short run in countries with high risk and high interest rates. That's because cash flows far out into the future have very low values. So, for example, it's harder to justify a large, costly aluminum smelter that takes years to build relative to a trading company that can be created quickly.

$25 million in the first year, Nike has only made $10 million and expects this trend to continue for the next four years.

Nike Factory Present Value 2

$$\frac{10}{(1.10)^1} + \frac{10}{(1.10)^2} + \frac{10}{(1.10)^3} + \frac{10}{(1.10)^4} = \$31.7M$$

The present value of the future cash flows of the Nike factory is now $31.7 million. What if a rival company approaches Nike and offers to buy the factory for $40 million after the first year's disappointing results? Should Nike take the deal? Remember that Nike spent $75 million to build the factory.

Nike should take the deal without hesitation. The factory's future cash flows are valued at only $31.7 million, so the $40 million offer is better. However, Nike will give up that sum in future cash flows in the process. The net present value of the offer—the value Nike will create for itself by taking the deal—is therefore $8.3 million. At this point, the $75 million paid to build the factory is a sunk cost—it's irrelevant to the current decision. Hopefully, Nike's rival has a plan to do better than Nike expects to do. Otherwise, it shouldn't have offered $40 million for the factory.

This Nike example generalizes to two of the most important equations in finance. First, the present value of any investment is the sum of all future cash flows discounted back to the present using an appropriate discount rate.

Present Value Equation

$$\text{Present value}_0 = \frac{\text{cash flow}_1}{(1 + r)} + \frac{\text{cash flow}_2}{(1 + r)^2}$$
$$+ \frac{\text{cash flow}_3}{(1 + r)^3} + \frac{\text{cash flow}_4}{(1 + r)^4} \ldots$$

The net present value of any investment is the sum of all current and future cash flows discounted back to the present using an appropriate discount rate.

Net Present Value Equation

$$\text{Net present value}_0 = \text{cash flow}_0 + \frac{\text{cash flow}_1}{(1 + r)}$$
$$+ \frac{\text{cash flow}_2}{(1 + r)^2} + \frac{\text{cash flow}_3}{(1 + r)^3}$$
$$+ \frac{\text{cash flow}_4}{(1 + r)^4}$$

If managers care about value creation, then the most important financial decision rule they should follow is to undertake only positive NPV projects.

Reflections

You are the general manager of a National Basketball Association team. After the 2018 draft, you find out that your first-round pick and tenth-round pick are equally good players. To whom would you give more playing time?

If they're equally good players, you should be indifferent and you should give them each equal playing time. However, a 1995 study published in *Administrative Science Quarterly*[1] found that NBA basketball teams give more playing time to players they drafted earlier in the draft who cost more and they retain those players longer even after controlling for performance, injuries, and position. Even in basketball, it is tough to ignore sunk costs.

IDEAS IN ACTION

Equity Analysis for Corning Glass

If you were an equity analyst or an investor, how would you figure out whether to invest in a company? Let's take a look at equity research analyst Alberto Moel's analysis of Corning

Glass, which demonstrates the mechanics of valuation and the power of applying it correctly.

Corning makes the glass for the displays on smartphones, televisions, and laptops. It is one of only a few companies that have mastered the manufacturing process for glass displays, which are extremely difficult to make. Because of this, the company has been able to dominate the market.

Corning grew rapidly in the early 2000s as the demand for flat-screen televisions and smartphones skyrocketed. Eventually, demand began to slow. The markets for TVs and smartphones weren't growing as fast, and therefore, growth in Corning's end markets was tapering off. Eventually, despite its technology, scale, and market leadership, Corning began underperforming the stock market as margins for the glass display business (Corning's customers) shrank.

Look at the market performance of Corning from 2008 to 2012 compared with the S&P 500, a measure of the market, and LG Display, one of Corning's customers. (See figure 2-10.)

The figure shows that, beginning in early 2010, as display margins at companies like LG Display began to shrink—panel prices had dropped 15 percent to 20 percent—the

FIGURE 2-10

Corning Glass's stock performance, 2008–2012

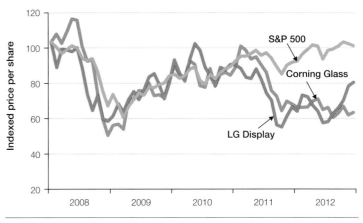

stock market began factoring those decreasing margins into the stock prices of their suppliers, including Corning.

Given all these factors, if you were Moel, would you buy or sell on Corning?

On the one hand, it looks as if Corning's customers are in trouble. LG's margins, and the margins of all display makers, are compressing, which is limiting their cash flow. But what does that mean for Corning?

In fact, glass prices—which impact Corning's margins—hadn't dropped in the same way that display prices had. That's because Corning's competitive edge has given it pricing power. Since display makers are beholden to Corning, the company can maintain high prices, even when the cost of displays decreases. So Moel realized that the market had overextrapolated the effects of declining end-market demand for Corning by ignoring Corning's pricing power.

Based on the discussion of Intel and Food Lion's profit margins in chapter 1 and Corning's activities, do you think Corning has high or low profit margins?

Corning's EBITDA margin was as high as 27 percent in 2012. Because Corning adds a great deal of value—it is essentially turning sand into glass—it should earn high margins.

Keeping Corning's growth in mind, would you expect a large or small difference between its EBIT/revenue margin and its EBITDA/revenue margin?

Corning grew rapidly in the 2000s by investing heavily in manufacturing facilities, so it had a large amount of depreciation, which reduced its EBIT. That would have resulted in a large difference between its EBIT/revenue and EBITDA/revenue ratios, making the EBITDA margin a more reliable measure of its performance. In 2012, Corning's EBIT/revenue margin was 14 percent compared to an EBITDA/revenue margin of 27 percent.

Forecasted Cash Flows

To start the process of valuing Corning Glass, the first thing Moel would do is to forecast cash flows. The next step is to take those forecasts and generate estimates of Corning's free cash flows. (See table 2-2.) Can you calculate the free cash flows for 2014? Hint: Look at the 2012 and 2013 free cash flows to see how to do that.

Using the free cash flow formula, we get: $2,195 + $1,108 − $1,491 − $50 = $1,762.

Now, discount the free cash flows to figure out a present value by creating discount factors. Discount factors come from the discounting formula; they correspond to how much $1 years from now is worth today. Once you've done that—equity analyst Alberto Moel used a discount rate (r) of 6 percent—multiply the free cash flows by the discount factor. Do that for 2015; look at the 2014 number for help. (See table 2-3.)

When you multiply the free cash flow by the discount factor, you get $1,381—the present value of the 2015 expected cash flow.

To value Corning, add the discounted values of all future cash flows, which is $18,251. (Tables 2-2 and 2-3 don't include all the relevant cash flows for reasons that will become

TABLE 2-2

Corning Glass valuation ($ millions)

	2012E	2013E	2014E	2015E	2016E	2017E
EBIAT	**$2,046**	**$2,136**	**$2,195**	**$2,144**	**$2,154**	**$2,126**
+ depreciation and amortization	983	1,056	1,108	1,169	1,238	1,315
– capital expenditure	1,775	1,300	1,491	1,615	1,745	1,864
– increase in working capital	112	32	50	53	46	47
Free cash flow	**$1,142**	**$1,860**	**?**			
Discount factor						
Present value of free cash flow						
Cumulative present value of free cash flow						
– debt	$3,450					
+ cash	$6,351					
Shareholder value						
Number of shares	1,400					
Implied share price (US$)						

apparent in chapter 5.) This represents the total value of the enterprise, but we want to know whether the stock is a good investment. To figure this out, we need to add the cash on the balance sheet (because, in addition to all the future cash flows, it belongs to the enterprise) and subtract the value of debt because shareholders get paid only after debt is retired. So Corning's equity valuation is $21,152 or, given the 1,400 shares outstanding, $15.11 per share. The stock price at the time of Moel's report was only $11, indicating that investors were overpenalizing Corning for the outcomes its customers were experiencing.

Moel recommended "buy" in his report dated December 2012. Look at Corning's performance over the next two years, compared to the S&P 500 and LG Display. (See figure 2-11.)

By understanding the source of Corning's profit margins, Moel knew that its cash flows would hold better than the display makers, even as the end market became tighter. He knew that EBITDA was a more reliable measure than EBIT or net profit. By using discount rates and the time value of money, he determined the current present value of Corning shares and made an excellent recommendation. That's what equity analysis, and investing more generally, is all about.

TABLE 2-3

Corning Glass valuation ($ millions)

	2012E	2013E	2014E	2015E	2016E	2017E
EBIAT	**$2,046**	**$2,136**	**$2,195**	**$2,144**	**$2,154**	**$2,126**
+ depreciation and amortization	983	1,056	1,108	1,169	1,238	1,315
− capital expenditure	1,775	1,300	1,491	1,615	1,745	1,864
− increase in working capital	112	32	50	53	46	47
Free cash flow	**$1,142**	**$1,860**	**$1,762**	**$1,645**	**$1,601**	**$1,530**
Discount factor		0.9434	0.8900	0.8396	0.7921	0.7473
Present value of free cash flow		$1,755	$1,568	**?**		
Cumulative present value of free cash flow						
− debt	$3,450					
+ cash	$6,351					
Shareholder value						
Number of shares	1,400					
Implied share price (US$)						

FIGURE 2-11

Corning Glass's stock performance, 2013–2014

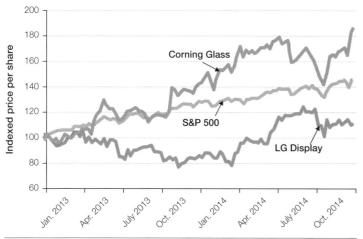

Hon Hai Sharp

Let's look at Japan's Sharp Corporation, which designs and manufactures electronic products such as TV sets, and Hon Hai Precision Industry Co. (known also as Foxconn Technology), the world's largest electronics contract manufacturer. As with the Corning case, we're going to examine it over the next few chapters.

The cornerstone of the case is Sharp's Sakai LCD plant. Sharp was the first company to make and commercialize flat-panel displays, and it had to decide whether to build even

Real-World Perspectives

Equity analyst Alberto Moel commented on the importance of cash flows in valuation:

The statement that cash is king is fundamentally true. All the investors are looking for is cash returns. You put in some money, you want your money back. So the only way you get your money back is if that amount is somehow turned into cash. Now if you are a shareholder and the share appreciates and you can sell it, you get your cash back. If you're a dividend investor, you will expect some cash back as a dividend. If you're a debt investor, you expect an income stream from whatever cash is coming through. So being able to return cash to shareholders or to the claim holders of the company is the key.

You can look at all kinds of metrics so you can see how the company is growing. Does that generate cash? If it does, you're good. If not, you've got a problem.

Cash is very, very important, and looking at those cash metrics is the key. Ultimately, it all ties into the fundamentals of valuation. Ultimately, valuation is all about discounted cash flow. It is not discounted earnings flow. It's cash flow. Because I put some cash in, I want it back with a return. That's why discounted cash flow is everything.

larger displays—think sixty-five-inch TVs—over time. LCD displays were once very small, and Sharp thought it could gain a competitive advantage through scale economies by making bigger displays. But this came with some manufacturing challenges, as large displays require massive sheets of glass, which require large factories.

In 2011, Sharp estimated that it would require an investment of $4.8 billion, spread over three years, to build the world's largest glass display factory in Sakai, near Osaka in Japan. Once the plant was commissioned in 2014, it would start generating cash for the company. Assuming a discount rate of 8 percent, let's calculate the net present value to decide whether Sharp should build the plant. Table 2-4 provides the spreadsheet of cash flows that allows you to determine the net present value (NPV) of the project by adding up all of the discounted free cash flows. (See table 2-4.)

The net present value for the Sakai plant was –$2,988.11 million. Should Sharp have built the plant? Everything we've just covered suggests that it should not.

Despite the negative NPV, Sharp decided to build the plant because it was so enamored with both the technological challenge and the desire to be on the cutting edge. Sharp's

TABLE 2-4

Sharp Corporation's projected free cash flows, 2007–2029 ($ millions)

Year	Free cash flow	Discount factor*	Discounted free cash flow
2007	−$1,378.00	0.93	−$1,275.93
2008	−3,225.00	0.86	−2,764.92
2009	−282.00	0.79	−223.86
2010	−430.35	0.74	−316.32
2011	−177.30	0.68	−120.67
2012	−83.33	0.63	−52.51
2013	6.83	0.58	3.99
2014	89.91	0.54	48.57
2015	166.32	0.50	83.20
2016	236.49	0.46	109.54
2017	300.80	0.43	129.01
2018	359.61	0.40	142.81
2019	413.26	0.37	151.95
2020	462.08	0.34	157.32
2021	457.46	0.32	144.21
2022	452.88	0.29	132.19
2023	448.36	0.27	121.18
2024	443.87	0.25	111.08
2025	439.43	0.23	101.82
2026	435.04	0.21	93.34
2027	430.69	0.20	85.56
2028	426.38	0.18	78.43
2029	422.12	0.17	71.89
NPV			**− $2,988.11**

*Discount factors have been rounded to two digits.

management, like many management groups, distrusted NPV analysis when it didn't provide the answer they wanted, and that distrust proved very problematic. Unsurprisingly,

Sharp soon ran into problems. It had hoped, against its forecasts, that consumer demand for very large TVs would be robust. It had hoped it could sell the TVs for a few thousand dollars each, which would have allowed for enough margin, EBITDA, and cash flow to make the investment worthwhile. But consumers thought the price was too high.

Sharp had no other choice but to lower the price, which shrank its profit stream. Its only hope, then, was to sell more televisions to make up the difference. But in order to attract enough customers, the company would have had to drop prices even more, which wasn't economically feasible. Unfortunately, because of the dynamics at play, the factory became a stranded asset. The company wasn't receiving a return on its investment, margins were compressing, and it was losing money. Shareholders were getting anxious as the stock price dropped and accounting considerations made the company anxious to divest the asset.

What is the minimum price Sharp should have accepted for the factory in 2011? To help you answer the question, consider the following:

- **Sharp spent $4.8 billion to build the plant.**
- **The project's original NPV was −$2.9 billion.**
- **Sharp calculated that the current present value of the cash flows from the plant in 2011 was $3.2 billion.**

Ultimately, Sharp was so desperate that it decided to sell 46 percent of the Sakai plant to Terry Gou, chairman of Hon Hai Precision, for $780 million. This transaction implied that the plant's value was just $1.7 billion. Although Sharp was happy to get rid of the plant, the company sold it for much less than its true value of $3.2 billion at the time. In effect, Sharp made two poor decisions—it should never have built the plant because it had a negative NPV; it should have tried harder to sell it for much more than it did because Sharp transferred a large amount of value to Terry Gou.

Quiz

Please note that some questions may have more than one answer.

1. **You oversee the purchasing department of Best Buy, the electronics and appliance retailer, and are concerned about the funding gap in your cash conversion cycle. Which of the following will *not* reduce the funding gap?**

   A. Increasing the payable period

   B. Increasing sales

   C. Decreasing receivables collection period

   D. Decreasing days inventory

2. **Which of the following is a disagreement between finance and accounting? (Choose all that apply.)**

   A. What constitutes economic returns (net profit or free cash flows)

   B. How to value assets (historical cost or future cash flows)

   C. Where to record inventory (on the income statement or on the balance sheet)

   D. How to value equity (book value or market value)

3. **In 2016, Pfizer invested $350 million in a new plant in China. For which of the following present values of the plant's cash flows does that decision make sense? (Choose all that apply.)**

   A. $300 million

   B. $400 million

   C. $500 million

   D. All of the above

4. **You are considering starting up a Five Guys Burgers & Fries franchise, which you estimate will cost $250,000. You expect to make considerable free cash flow for the next five years, after which you will sell off the franchise for $200,000. The discounted values of those cash flows are $90,000, $80,000, $70,000,**

$60,000, and $180,000 (which includes the fifth-year cash flow, as well as the proceeds of the sale), respectively. Which of the following is likely to be the net present value of your investment?

A. $180,000

B. $230,000

C. $480,000

D. $600,000

5. **Why does finance add back depreciation and amortization in its measure of economic returns?**

   A. Depreciation is highly uncertain and should not be counted.

   B. Companies often overspend for assets, leading depreciation to be too high.

   C. Depreciation isn't a cash expense.

   D. Depreciation appears on the balance sheet, not the income statement.

6. **One share of Facebook stock is being traded at $150. If so, which of the following does the stock market believe to be true?**

   A. The present value of all future free cash flows from Facebook's business, after netting out cash and debt, implies a Facebook stock value of $150.

   B. You can always sell a share of Facebook stock for at least $150.

   C. The net present value of buying one unit of Facebook stock is $150.

   D. The discount rate on future cash flows used to value Facebook stock is 15 percent.

7. **United States Steel Corporation has a receivables collection period of thirty-three days, a days inventory of sixty-eight days, and a payables period of forty-nine days. How long is its funding gap?**

   A. –14 days

   B. 52 days

   C. 84 days

   D. 150 days

8. **If your supplier offers you a 2 percent discount if you pay twenty days earlier than you would have otherwise, how much is the supplier implicitly charging you for a twenty-day loan?**

   A. 0 percent

   B. 1 percent

   C. 2 percent

   D. This is a discount, not a loan, so there is no implied interest rate.

9. Your company builds a new plant with an investment of $100 million and an expected present value from its future cash flows of $150 million. Two years later, it becomes apparent that the new product isn't selling as well as expected, and the present value of future cash flows at that point is only worth $50 million. Should the company shut down the plant?

    A. Yes, the net present value is now negative.

    B. No, the present value is still $50 million.

10. Which of the following is true about free cash flow?

    A. It is for equity providers only and is tax adjusted.

    B. It is for all capital providers and is tax adjusted.

    C. It is for equity providers only and is not tax adjusted.

    D. It is for all capital providers and is not tax adjusted.

Chapter Summary

In this chapter, we explored two core finance principles. First, cash is a better measure of economic returns relative to profits. "Cash" is a somewhat ambiguous term, but it can be sharpened by thinking about EBITDA, operating cash flow, and free cash flow—finance nirvana. The emphasis on cash explains why companies that generate profits but no cash might be unsustainable and why companies that generate no profits but lots of cash might be valuable. Second, cash earned today is more valuable than cash earned tomorrow because of the opportunity cost of capital. Ignoring that opportunity cost can lead to value destruction or value transfers. All value comes from future cash flows, and making positive net present value decisions is the hallmark of a good steward of capital and manager. Everything else in the remainder of this book will build on those core ideas.

3

The Financial Ecosystem

Understanding the who, why, and how of capital markets

In the summer of 2018, Netflix, the online video streaming service, announced that it had added 670,000 new domestic subscribers to its service and 4.5 million international subscribers (in addition to the 125 million subscribers it already had). The stock fell by 14 percent in after-hours trading. Why? How could a large increase in the total subscriber numbers translate to a 14 percent stock price drop?

In 2014, activist investor Nelson Peltz took a large stake in PepsiCo and began demanding that it split its snack foods division (Frito-Lay) from its soft-drink division. PepsiCo responded by saying, "We trust that you appreciate the seriousness with which we have examined your observations and proposal and the firmness with which we reject the proposal to separate the businesses."[1] Peltz then took his complaint to other shareholders, leading to a lengthy shareholder revolt that ended two years later when Peltz sold his stake in the company. Why would an activist shareholder fight with a company's upper management?

In our retirement accounts, we face choices between different kinds of funds, including active and passive mutual funds? What does that mean? What are mutual funds and how are they different from those evil hedge funds?

In this chapter, we'll come to understand the who, why, and how of capital markets. These markets are critical for the growth of the economy and increasingly guide policymakers and managers. But, these markets have also engendered great skepticism about their value and wisdom. Regardless of your views on these markets, you will interact with them more and more as a rising manager, a saver, and a citizen. Here, we'll explore and demystify capital markets.

Most broadly, we're going to ask what role finance plays in society and how to restructure that role. In the process, we'll confront the prevailing skepticism on the value of financial markets and discover that finance is about much more than money.

Why Can't Finance Be Simple?

Why can't the world of finance be simpler? Let's think about a simple version of capital markets. On one side, there would be individuals and households that have savings that they want to invest. These are people like you and me who want to save for college or retirement and want to use that money to generate a return. On the other side are companies that need capital to build new projects and grow. So a simpler financial world would just have the savers and firms, and we wouldn't need the mess of finance that exists in the middle. (See figure 3-1.)

So why doesn't the world work this simply? Why can't individuals just give their money directly to companies and be done with it? In fact, the world of finance looks considerably more complex. (See figure 3-2.)

FIGURE 3-1

A simpler financial world

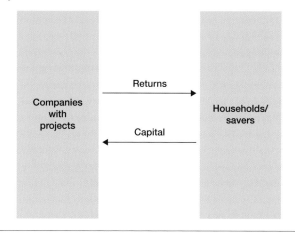

Why are capital markets so complex? Why do we have so many intermediaries, such as investment banks, funds, and analysts who stand between savers and firms? When most people look at the mess of capital markets, they conclude that it is a rigged system filled with leeches that extract value from all the real people in the economy. Indeed, in the wake of the financial crisis, this view prevails more and more. As we explore this terrain, we'll try to figure out why the financial world is as complex as it is and whether it really needs to be.

FIGURE 3-2

The reality of capital markets

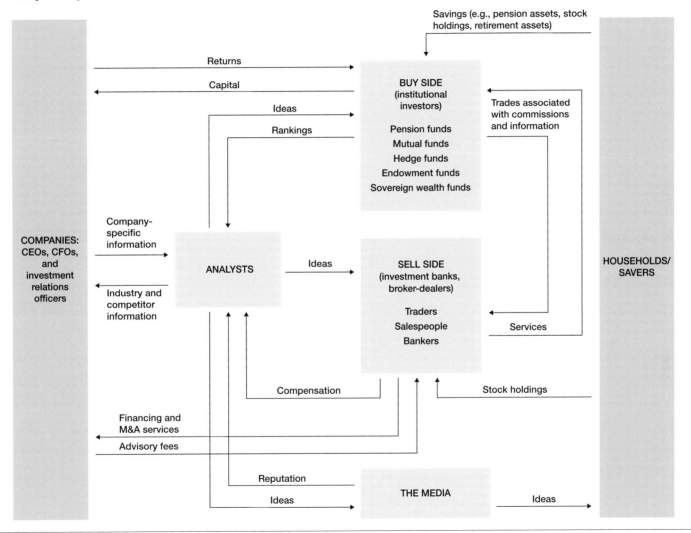

Who's Who in Capital Markets

To examine all this complexity, let's use the person at the center of it all—the equity research analyst—as a guide. The analyst's job is to value companies by creating forecasts and then make recommendations to investors. Alberto Moel, the equity analyst who examined Corning Glass in chapter 2, did exactly this. Analysts spend most of their days, and sometimes nights, talking to people. Mapping Moel's conversations can help us begin to understand this world.

The Companies

First and foremost, Moel wants to talk to the companies he's evaluating (such as Corning), and within those companies, he'll talk to anyone he's allowed to. At a minimum, he'll have conversations with CEOs and CFOs (like Laurence Debroux of Heineken and Paul Clancy of Biogen), whom he'll ask about new product launches, strategy, and forecasts. Basically, Moel looks for information, beyond the raw numbers, that will tell him how a company is performing, which is a critical ingredient for formulating forecasts that will guide his recommendations.

Since finance is always a two-way street, CFOs such as Debroux and Clancy will have their own questions and want

to pick Moel's brains, which can be a valuable source of industry knowledge and provide a better understanding of the competitive landscape. This exchange of information is one of the first key insights about capital markets—often, their interactions take the form of trades, and these trades may not only be in capital. Often, these trades are for information or knowledge.

Institutional Investors: The Buy Side

Moel shares his analysis of the companies he covers with a broad array of investors. These are not just any investors but rather they are institutional investors, including people like Jeremy Mindich of Scopia Capital. People in finance use a lot of different labels for institutional investors—money managers or asset managers—or, more generally, they might refer to them as the buy side. But, despite the different nomenclature, institutional investors are simply entities that invest large amounts of capital on behalf of others and allocate it in ways that they feel will best support their clients. There are several different kinds of funds, including mutual funds, pension funds, foundations and endowment funds, sovereign wealth funds, and hedge funds.

The rise of institutional investors has been one of the most important developments in modern capitalism, so let's take a closer look at specific types of institutional investors so they won't seem so foreign when you encounter them. We'll discover some of the biggest ideas in finance as we trace through Moel's interactions with these investors.

Mutual funds. Mutual funds manage money on behalf of individuals and invest those funds in diversified portfolios of stocks or bonds. To give you a sense of their enormity, Fidelity and Black Rock collectively manage nearly $10 trillion through various mutual funds. There's a good chance you're invested in mutual funds through your retirement accounts. Because mutual funds invest on behalf of individuals with varying amounts of wealth and sophistication, they are tightly regulated.

Given their exposure to risky assets like stocks, they need to manage those risks. Their method for managing risks is an example of a fundamental lesson of finance. They hold a wide selection of stocks, rather than a few, so that the funds are not overly exposed to any one stock. That process of diversification limits their exposure. More important, since the stocks don't all move together, their movements can offset each other and reduce the overall riskiness of the portfolio without sacrificing return. So diversification has the virtue of insulating against risk without giving up that much return; this is why diversification is so strongly recommended.

In chapter 4, we'll return to the idea of diversification to talk about how risk is priced.

Mutual funds are often classified as active—meaning a manager personally decides which stocks to hold in the portfolio—or passive. The growth of passive mutual funds (index funds and exchange traded funds) has been one of the most important developments in capital markets. Between 2011 and 2018, passive mutual funds grew from one-fifth to one-third of the total money managed by professional investors. In 2017 alone, $692 billion flowed into passive mutual funds.

Passive funds aren't actively managed by someone who tries to time the market or select underperforming stocks that will eventually rise. Instead, passive funds simply invest in all the stocks in a broad market index such as the S&P 500, which tracks five hundred of the world's most valuable companies. Given their mechanical nature, passive funds are relatively cheap to invest in. But it's not just that they're cheap. Passive funds are a manifestation of a Nobel Prize–winning idea known as the "efficient market theory." This theory suggests that if information is widely available to investors, then it's impossible to outperform the market because prices already reflect that available information. So trying to beat or time the market over the long term is a useless endeavor. From this perspective, why pay active managers lots of money to do something that isn't possible?

There is considerable debate over the efficient market theory. However, the underlying logic that it's difficult to beat the market on a sustainable basis, combined with the promise of increased gains from diversification, has proven true and has driven the rise of low-cost, passive investing at the expense of actively managed funds.

Pension funds. These funds are large pools of money that represent the retirement assets of workers from a particular company, union, or government entity. As one example, the California Public Employees' Retirement System (CalPERS) manages over $320 billion of pension assets on behalf of the public employees in California. Generally, pensions can take one of two forms. In defined benefit (DB) plans, employees receive payments after retirement from their employers, which are funded by pension plans run by those companies or organizations (such as CalPERS). In contrast, companies with defined contribution (DC) plans simply contribute to individual pension accounts that the employee manages. While many public employees have DB plans, pensions have shifted dramatically away from DB plans and toward DC plans during the last fifty years. This shift, in turn, has fueled massive growth in mutual funds.

Reflections

Which of the following portfolios do you think is best diversified?

- Google, Yahoo, Microsoft

- Merck, Pfizer, Biogen

- Google, Caterpillar, Merck

The portfolio of Google, Caterpillar, and Merck is the most diversified of the three. The objective of diversification is to have a collection of stocks that do not move together and do not share the same risks. For example, when Google does poorly, Caterpillar might do well. The risk of having a portfolio concentrated in a single industry is that often industry stocks tend to move together, which is less likely if the companies are from different industries.

Foundations and endowment funds. Not-for-profit foundations and organizations sometimes retain and invest funds over long periods to create more stability for their operations. These foundations and endowments, which have grown over the last several decades, are now large, innovative players in capital markets. For example, Harvard University controls a $37.1 billion endowment as of 2017.

Sovereign wealth funds. Countries with excess savings—typically stemming from natural resources—often invest those savings through a sovereign wealth fund. These funds have grown dramatically over the last several decades and have become more experimental in their investment strategies. The Norwegian sovereign wealth fund, for example, manages a sovereign wealth fund of over $1 trillion as of 2017.

Hedge funds. The final institutional investor is the most controversial—hedge funds have grown from $260 billion in assets in 2000 to $3 trillion in 2017. Although they are similar to mutual funds, they are differentiated by their lower level of regulation and use of leverage and their different approach to managing risk.

Hedge funds, which include many pension, endowment, and sovereign wealth funds as customers, have lower levels of regulation because only so-called sophisticated investors (which just translates to "rich") can buy them. Accordingly, their managers are less constrained in their attitude toward risk. For example, a hedge fund may amplify its buying power by buying shares using borrowed funds. So instead of investing $10,000 of a client's money, it will borrow additional amounts from a broker and then invest, for example, $20,000. Leverage will amplify the returns, as we saw in chapter 1. Unlike mutual funds, hedge funds can also take more concen-trated positions in companies, which allows them to become "activist" shareholders that promote the policies and strategies most beneficial to their investors.

Although hedge funds are willing to assume risk by taking significant stakes in individual companies with leverage, they attempt to manage this risk by, unsurprisingly, *hedging*. While hedge funds are demonized as being risky, they argue that they are *less* risky because of this risk management. Mutual funds manage risk by diversifying across stocks, but that still leaves them vulnerable to overall stock market movements. Hedge funds attempt to manage risk better.

How can a hedge fund that invests in Merck, a global pharmaceutical company, manage the risk of that investment? A mutual fund would limit its investment in Merck by buying many other stocks, but a hedge fund would rather focus its efforts on a company it really likes. A "hedge" (as in real life when you want to "hedge your bets") is another investment that moves the opposite way that Merck does so that it provides a return when Merck falls. For these purposes, let's consider another pharmaceutical company, Pfizer. A hedge fund will "go short" Pfizer to manage its exposure because it "went long" Merck.

What does all that mean? "Going long" is relatively simple—it just means you buy the stock. "Going short" is more complicated. To short a company's stock, you borrow shares from another investor, such as a mutual fund, which charges a fee for lending the shares to you. Once you've borrowed the shares, you sell them. At some point in the future, you buy back the shares (hopefully at a lower price) and return them to the institutional investor whom you borrowed the shares from.

Imagine you go short Pfizer at $40, and Pfizer then drops to $20. How have you done? You borrowed shares of Pfizer, sold them, and received $40; later, you bought shares at $20 and then returned the shares, leaving you with a gain of $20 per share. This means that you'll make money when Pfizer declines. If Pfizer went up to $80 or $120, you would actually end up losing a fair amount—in fact, you could lose far more than you had initially committed. (See figure 3-3.)

How does all this relate to hedging? Let's imagine that both Merck and Pfizer are selling at $100. You decide to go long Merck, but how can you manage that risk? You don't want to buy other pharmaceutical companies or other types of companies as mutual funds do. Instead, you go short Pfizer for the same total dollar amount as your long position in Merck. How does your investment strategy perform?

Let's look at real data from 2012 to 2014. (See figure 3-4.) During 2012, both Merck's and Pfizer's stock were moving together quite tightly. By December, they'd both gone up by 20 percent. If you sold your Merck shares and repurchased

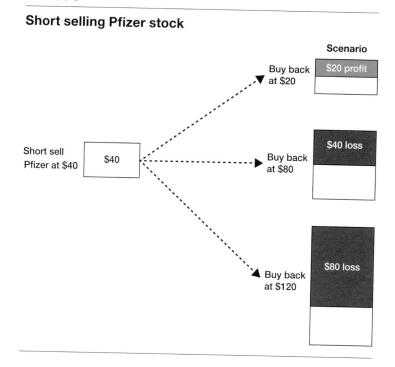

FIGURE 3-3

Short selling Pfizer stock

Pfizer shares at year end, thereby closing out your position, you would end up at the same place where you started. The gains on your long position (plus 20 percent because Merck went up) are offset by your losses on your short position (minus 20 percent because Pfizer went up too).

Now let's look at 2013. By the end of 2013, Pfizer had outperformed Merck. By December, Pfizer was up 50 percent and Merck was only up 40 percent. Because your Pfizer stock

FIGURE 3-4

Comparison of stock prices for Merck and Pfizer, December 2011–December 2014

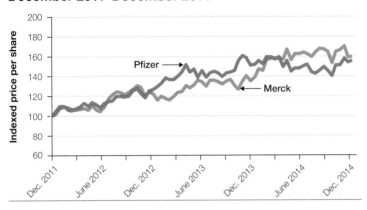

went up by more than your Merck stock went up (your short outperformed your long), you lost money. Finally, let's look at 2014. During that year, Merck outperformed Pfizer. By December, Pfizer had risen a total of 60 percent and Merck had risen a total of 70 percent. Because your long outperformed your short, you made money.

So hedging can help insulate an investor from sectorwide or marketwide movements and isolate the relative performance of a given company. In that sense, you have managed risk because you are now exposed to only the relative outperformance (or underperformance) of a given company's stock.

Hedge-fund managers also receive carried interest, a compensation model that allows them to participate in the economic returns of their funds. The combination of leverage and carried interest means that fund managers are particularly attracted to outsized returns and will go to great lengths to find investment opportunities. As one example, consider a fund manager looking to see if JCPenney will have a good holiday season. Rather than talking to analysts such as Moel or building the models we saw in chapter 2, they may go to much greater lengths, such as taking satellite images of JCPenney's parking lots on Black Friday to get an early sense of the store's quarterly results or hiring former counterintelligence officials to verify the validity of its executive's statements. And if a hedge fund is shorting a stock, it may be willing to publicly attack a company. These aggressive maneuvers attract supporters who appreciate the work hedge funds are doing and produce detractors who consider them vaguely evil for attacking companies.

Equity research analysts such as Moel pitch ideas to these varied institutional investors, but what do they get in return? Institutional investors don't actually pay analysts directly for their ideas. Instead, institutional investors rank analysts based on the quality of their recommendations. These ratings are a critical component to the analysts' compensation. Indeed, being the number one–ranked equity research analyst can yield compensation that is several times that of a number ten–ranked analyst.

Real-World Perspectives

Jeremy Mindich, founder of Scopia Capital, a hedge fund in New York City, commented on the hedge fund business model:

Scopia's basic investment philosophy is that we should be able to find great longs and great shorts at any moment in time so that the disparity of returns between those long positions and those short positions should be the source of our return stream. We're not looking for short-term trades; we're not looking to invest in companies because of their quarterly earnings.

So we always had the idea that you can find, in any market environment, companies that are grossly mispriced, both undervalued and overvalued, to construct a long or short value portfolio. We call ourselves a market-neutral fund, which means that we have little or no net exposure to the stock market. Generally, market-neutral funds are quantitatively driven, so they tend to be collections of stocks driven by a quantitative algorithm that creates a basket of two hundred to three hundred undervalued long ideas (by whatever factor criteria) and another couple of hundred short ideas that are, for whatever reason, considered overvalued. The hope is that by leveraging that portfolio and squeezing out small differences in returns, you can create an interesting return stream.

At Scopia, we're trying to have a concentrated portfolio of roughly twenty to twenty-five long ideas and roughly thirty to forty short ideas. The long ideas are deeply researched, significantly mispriced, undervalued companies, and the short ideas are also deeply researched, significantly mispriced companies. The vision we have for the future of those businesses creates the investment opportunity.

Taken together, these institutional investors make up "the buy side," a collection of organizations that accumulate funds—often from individuals—and use them to buy assets in the financial markets. Who is the buy side buying from? Mutual fund managers don't typically knock on the doors of companies and offer to buy their stock directly. For that, they reach out to someone on "the sell side."

The Sell Side

Equity analysts make significant amounts in compensation, but we haven't yet identified any dollars being paid to anyone. So where's the money? Analysts such as Moel typically work for investment banks that constitute the sell side. Within these banks, equity analysts speak to three constituencies—

Is Short Selling Evil?

Shorting is a controversial activity and leads to many questions. Is it proper to benefit when companies do poorly? Or is that just evil? Should we ban that activity?

Despite these concerns, short sellers do play a positive role in markets, as they often highlight what is going on in companies that are not doing well. For example, short sellers discovered the wrongdoing at the likes of Enron and WorldCom, both of which participated in the largest corporate governance scandals we've seen. Since short sellers are incentivized to look for flaws, weaknesses, and discrepancies, they see things that others don't see. Given that, one could make the argument that short sellers are a force for positive social good, as opposed to something evil.

---

traders, salespeople, and investment bankers—to provide ideas about the companies they cover.

Traders

Traders, sometimes known as market makers or broker-dealers, ensure that there are buyers and sellers for various financial instruments. They make money largely from the gap known as the bid-ask spread. A bid is the highest price an investor is willing to pay for a share, while the ask is the lowest price that a seller is willing to sell a share for. Those on the buy side don't pay analysts directly for their reports; rather, they can choose to trade through the broker-dealer associated with the equity analyst they like, who then makes commissions on those trades. This is one way the buy side can show appreciation for the equity analyst's work. However, these commissions have narrowed significantly over time, so they're a relatively small part of the puzzle.

Even in the face of declining commissions, it is quite valuable for broker-dealers to process trades. If you've ever been on a trading floor, you know that traders deal in the short term, where the decisions of the large institutional investors is what matters. Traders find it quite valuable to know the trading activity of these investors because the transactions contain information. Are large funds buying? Are they liquidating? This is valuable information for traders, so good equity research analysts ensure that their traders get a share of trade flow.

Salespeople

Unsurprisingly, salespeople sell financial instruments to investors on the buy side. Analysts might talk directly to the larger institutional investors, but salespeople disseminate the analyst's ideas to the broader community to woo the buy side more directly. This can generate commissions and trade flow, but it isn't where the big money really is.

Investment bankers

Unlike the commercial bankers you interact with for loans and deposits, investment bankers work with companies that either want to raise capital or want to buy or sell operating assets. Financing arranged by investment banks, such as initial public offerings (IPOs), equity offerings, and debt offerings, allows companies to access new funding. The mergers and acquisitions (M&A) departments of investment banks help companies divest portions of their businesses or acquire new businesses. In effect, investment banks are brokers for businesses. Both IPOs and M&As are extremely lucrative. Fees for equity financings can be as high as 7 percent of the proceeds for an IPO. Similarly, advisory fees on M&A can be close to 1 percent, so a $10 billion transaction can deliver $100 million in fees. These fees typically dwarf other trading revenue streams.

The Media

Moel's final set of conversations allow him to broadcast his ideas to an even larger audience. Equity research analysts use the media (e.g., the *Wall Street Journal*, Squawk Box on CNBC, or Bloomberg TV) to disseminate their ideas to a broader audience, including households that invest directly. Often, analysts provide commentary on the latest developments and will use those occasions to communicate their more general views of a company.

Incentives for Equity Analysts

The conversations of equity research analysts such as Moel span the capital markets depicted in figure 3-2. They speak to companies that need capital, the buy side that pools the capital of the households, the sell side that intermediates the markets for stocks and companies, and the financial media. In effect, equity research analysts are at the center of the capital markets. Capital markets are important for capitalism, so it's worth thinking through what incentives exist for the individuals who stand in the middle of these markets. And assessing their incentives is critical for figuring out what this high-priced talent in capital markets is getting paid for and whether they are really worth it.

As we saw, a critical component of analyst compensation is a ranking system deployed by the buy side to signal sentiments about which analysts provide the best advice. This ranking results in a tournament-like labor market where the best analysts do very well, while lower-ranked analysts don't do as well—compensation drops sharply as they move down in the rankings. How does an analyst get a good ranking? If rankings are everything, then analysts should supply the buy side with the best analysis possible, presumably through hard work and creativity. In short, analysts should focus mostly on doing their job well. If this were the whole story, we could rest assured that capital markets were working well.

In fact, evidence shows that analysts can be biased, often strongly, toward being positive, meaning they rarely tend to issue "sell" recommendations and instead issue a disproportionate share of "buy" recommendations. Why?

Think about what happens when an analyst issues a negative report on a stock, which says that a company is overvalued. Ultimately the investors will appreciate the truth and rank the analyst highly. But, what else might happen along the way? First, the CEO and CFO of the company will not appreciate the lack of confidence and may try to shut out the analysts by not engaging with them or not taking their questions on the next conference call. If the CEO and CFO are really angry, they could call the analysts' investment banker colleagues and signal that they won't work with the investment bankers on future M&A and financing deals. Given the relative magnitude of the revenue streams, this could be disastrous. As a result, analysts find it very hard to say "sell" and instead say things like "market perform" or "neutral," which really means "sell."

The rankings system itself creates additional problems. What would new, young research analysts at a less prestigious investment bank do? With nothing to lose, they often say crazy, extreme things; if they're right, they shoot up in the rankings for being brave, and if they're wrong, no one was paying attention anyway.

For higher-rated analysts, there's a different pathology. If you're the number one analyst, how do you make sure that the number two and number three analysts never overtake you? You "herd" alongside them. If you estimate earnings to be precisely in between the estimates of the number two and number three analysts, it's unlikely that you can be unseated by those analysts. Of course, just herding and copying what other people are doing is precisely what analysts should not be doing.

Thus, the incentives for the people at the center of the capital markets are considerably more complicated than you might hope. It would be wonderful if the only incentive for analysts was to work hard and do their job. Unfortunately, that's not the case—they tend to be positively biased, and some "herd" by copying other analysts while others say extreme things.

Hopefully, now you can review the diagram shown in figure 3-2 and really understand the complexities of capital markets. But these complexities still leave a central question unanswered: Why are all the people in the middle making so much money? Are they doing anything of value? Why can't the people who have the capital—you and me, as households—get together with those needing the capital—companies—and get rid of everything in the middle? Why can't the world of finance be simpler?

The Problem at the Heart of Capital Markets

Reviewing the mess in figure 3-2 might just intensify your skepticism about the value of capital markets. It can appear that all of finance just extracts value from the companies and savers who make up the "real" economy. So let's explore whether capital markets are, in fact, solving a deep and diffi-

cult problem and what that problem might be. Why is bringing together savers and companies so complicated?

What's the deep problem that capital markets—and much of finance—solves? Let's begin with a simpler question: Who has all the information about the future of companies that we as investors want to know? Clearly, the managers of the companies do. But can I trust the managers when they share that information? The problem is that we can't necessarily trust what managers tell us. They want something from us—our capital—so they may tell us things that aren't true in order to get it. The inability to credibly share information is called asymmetric information; it's a deep and hard problem that all the people in the middle of figure 3-2 are

FIGURE 3-5

The problem of asymmetric information

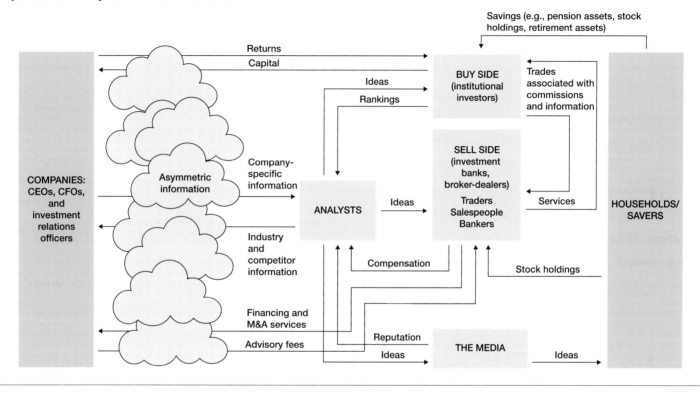

trying to solve. While some CFOs—like Paul Clancy and Laurence Debroux—are good people, some will inevitably shade things to their advantage.

In a world of perfect information, capital markets are relatively simple—they just need to pool resources and price risk (something we'll turn to in chapter 4). But in a world of asymmetric information, capital markets need to figure out how to allocate capital when you don't know whom to believe. The clouds in figure 3-5 represents that problem.

The problem of capital markets is a manifestation of an even more general problem known as the principal-agent problem. Historically, many individuals worked for themselves in trade or agriculture—they both owned and managed their businesses. In modern capitalism, the scale of enterprise has grown and owners are no longer managers; now owners (the principal) have to monitor managers (their agents) to ensure that they're not misbehaving. The separation of ownership and control creates the problem of corporate governance: How do shareholders ensure that managers are pursuing their interests? Finance is all about trying to help solve that monitoring problem.

For example, let's say that the CEO of a company is contemplating a large acquisition. She shares her forecasts for the company to be acquired and advises the owners that the acquisition is a great idea. But, what if she just wants to run a larger company and her ability to lead a transformational acquisition could place her in a higher echelon among CEOs? She could get a better job with more pay. So is the acquisition great for the company or for the CEO? What about plans for a new headquarters? Is the move to attract talent, as the CEO says, or just managers padding their compensation with an on-site five-star gym facility and a better breakfast buffet than you can get at the Four Seasons?

This problem pervades all of a company's interactions with financial markets. The CEO misses an earnings forecast by a penny and attributes it to bad weather conditions. Is it true or does the mistake signal the beginning of the end for the company? Suspicion by investors about the company helps explain the large price drops associated with small earnings misses because those misses may be for more than one quarter. It's about credibility and asymmetric information. When a CEO announces that she is divesting part of her shareholding in a so-called normal portfolio rebalancing plan, it could be true. But the reality is that someone who knows much more than you do about the future of the company is selling shares. That can be alarming.

Managers and owners engage in a complex communication game where every signal coming from a manager is reevaluated with suspicion in the background. For companies, the problem of asymmetric information can also affect whether they finance their projects through equity, debt, or internally generated profits. Each method signals a different message to investors. For example, an investor may balk at a company using equity. If the project is so great, why issue new shares? The questions become: Why are the owners, if they're so confident about the future, willing to share the upside? Why wouldn't they keep the upside for themselves by issuing debt? This is the reason equity issuance is usually associated with stock price declines. It's not because of dilution or an accounting argument. It's because the stock issue sends a negative signal. To some investors, the company looks as if it is unwilling to finance the project internally and, therefore, the project isn't as great as it seems. Equity becomes the most expensive source of financing.

Debt seems a little better. Although a company is still relying on external capital providers, at least it's not giving up ownership. But, whenever a company goes to outside sources for funding, investors will always ask why. The best source of financing is internally generated funds. There's no informational cost associated with it, but it can be a limited source.

One last thing to consider is stock buybacks, an increasingly important phenomena we'll return to in chapter 6. When a CEO announces a stock buyback, she's implicitly telling investors that she thinks the stock is undervalued. That's why share buybacks are often greeted as good news, again, not because fewer shares are outstanding. Instead, stock buybacks can send a powerful signal of confidence from the managers who know more than the investors.

The Persistence of the Principal-Agent Problem

If finance is meant to ameliorate the principal-agent problem, how is it doing? Given the repeated crises in corporate governance, it's easy to conclude that the financial markets aren't doing their job well, so their promise is unfulfilled.

But first, it's important to consider how we could intervene to improve corporate governance. If you were in charge of the world, how would you try to solve this problem?

Here are a few possibilities. First, could we punish managers more when they lie? This is tempting, but it can lead them to say less and less, thereby increasing the level of asymmetric information. Second, we could pay managers with more equity so they behave like owners want them to. Equity compensation has become much more common in the last several decades but comes with its own issues. Managers may orient their performance to short-term results and then sell shares at their peak level. Could we create a board of directors above the managers to monitor them and represent owners? Well, who's going to pick those directors? Often, it's the managers themselves. And to complicate matters, they may serve on the board of the CEO who sits on their board. Every potential solution leads to collateral consequences that can amplify, rather than ameliorate, the problem.

Finally, private equity can help by effectively replacing dispersed owners with one large owner who carefully monitors, and uses leverage to constrain, management. But private equity also creates its own issues—these investors realize profits by issuing stock to capital markets and have incentives to make their companies appear better than they are prior to going public.

Hopefully, this will help you make sense of other things happening in capital markets. Hedge funds often take activist positions and try to influence managers to make significant changes. They are often maligned as irksome troublemakers. But maybe they're correcting against some of the biases in the markets that give managers too much power. Maybe short-sellers, who are also maligned, aren't evil but are actually heroes for fighting the tide of excess optimism that managers and analysts often create. Finally, it shows you that the capital markets are not a perfect solution to this problem but finding a way to make progress against this problem is not straightforward at all. The separation of ownership and control demanded by the scale of modern enterprise means that the principal-agent problem is here to stay—and that is in part what makes finance so fascinating.

If, as a CEO or CFO, you know about these problems with capital markets, how would it affect the way you run your company and the way you communicate with the

Used-Car Markets

The problem of asymmetric information and the phenomenon of signaling are not concerns for capital markets alone. We see these concepts in our everyday lives.

Think about the used-car market. Let's say you go to the Volkswagen dealer and buy a new car for $50,000. After a few days, you decide that you don't want the car. If you put it on the market, how much will you get? The answer is likely not nearly the depreciated value, which would be close to $49,999. It will be closer to $45,000 or $40,000. Why is that? Because potential buyers will be skeptical and think there's something wrong with the car that you're not revealing. After all, the person with all the information about the car—you—is selling. In order to deal with their skepticism, you'll need to cut the price to a point where buyers would be more willing to take on the risk.

Things can get worse. Imagine that some people really do have good cars, but just need to sell because they're moving across the country. And imagine that some people actually got lemons when they bought the cars and now are trying to sell to somebody who's unsuspecting. What happens when the buyer reduces his price to $45,000 or $40,000? The answer is that people with good cars say, "I don't want to be in this market anymore," and they leave. The average quality of the used cars goes down. The buyers reduce their price even further. More good cars leave the market, and the market unravels. That's why asymmetric information is so destructive.

capital markets? CEOs and CFOs need to manage their credibility with capital markets because the loss of investors' faith can be particularly problematic. As such, overpromising is particularly dangerous. At the same time, underpromising and overdelivering can cause investors to expect surprise performance—an expectation that you won't be able to live up to.

IDEAS IN ACTION

The pursuit of three investment ideas demonstrates some of the concepts from our exploration of capital markets. We'll return to the aftermath of the Sharp Sakai plant investment, consider a short investment in a wire manufacturer, and examine a leveraged buyout (LBO) by Morgan Stanley Private Equity.

Hon Hai Sharp and the Sakai Plant

In the case study in chapter 2, I introduced Sharp's Sakai plant, a factory designed to make large glass displays for televisions. Sharp's large investment in the new factory was unwise and proved untenable, and Hon Hai chairman Terry Gou personally purchased a stake in it. There are some more interesting wrinkles to this story, which will exemplify the principal-agent problem.

Gou's investment in the Sakai plant was one of two moves jointly announced in March 2012. The other was that Gou's company, Hon Hai, which assembles glass displays for the likes of Apple and Microsoft, would buy more than US$800 million in equity from Sharp, which would make it Sharp's largest investor.

When equity analyst Alberto Moel heard the news from one of his clients, he was puzzled. He'd followed Hon Hai throughout his career. The company had a reputation as being opaque, and the dual transaction in this case was puzzling. Why would Hon Hai buy a large stake in Sharp while its chairman used his own personal wealth to buy a 46 percent stake in the Sakai plant.

If both transactions were completed, Hon Hai would own Sharp, and at the same time, Sharp would sell an asset to Gou, Hon Hai's chairman. As we saw in chapter 2, the sale to Gou appeared to be happening at a fire-sale price, creating a great amount of value for Gou. But where did that value come from? In effect, Gou was taking value from Sharp shareholders—but that included Hon Hai, the company he ran! Market commentators speculated that Hon Hai's promised investment in Sharp was just designed to facilitate the sale of the Sakai plant to Gou at a rock-bottom price.

After the deals were announced, Sharp's stock price dropped and kept dropping because the company had received so little for the plant from Gou. Hon Hai attempted to renegotiate for a lower price, but when that failed, Hon Hai withdrew its offer. The chairman, however, kept his side of the deal and bought a large stake in the Sakai plant.

What do you think about Terry Gou's actions? Your answer depends on your views of the Sakai plant. If you agree with the argument that the plant had significant value, then the chairman was effectively preparing to take value from Hon Hai's shareholders. As a major shareholder in Sharp, Hon Hai was giving its chairman an underpriced asset, removing a Sharp asset worth $3.2 billion for only $1.7 billion, an incredible deal. In other words, why not let Hon Hai shareholders participate in the great deal that the Sakai plant turned out to be? That's the uncharitable view. On the other hand, if you think that the plant was very risky, then the chairman was committing his own money to shield his company from additional risk.

Short Selling Bekaert

In 2010, Jeremy Mindich's hedge fund, Scopia Capital, decided to short-sell Bekaert, a company that makes steel wire. After gaining significant expertise in steel wires, Scopia thought that Bekaert was overearning relative to its historic margins because it manufactured wires that went into radial tires used in industrial machinery. Most companies at the time were focused on electrical wires for the housing market, which left Bekaert as one of the only companies focused on the industrial market. As a result, it was earning outsized returns that were likely unsustainable. Mindich believed that Bekaert's earnings would revert to the mean as its competitors looked toward the industrial market.

Scopia further examined the numbers and saw that earnings had been steadily climbing from 2006 to 2008, and then dropped because of the global financial crisis. The question was, would growth resume? The consensus from analysts was yes. The next step was trying to find competitors and gauge how they were doing. Scopia discovered that a number of Chinese competitors were looking to enter Bekaert's most profitable customer segment.

What would you want to know about the Chinese competitors in order to determine if Bekaert will be able to maintain its high margins?

Two members of Scopia's team visited the Chinese wire companies and tried to answer the following questions:

- What were their expectations for the new wire plants?

- What were their expected margins?

After talking with representatives from the companies, the analysts at Scopia decided that their expectations for future profits were much lower than the market's.

From this information, Scopia was able to deduce that Bekaert shareholders were in for a nasty surprise, although it wasn't sure when. While people were arguing about whether the industry's growth was going to continue or stall, Scopia saw something much worse: earnings were going to be cut in half. "In the case of Bekaert, we saw this industry returning to sort of normal margins," recalled Mindich. "An industry that had been enjoying outsized returns was heading toward a more normal environment." So Scopia decided to short the stock.

Assuming you want to short Bekaert, what are the risks of doing so?

Figure 3-6 shows the price of Bekaert's stock from 2006 to 2013. The price rise through late 2010 reflected the unsustainable optimism that Mindich was hoping to capitalize on. Although Scopia's predictions turned out to be right, it ended up shorting the stock too early and had to endure a year's worth of losses while Bekaert's stock price rose about 30 percent. Mindich said, "That's not the goal. We're not hoping to find ideas that are going to cause us so much pain before they work out. But because we had

FIGURE 3-6

Bekaert stock price, 2006–2013

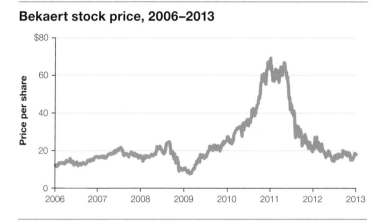

done so much work and we were so convinced about the ultimate fundamental case for the business, we were able to wait out the storm because we were sure that it was not sustainable."

You can imagine how painful it was for Scopia to watch its investment thesis go wrong for the first year as Bekaert stock rose and stayed high. With short sales, there is unlimited potential loss because the stock price can continue to rise, possibly catching investors in a "short squeeze," where short sellers are forced to buy their share back while the stock price continues to rise. Mindich's analysis and determination allowed Scopia to see the investment thesis through to its conclusion.

The Leveraged Buyout of Tops Friendly Markets

In 2007, Morgan Stanley Private Equity purchased Tops Friendly Markets, a supermarket chain in upstate New York, in a leveraged buyout (LBO). Private equity firms purchase companies using debt, improve operations, and then sell the company to the public markets or to a strategic buyer. The leverage can substantially increase their returns.

Morgan Stanley jumped at the opportunity to buy Tops for a few reasons. First, Royal Ahold, a Dutch grocer that owned Tops, was a distressed seller with a firm objective: it wanted its US asset off its balance sheet by the end of 2007, which meant that its move was more about timing than about trying to sell at full value. In this type of situation, managers may be somewhat irrational in their desire to sell an asset quickly.

Since Royal Ahold was in a rush, the current management team at Tops was likely to stay on with the parent company, which would allow Morgan Stanley to hire its own CEO. The team hired Frank Curci, who had led Tops five years before Royal Ahold took over. Curci's knowledge and expertise, the team surmised, would be invaluable in helping the team return the company's operations to their previous condition.

According to Morgan Stanley's Alan Jones, one of Tops' most attractive characteristics was that it was a "classic corporate orphan." Since Royal Ahold's headquarters were geographically distant from the Tops stores, it had trouble managing the business, a common problem. So even though the operating margins and the return on capital were much lower than that of other comparable companies in the supermarket business, Morgan Stanley thought that, with better management, the business could thrive again. The next step was to look at the financials and highlight areas for improvement. The team took a three-pronged approach: change its pricing strategy, improve its technology, and reconnect with its customers.

At the time, Tops was trying to compete against two very different competitors: Walmart, a low-end, big-box chain, and Wegmans, a regional, high-end grocery chain. Competing with Walmart on pricing was an impossible feat. So early on, the team decided to position Tops between the two. This would mean adopting a more traditional, high-low supermarket model, which entails pricing common items such as bread at a competitive price and then pricing other merchandise at a higher one. The team thought this pricing model would be a key to Tops's success.

Curci noticed right away that Tops seemed to have lost its connection to its customers. For example, many Tops stores are located in the Buffalo area of western New York, the birthplace of buffalo wings (deep-fried chicken wings). Curci noticed that the wings were conspicuously absent from the stores. He thought this pointed to a much larger oversight of a basic retailing rule: give the customers what they want. It also reinforced the need for a better technology system. The old system meant that the previous management team was unable to respond to customer needs and inventory changes. With an assist from new point-of-sale technology, Tops began to cater more to the local customers, many on tight budgets. It replaced all the gourmet food with more basic staples. With this in mind, Curci left the merchandising decisions to the managers at individual stores, after Morgan Stanley put them all through an extensive capital expenditure program. This step was crucial in positioning Tops between Walmart and Wegmans because it allowed managers to respond more quickly to local demands and fluctuations.

In order to fulfill its plan for selling Tops, the team calculated that it would have to increase its leverage by taking on more debt, which would have raised the debt of Tops to 96 percent of assets. This much leverage was unusual and potentially risky for Morgan Stanley. But after much analysis, working closely with the management team, and hiring a consultant to gauge whether the company could thrive at that debt level, Morgan Stanley decided to proceed. One thing that made the decision easier was that, due to quick inventory turnover, supermarkets are very capable of generating cash flows.

After increasing its leverage, 30 million shares remained. Since the top managers had done so well in turning the company around, Morgan Stanley gave them the opportunity to buy in. In the end, Morgan Stanley made about 3.1 times its original investment, the management team at Tops was able to independently operate its stores, and Tops thrived through the transaction.

Quiz

Please note that some questions may have more than one answer.

1. **You are the manager of a hedge fund and believe that General Motors (GM) is going to do really well next year. Specifically, you are certain that GM is going to outperform Ford Motor Company, a rival car company, and you wish to set up a trade. Which of the following is an investment strategy that will make money if you are right?**
   A. Long GM, short Ford
   B. Long GM, long Ford
   C. Short GM, long Ford
   D. Short GM, short Ford

2. **What is the main benefit of diversification?**

   A. It increases the amount of risk in your portfolio, relative to the amount of return.

   B. It decreases the amount of risk in your portfolio, relative to the amount of return.

   C. It increases the amount of risk and return for your portfolio.

   D. It decreases the number of stocks in your portfolio.

3. **When companies report earnings that are only a few cents below their previous estimates, why do their stock prices go down by so much?**

   A. Even a few pennies can make a huge difference when multiplied over millions of shares.

   B. Accounting earnings are inaccurate.

   C. Such an earnings miss indicates the possibility of a future dilution.

   D. Investors can't be certain if the company failed to meet its estimates because of coincidence or bad luck, or if the missed estimate is a signal that management is obscuring deeper problems.

4. **You are excited about an investment opportunity in Dow Chemical, a multinational chemical corporation, because it is undervalued relative to peers. Which of** the following companies should you short to better capture the potential outperformance of Dow?

   A. Bayer, a multinational chemical and pharmaceutical company

   B. British Airways, an airline

   C. Consolidated Edison, a power company supplying electricity to the New York City region

   D. Not any one particular company; you would want to diversify to gain an advantage

5. **Which of the following is an example of a bad incentive?**

   A. Investors want to make money so they invest in companies that are doing well.

   B. Analysts are afraid to recommend "sell" for a company's stock because that company may not do business with their employer in the future.

   C. CEOs take large risks with their companies, because a great deal of their personal wealth is tied up in stock options.

   D. Pension funds invest in high-quality companies because they want to take care of their retirees.

6. **Most equity research analysts are employed by (and receive their paychecks from):**

   A. Individual households

   B. Industrial companies

C. A sell-side firm

D. The media

7. **Which of the following are possible consequences of the usual compensation model and industrial structure for equity analysts? (Choose all that apply.)**

   A. Analysts will work hard to provide accurate valuations for companies.

   B. High-ranking analysts may "herd" by choosing valuations similar to other analysts to protect their position in the rankings.

   C. Analysts will always recommend "sell" in order to gain profits from selling short.

   D. Low-ranked analysts may make outlandish and contrary predictions, hoping that a lucky break will propel them to the top of the rankings.

8. **In 2012, Facebook conducted its initial public offering and sold 421 million shares to the public for the first time. Which player in the capital markets helped it sell these shares?**

   A. Analysts

   B. The buy side

   C. The sell side

   D. The media

9. **In 1989, the private equity firm KKR was involved in a famous $31 billion deal with RJR Nabisco. What does private equity do?**

   A. Invests in private pension funds on behalf of companies

   B. Buys companies, improves them, and then sells them to another private investor or the public markets

   C. Combines the private equity assets of thousands of investors and invests those assets in a broad portfolio of diversified assets

   D. Advises companies on private investors who may be interested in buying bonds from them

10. **In *Freakonomics*, authors Steven Levitt and Stephen Dubner note that professional realtors sell their own homes for 10 percent higher prices, on average, than comparable homes they sell for others. Which problem of capital markets might this be a manifestation of?**

    A. The buy side

    B. Board oversight

    C. Herding

    D. The principal-agent problem

Chapter Summary

I hope this whirlwind tour of the capital markets has demystified the complex world of institutional investors, analysts, and investment bankers for you. Many people see the world of finance that sits between savers and companies as a group of leeches subtracting value from the real economy. But capital markets are trying to solve, albeit imperfectly, the deep problem of capitalism—the principal-agent problem that arises when owners are no longer managers, and asymmetric information makes monitoring and communication difficult. As a result, it becomes clear that finance isn't really about money and cash. Ultimately, it's all about information and incentives.

With asymmetric information and principal-agent problems at the forefront of your mind, you can make more sense of Netflix's sharp stock price drop because of a small subscriber shortfall. Any unexpected departure from expectations can prove very costly because that departure can magnify investors' concerns about managers. And you can see that the battle between Nelson Peltz and PepsiCo's management is an effort by an activist shareholder to make sure that management is pursuing what's in the best interest of shareholders. However, Peltz has his own agenda that may not align perfectly with other shareholders, creating yet another incentive problem.

Now that we have examined the informational problem at the heart of capital markets, we can turn to an even bigger question: What is a company worth? We will next address how firms create value, how they are valued, and how they should make investment decisions based on their cost of capital.

4

Sources of Value Creation

Risk, costly capital, and the origins of value

n chapter 1, we discussed how creating value for share-holders is an important goal for managers. But what does it mean to "create" value? And how do you do it? Let's take a look at two extreme examples to better understand how value can be created or destroyed. For value creation, let's take a look at Apple's stock price performance for the last thirty years. (See figure 4-1.)

As you can see from the chart, Apple wasn't creating much value for its shareholders for the majority of its life as a public company. The company existed, but it might as well not have bothered; while expending a great deal of effort to compete with IBM and Microsoft, it was essentially treading water in terms of value creation.

Beginning in the early 2000s, things changed dramatically. Apple started creating value, and a great deal of it. Apple stock was worth more than $1 trillion by mid-2018. What changed? What did Apple do differently that changed its fortunes? The short answer is it created a new generation of products ranging from the iPod to the iPhone to the iPad. But the better question is, why did the inception of the iPhone cause Apple to create value when years of creating Macintosh computers did not?

What about the opposite—value destruction? For that, let's take a look at the stock price chart of Avon Products, a cosmetics company, from January 2009 through October 2018. (See figure 4-2).

FIGURE 4-1

Apple Inc.'s stock price, 1988–2018

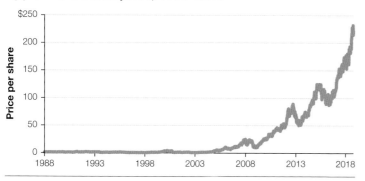

FIGURE 4-2

Avon Products Inc.'s stock price, January 2009–October 2018

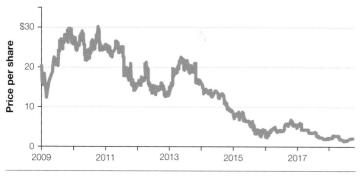

During the nine-year period, Avon lost 90 percent of its value. Why? Clearly, there were failures to innovate and to create a sustainable business model. But how can a company lose so much value so quickly?

These two examples of extreme value creation and destruction provide two lessons. First, value creation is neither simple nor straightforward. Second—and this is the brutal truth—finance is hard, and sometimes the best equity analysts and investors get it wrong. Avon was significantly overvalued for many years and, as investors realized their mistake, the price fell to reflect its more accurate value.

In this chapter, we're going to take a closer look at how companies can create and maximize value. In particular, the recipe for value creation hinges on the idea of costly capital. As stewards of the capital entrusted to them by equity and debt holders, managers must consider the cost of that capital, even if that cost is not explicit. In effect, the returns demanded by capital providers become the costs of capital for managers. Finally, we need to settle on a way to define and measure risk because the returns demanded by capital providers will be a function of the risk these providers of capital bear.

By the end of this chapter, we'll be ready to combine the ideas about free cash flow from chapter 2 with the ideas of costs of capital, expected returns, and risk from this chapter to undertake the process of valuation. In some ways, this chapter is the toughest one in this book, but if you emerge from it with the core intuitions provided in the figures, then you're winning.

How Is Value Created?

Our first measure of value creation compares a company's book value and its market value via the market-to-book ratio. Book value is simply an accounting of the capital that shareholders have invested in a company, whereas market value measures how much a company is worth according to the financial markets—and, as we saw in chapter 2, market values are a forward-looking assessment of the value of a company.

Since book values are derived from accounting-based balance sheets and solely focus on the dollars invested in a company, they provide an incomplete picture of value. For example, take a look at table 4-1 for Facebook's balance sheet at the end of 2017 based on book values and market values.

While the market value of Facebook's equity is $512.8 billion, its book value is much lower, $74.3 billion. This yields a market-to-book ratio of 6.9. Given that market values emphasize future cash flows (see chapter 2), the market thinks highly of Facebook's prospects and its ability to create value.

We're going to do a few exercises to puzzle through the sources of value creation, as we did with financial analysis in chapter 1. Like that exercise, these may be tough but have a considerable payoff.

TABLE 4-1

Facebook's balance sheets, 2017 ($ billions)

Accounting balance sheet

Assets		Liabilities and shareholders' equity	
Cash	$41.7	Operating liabilities	$10.2
Operating assets	$42.8	Shareholders' equity	$74.3
Total	**$84.5**	**Total**	**$84.5**

Market value balance sheet

Assets		Liabilities and shareholders' equity	
Cash	$41.7		
Enterprise value	$471.1	Shareholders' equity	$512.8
Total	**$512.8**	**Total**	**$512.8**

Let's consider a company that relies solely on equity financing:

- The firm has a book value of $100, as it has just been capitalized with $100.

- The return on equity is projected to be 20 percent.

- The company is expected to reinvest 50 percent of its profits in the company. These reinvestments represent growth opportunities and earn similar returns to its current return on equity (ROE).

- The company will end its operations after ten years, and anything that's left will be distributed to the shareholders. It will sell all of its assets for a onetime cash flow (assume it can do so at the book value of those assets at that time).

- Future cash flows will be discounted at a rate of 15 percent because shareholders expect a return of 15 percent.

So what should this company's market-to-book ratio be? That is, is the company creating value? To make things simpler and more concrete, is your intuition that the market-to-book ratio is greater than 1, equal to 1, or less than 1?

To determine its market-to-book ratio, we need to figure out its book value and its market value. The book value is $100 as given above. Its market value, however, requires forecasting and discounting future cash flows, as we saw in chapter 2. While there's a simpler way to figure this out, let's try a more roundabout way first.

Take that initial book value of $100, apply the 20 percent ROE, and then distribute half to shareholders and reinvest the other half in the company. Then apply the 15 percent discount rate to those dividends. Do this for the first year until the tenth year, when whatever is left in the company is liquidated and returned to the shareholders. (See table 4-2.)

In this particular case, today's market value, based on those expectations of what's going to happen in the future,

is greater than 100, which leads to a market-to-book ratio greater than 1.3.

Is there a simple way to conclude this without creating a full spreadsheet? To think this through, let's say the company's ROE drops from 20 percent to 15 percent and everything else stays the same. What would happen to the market-to-book ratio? Your instinct is likely that the ratio will go down given that a lower ROE is not as good for shareholders. But how far will it drop?

If you create a spreadsheet as in the previous example, you'll see that the market value will drop to 100, which is the same as its book value. To be clear, it drops to *exactly* 100; that is no coincidence. You might think that earning an ROE of 15 percent is quite good. But, in fact, the company has merely met expectations. This is the harsh logic of finance. If the ROE is the same as the cost of capital, nothing else matters—the company is not creating value. You could have stayed in bed.

This comparison teaches us that the *sine qua non* of value creation is beating the cost of capital. In the first example, equity is earning 20 percent, and shareholders are only discounting future cash flows by 15 percent. That simple comparison—expected returns on an investment versus the cost of capital—is all you need to know to think through whether or not a company is creating value.

Value Creation or Value Destruction?

Avon and Apple are pretty clear examples of value destruction and value creation, respectively. But what if the distinction is not so clear? How can we understand the data to be sure a firm is creating or destroying value?

Let's look at a less clear-cut case. The graphs show the stock price and return on capital for British Petroleum (BP) since 2000.

Is BP creating value? The stock price has increased from $20 to $46, so that's good, right? It must be creating value. Taking a closer look, that price increase took place entirely from 2003 to 2008, and the stock price has stagnated since then. So let's examine those periods separately.

Did BP create value from 2003 to 2008? There the answer is clear; it shows up where we'd expect it to be in its operations—in its return on capital. BP had a return on capital well over 10 percent and was significantly outperforming its cost of capital, thereby creating value—and this showed up in a rising stock price.

After 2008, BP's return on capital declined significantly to levels well below its cost of capital. That value destruction is apparent in the stagnant stock price. You might think that this has been neither bad nor good for BP shareholders (and maybe even good, if you consider that BP gave a 4 percent dividend), but that's not the right way to think about it. BP shareholders had expected higher returns when they bought those shares, given competing opportunities. BP didn't deliver those expected returns, so its shareholders suffered during this period by earning a return much lower than their expected returns. By failing to beat its cost of capital and thus failing to produce the expected return of its shareholders, BP provides an example of value destruction.

BP's stock price, 2000–2018

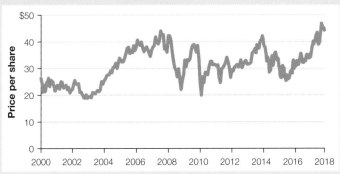

BP's annual return on capital, 2003–2017

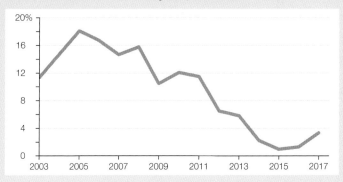

TABLE 4-2

Sources of value creation

Initial book value	$100.00	Discount rate	15%
ROE	20%	Earnings retention rate	50%

Year	Book value of shareholder investment	ROE achieved	Profit after tax	Earnings retention rate	Earnings retained	Cash returned to shareholder	Present value factor	Present value
1	$100.00	20%	$20.00	50%	$10.00	$10.00	0.87	$8.70
2	110.00	20	22.00	50	11.00	11.00	0.76	8.30
3	121.00	20	24.20	50	12.10	12.10	0.66	8.00
4	133.00	20	26.60	50	13.30	13.30	0.57	7.60
5	146.40	20	29.30	50	14.60	14.60	0.50	7.30
6	161.10	20	32.20	50	16.10	16.10	0.43	7.00
7	177.20	20	35.40	50	17.70	17.70	0.38	6.70
8	194.90	20	39.00	50	19.50	19.50	0.33	6.40
9	214.40	20	42.90	50	21.40	21.40	0.28	6.10
10	235.80	20	47.20	50	23.60	23.60	0.25	5.80
						259.40	**0.25**	**64.10**

Present/market value	$135.89
Market-to-book ratio	1.36

If the ROE were to drop even more, from 15 percent to 10 percent, the market value would dip below 100, making the market-to-book ratio less than 1. This is an even worse scenario. It means that the company is not providing returns commensurate with the capital providers' expectations and, as a consequence, is destroying value. You may feel that a 10 percent ROE is pretty good, but the company is returning less to capital providers than they demand given the risk they assumed. It's not just that you *could* have stayed in bed, but you *should* have stayed in bed.

What Else Matters in Value Creation?

The relationship between returns on investments and costs of capital isn't the only factor that will have an impact on the amount of value creation. Let's consider other factors. We'll vary the ROE (as we did before), the duration of the project, and the amount of profits reinvested in the business, but not the discount rate, which will stay fixed at 15 percent. How do you think ROEs, durations, and reinvestment rates will change market-to-book ratios, with other factors constant?

TABLE 4-3

Sources of value creation

Duration	Future return on book equity				
	10%	15%	20%	25%	
5 years 10 years 20 years 30 years					} 30% of earnings are reinvested
5 years 10 years 20 years 30 years					} 70% of earnings are reinvested
5 years 10 years 20 years 30 years					} 100% of earnings are reinvested

You might quickly surmise that higher ROEs will increase market-to-book ratios. But what happens as the hypothetical company lives for 30 years instead of 10 years? What happens as more and more earnings are reinvested? And is the effect of duration and reinvestment on market-to-book ratios a function of the ROE?

Table 4-3 is a blank table with different variations of ROEs, horizons, and reinvestment rates. Before you peek ahead, let's focus on the first panel—with a 30 percent reinvestment rate—and answer two questions: Where will the

highest and lowest market-to-book ratios be? Are there any situations when the ratio is exactly 1?

Table 4-4 provides the answers for the first panel. The highest market-to-book ratio is at the bottom right. The company would be earning its highest ROE, which would lead to higher market values, and it would be doing it for the longest period of time. High ROEs over a long time span: that's what makes market-to-book ratios and value creation significant.

It's tempting to guess that the smallest market-to-book ratio will be in upper left corner as that is the opposite circumstance. In fact, the smallest market-to-book ratio is in the lower left. In this scenario, the company's ROE doesn't beat its cost of capital (its discount rate), but despite this, the company persists for thirty years, resulting in a great deal of value destruction. Finally, look at the column in which the ROEs are 15 percent. No matter the time horizon, the market-to-book ratio will always be 1. A company could go on for five years or thirty years or a hundred years. It doesn't matter. Since its ROE is the same as its cost of capital, it's not going to create value, no matter how long it operates. Now let's return to the blank table in table 4-3 and consider the effects of varying reinvestment rates from 30 percent to 70 percent to 100 percent. Let's ask the same questions but for the whole table: Where will the highest and lowest market-to-book

TABLE 4-4

Sources of value creation

Duration	Future return on book equity				
	10%	15%	20%	25%	
5 years	0.8	1.0	1.2	1.4	} 30% of earnings are reinvested
10 years	0.7	1.0	1.3	1.7	
20 years	0.6	1.0	1.4	2.0	
30 years	0.6	1.0	1.5	2.2	

TABLE 4-5

Sources of value creation

Duration	Future return on book equity				
	10%	15%	20%	25%	
5 years	0.8	1.0	1.2	1.4	} 30% of earnings are reinvested
10 years	0.7	1.0	1.3	1.7	
20 years	0.6	1.0	1.4	2.0	
30 years	0.6	1.0	1.5	2.2	
5 years	0.8	1.0	1.2	1.5	} 70% of earnings are reinvested
10 years	0.7	1.0	1.4	2.0	
20 years	0.5	1.0	1.8	3.1	
30 years	0.4	1.0	2.2	4.6	
5 years	0.8	1.0	1.2	1.5	} 100% of earnings are reinvested
10 years	0.6	1.0	1.5	2.3	
20 years	0.4	1.0	2.3	5.3	
30 years	0.3	1.0	3.6	12.2	

ratios be? Are there any more situations when the ratio is exactly 1?

As table 4-5 reveals, the highest market-to-book ratio is in the bottom right corner of the entire table, and it's very large. The company is beating its cost of capital by a wide margin for thirty years, and it is reinvesting all those profits at this higher rate for the whole thirty years.

The worst scenario is at the bottom left. The company is destroying value because it's not meeting the cost of capital. It's doing so for a long period of time, thirty years, and it never distributes any money until the very end. So even more value is being destroyed when the company invests more profits at that relatively low rate of return.

Where are the rest of the 1.0s? Sure enough, the 15 percent ROE scenarios always give a 1.0 market-to-book ratio because the company is just meeting its cost of capital. It can keep cash inside or release it, and it can do so for many years or just a few; it just doesn't matter because value is being neither created or destroyed.

Three Ways to Create Value

This exercise provides finance's basic recipe for value creation. To create value, companies must do three things. First and foremost, they must beat their cost of capital. If they don't, nothing else matters. Second, they must beat their cost of capital for many years. And, third, they must reinvest additional

Real-World Perspectives

While it's one thing to see this play out in a spreadsheet, these measures of value creation are exactly what equity analysts like Alberto Moel, formerly of Bernstein, look at in the real world. Moel commented:

So if a company is generating excess returns on its capital, over a long period of time, you will see that in the shareholder return. Of course, over the short term, it is all over the place, but in the long term, that's the key. So if you find a company that has excess returns, meaning that it's generating more than its cost of capital consistently, or at least over many years, then you know that company will generate excess returns to the shareholder, so that's how we approach it.

profits at high rates through growth. These prescriptions also correspond to business strategy. Beating a cost of capital is all about creating a competitive advantage through innovation. Keeping the gap open between returns and costs of capital for longer periods is what barriers to entry, brands, and intellectual property protection are all about. Finally, reinvesting more profits is all about growing an opportunity through expansions, adjacencies, or integration.

A Deeper Dive into Costs of Capital

This exercise shows that the cost of capital is critical to value creation. Managers apply discount rates to penalize future cash flows, as we saw in chapter 2, because there is an opportunity cost to any investment. Those discount rates are often referred to as costs of capital because they refer to the penalties (costs) associated with deploying that capital. Where do those discount rates and costs of capital come from?

Recall that firms have two types of capital providers—lenders who provide debt capital and owners who provide equity capital. The key insight is that the costs of capital are a function of the returns that investors expect. In short, an investor's expected return becomes the cost of capital for managers. The costs of debt and equity will be different; equity is a residual claim with a variable return, whereas debt has a fixed return that has priority for repayment.

So where do these expected returns (that become costs of capital) come from? Providers of capital will measure the risk that they are exposed to and expect returns to compensate for that risk. The demand for additional returns to bear risk is a foundational idea in finance and relates to risk aversion. Would you prefer a sure $1 million or a 50/50 chance at

An Introduction to Risk and Return

Investors demand higher returns from companies that they consider to have greater risk, as we saw in chapter 2. Those demands for higher returns translate into higher costs of capital.

Investors, like most of us, are risk averse. It's human nature. As a consequence, if they are forced to bear risk, they will demand something in return. Think about labor markets. When people take jobs in riskier industries such as construction, they demand higher wages. That same thing is true in finance.

Consider four types of assets in which people can invest: obligations of the US government that mature

in thirty days, obligations of the US government that mature in thirty years, common stocks for small companies, and common stocks for large companies.

The table gives the annual average returns for those four asset classes, from 1926 to 2010, compiled from the Ibbotson *SBBI Yearbook*. Alongside the returns, a standard deviation of returns is listed. A standard deviation is a measure of the dispersion of returns around that average return. A zero standard deviation would indicate that each year had exactly the average return. Higher standard deviations correspond to more variable returns.

One helpful rule of thumb is that two-thirds of observations will fall within one standard deviation of the average. For example, the average adult height in your town might be five feet six inches, and the standard deviation might be four inches. In this example, two-thirds of the adults would be between five feet two inches and five feet ten inches.

The table indicates that on average, investors will earn 9.9 percent on large company common stocks, and in two of three years, their return will fall between −10.5 percent and 30.3 percent (that's 9.9 ± 20.4 percent). Contrast that with government bonds, where

$0 or $2 million? While it's tempting to think otherwise, if this were a real situation, most of us would choose $1 million, which shows a preference for a certain amount relative to a probability-weighted amount.

But how do we actually operationalize the idea of cost of capital? How do we measure the appropriate amount to charge for risk? These questions lead us to some of the most elegant ideas in all of finance.

Returns for four asset classes, 1926–2010

Asset class	Annual average return	Annual average standard deviation
Short-term government bills (30 days)	3.6%	3.1%
Long-term government bonds (30 years)	5.5	9.5
Common stocks (large companies)	9.9	20.4
Common stocks (small companies)	12.1	32.6

Source: SBBI Yearbook.

In order to measure the reward for bearing risk, investors often divide the returns of an asset class by the associated standard deviation. In other words, this ratio enables investors to determine how much return they receive per unit of risk. This measure is called the Sharpe ratio, one of the key ways investors measure risk. As seen in the table, long-term government bonds have a Sharpe ratio of 0.58 (5.5 percent/9.5 percent), whereas common stocks from small companies have a Sharpe ratio of 0.37 (12.1 percent/32.6 percent).

investors will earn an average return of 5.5 percent, and in two or three years, the return will be between −4.0 percent and 15 percent.

As this table demonstrates, returns are related to the risk a given investor bears. In particular, equities give a higher return, but they also make you bear more risk because returns can fluctuate greatly; returns may be very high one year, and very low or negative in another year.

The Weighted Average Cost of Capital

The weighted average cost of capital, or WACC, is the most common way to discount future cash flows but is also one of those mysterious phrases that people in finance like to throw around to intimidate others. But it's really quite transparent if we break it down and use pictures to think it through. The phrase implies multiple sources of capital, and we know there are two types of capital that must be associated with two different costs: the cost of debt and the cost of equity. We can't simply add them but should average them to account for their relative proportions.

The formula for a WACC features the two costs of capital, two weights to account for their relative proportion, and a tax term.

Weighted Average Cost of Capital

$$\text{WACC} = \left(\frac{D}{D+E}\right)r_D\,(1-t) + \left(\frac{E}{D+E}\right)r_E$$

r_D = cost of debt

r_E = cost of equity

D = market value of the firm's debt

E = market value of the firm's equity

$D+E$ = total market value of the firm's financing (equity and debt)

t = corporate tax rate

The costs of debt and equity are their expected returns. For now, simply think about the weights as a share of the total financing needs that come from debt and equity.

The tax term requires a little more explanation. Interest payments are typically deductible expenses that can lower a firm's tax payments. In effect, these interest payments shield a company from paying more taxes and are known as "tax shields." How much benefit the interest payments provide because of their deductibility depends on the tax rate. If tax rates are high, the ability to deduct interest payments is very valuable. If the tax rate is 40 percent, and a company has to pay $10 in interest payments, how much does it actually cost to pay $10? The company is out $10, but its pretax income is lower by $10, and that lowers their tax bill by $4, so the true cost is $6.

The actual calculation of a WACC is straightforward. If 20 percent of a company's financing is debt that costs 10 percent, 80 percent of its financing is equity that costs 20 percent, and the tax rate is 10 percent, calculating the WACC of 17.8 percent is fairly simple.

The deeper questions are: Where do the weights come from? Where do those costs of debt and equity come from? If equity is a residual claim, how can you capture the cost of equity? Which is more expensive—debt or equity? We're going to construct a WACC because it builds important finance intuitions, and the idea of WACC is best demystified by having to actually do it.

The cost of debt

Determining the cost of debt is the most straightforward element of this calculation. Because debt has a fixed return, the cost of capital is simply the interest rate that a lender will charge you when you are undertaking a project.

Real-World Perspectives

Once again, these calculations aren't just theory. Heineken CFO Laurence Debroux looks at her cost of capital every day:

In explaining cost of capital, you have to come back to a single concept. In order to build your business, you use money. Who is lending or investing this money with you? You have shareholders and banks or bondholders; you need to give a fair remuneration to all those people. And depending on the structure of your capital, of your financing, then you have an average cost of capital, which is basically what it costs you to be in business; this is very sound. No one would invest their own money to get an unreasonable return. It is very sound to give those stakeholders a return that they are expecting.

To arrive at an interest rate, a bank will examine the riskiness of the underlying business, the stability of its cash flows, and its credit rating. Then, it'll charge an interest rate commensurate with that risk. (Technically, that interest rate is the *promised* return and there is a probability that the issuer will default, meaning that the expected return is slightly lower.)

That interest rate has two components that correspond to the reasons we penalize cash flows for making us wait:

$$r_D = r_{\text{risk-free}} + \text{credit spread}$$

where $r_D = \text{cost of debt}$ and $r_{\text{risk-free}} = \text{risk-free rate}$

The risk-free rate. Investors will demand, at a minimum, the rate on a risk-free investment; this idea of a risk-free investment is approximated by the interest rate on government securities such as US Treasury bonds. At a minimum, the logic goes, any risky project should provide what we demand from a risk-free asset. Why do investors charge a cost of capital in the absence of risk? We as investors don't just dislike risk; we also like things now rather than later, and we need compensation for delaying the enjoyment of our wealth. More specifically, we prefer money now rather than later because we are impatient and we want to be compensated for any expected inflation because that inflation will reduce our purchasing power.

Credit spreads. A credit spread reflects the additional cost associated with the riskiness of the debt. As you might expect, riskier companies feature higher credit spreads. In mid-2018, US Treasurys with a maturity of ten years were yielding (i.e., providing a return of) 2.96 percent. At that time, Walmart, an AA-rated company (the typical rating system begins with AAA (close to risk-free) and descends to A, to BBB and then B, and then to CCC and C), issued $16 billion of debt to finance its acquisition of Flipkart in India and paid an interest rate of 3.55 percent, implying a credit

Yield Curves

Costs of debt comprise the risk-free rate plus a risk premium for credit risk. Rates are also influenced by the amount of time until the bond will be paid, also known as the bond's maturity date. We can visualize these effects through the yield curves shown in the figure.

The curves plot interest rates for various bond maturities, from very short-term debt to bonds reaching decades into the future. The horizontal axis shows the time between now and the bond's maturity date. The scaling is not uniform; the vertical axis shows the corresponding interest rate.

First, notice that the yield curve normally slopes upward. Longer-term debt typically, but not always, needs to offer a higher interest rate than short-term bonds. Why? In part, the steepness of the yield curve reflects expectations of future interest rates. A steep curve reflects that future interest rates are expected to be higher and longer-term bonds must compensate investors for fixing their interest rates for a longer period. Future interest rates might be expected to be higher because of future growth or inflation expectations. Second, notice the difference between the treasury rates and the corporate AAA and CCC bonds, whose yield curves lie above the treasury curve. This is the result of the risk premium increasing the cost of the debt, as discussed earlier.

Bond yield curves change constantly in response to market expectations about the future. Traders often speculate about changes in the curve, from shifts of the full curve higher or lower, to changes in the slope of the curve, to changes in the convexity (the amount by which the curve bends).

Yield curves for bonds with varying risk and maturities, July 30, 2018

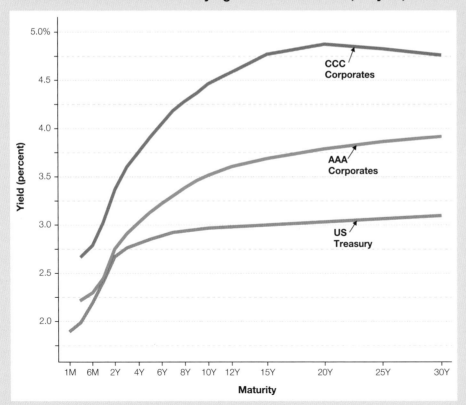

Debt and Financial Distress

The likelihood of, and the costs associated with, financial distress are two factors that limit how much debt a firm should take on. Firms can lose between 10 percent and 23 percent of their value prior to bankruptcy as a result of unexpected cuts in capital expenditures, undesired asset sales, and costly managerial myopia. Bankruptcies induced by financial distress can be extremely costly; as one example, the fees associated with Lehman Brothers' bankruptcy exceeded $2 billion.

Let's look at three companies: NextEra Energy Resources, a wholesale electricity supplier based in Florida; AbbVie, a mature pharmaceutical company; and TripAdvisor, a young travel website company. Which one do you think has the most leverage, which has the least, and which is in between?

Energy companies like NextEra have stable, predictable cash flows and worry less about a sudden change causing financial distress. You might think that the pharmaceutical industry is risky—and it is—but more mature companies have patents and stable cash flows. Internet companies like TripAdvisor operate in an environment with less stable cash flows, so both the likelihood and costs of financial distress are much larger.

AbbVie has a higher amount of debt, but it's useful to remember what we went over regarding Merck and Pfizer in chapter 1: companies in the pharmaceutical industry, in general, have been increasing the amount of debt they have on their books. This likely means that they consider the likelihood and costs of financial distress to be diminishing, an indication that perhaps this industry is taking fewer risks and producing more stable cash flows.

spread of 0.59 percent. At the same time, CVS, a BBB company, issued debt to finance its acquisition of Aetna with an interest rate of 4.33 percent, implying a credit spread of 1.37 percent. Cequel Communications, a cable company, issued CCC debt at 7.5 percent, implying a credit spread of 4.54 percent. That's a pretty straightforward relationship between risk and return.

Optimal capital structure

The relative use of debt and equity in a company is referred to as its capital structure. The right capital structure varies by industry and by the relative riskiness of those industries (as we saw in chapter 1 with Carolina Power & Light vs. Intel). Regulated monopolies like power companies often

FIGURE 4-3

Optimal capital structure

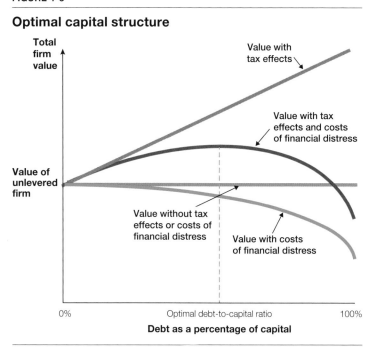

This figure depicts the relationship between capital structure and overall firm value. As the relative use of debt increases, what happens to firm value? The first insight from the blue line is that, ignoring the effects of taxation and the costs of failure, all value comes from the real operations of a firm, so value should be invariant to capital structure. This assessment is an important starting point, as it's a reminder that the deployment of assets—not financial engineering—is the source of all real value creation. But it also suggests that capital structure doesn't matter.

As noted previously, because they are deductible, interest payments allow you to shield income from taxation. As you take on more debt relative to equity, you shield more income from the government, and value increases, as shown by the orange line. Indeed, it would make sense to use all debt and no equity because with every additional dollar of debt, you are saving more money with taxes.

Now let's consider the effects of too much leverage on business operations. If you've ever been in a company that's gone bankrupt or approached bankruptcy, you know that it incurs significant operational costs. Customers leave, employees leave, and financing becomes more of a strain. So, as leverage goes up, it's more likely that firms will experience these operational costs and value will decrease, often very quickly given the precarious status of the firm. And the way these

have capital structures heavily weighted toward debt because of their steady cash flows; high-risk companies with unpredictable futures are weighted toward equity.

One way to envision the decision about capital structure is to consider the offsetting incentives to use debt based on taxation and the costs and probabilities of failure. The theory of optimal capital structure, as depicted in figure 4-3, tries to do that by first counterintuitively ignoring these effects and then layering them on.

Capital Structure across Countries

If you look at three companies in different parts of the world—say, NextEra, an energy company in the United States; Tractebel Energia, one of the largest electricity companies in Brazil; and Electric Ireland, an electricity company in Ireland—you won't see the same capital structure in each country.

Different countries have different tax rates, which influence the attractiveness of their debt. Additionally, the stability of cash flows to the businesses in these countries may be different, which will affect the costs and likelihood of financial distress. Companies need to consider the local conditions of the country they are in and balance the tax benefits of debt with the risks of financial distress in order to determine their optimal capital structure.

costs begin destroying value, shown by the green line, will vary by the nature of the business. Very stable businesses won't incur those costs until they're at really high levels of leverage. In contrast, very risky businesses could incur costs of financial distress early on.

When we combine tax effects with the costs of financial distress with the red line, it becomes clear that weighing the tax benefits relative to the costs of financial distress will provide the value-maximizing capital structure. By implication, firms from different industries will have different capital structures that reflect a trade-off between tax benefits and the costs of financial distress associated with that underlying industry. That optimal capital structure for a given industry will provide the weights for costs of equity and debt we'll use in the WACC calculation.

The cost of equity

Isolating the cost of equity is a little harder. We can't just ask equity holders for the return they'd like as we did with debt—most equity investors would only answer, "a lot." If we can't actually ask equity holders what their expected return is, how do we figure it out? Fortunately, there's an elegant Nobel Prize–winning theory that contains many important intuitions to help us think through the cost of equity—the capital asset pricing model. This model follows the same logic as the cost of debt: a risk-free rate plus a risk premium. The amount equity investors charge for risk has two components: the quantity of risk of a given stock and the price of that risk. But how do we think about risk in this setting? Indeed, what is risk?

Myths About Costs of Equity

Two important myths are often repeated when people talk about costs of equity. One is that equity is relatively cheap compared to debt. That myth goes like this: "Well, if I don't pay my debt holders, I go bankrupt. That's expensive. If I don't pay my equity holders, nothing happens. So equity is cheap." The second, related myth says that equity is free: "I don't have to give equity holders anything, so the cost of equity is zero."

Those two myths, while remarkably pervasive, are wrong because they don't manifest some central intuitions on the relationship between risk and return. Which is riskier, equity or debt? When a company fails, debt holders get paid first and equity holders may get nothing. So equity holders are in a considerably riskier position. As a consequence of being in a riskier position, they're going to demand a higher return, and it certainly won't be zero. That's the underlying intuition of the relationship between risk and return.

What is risk? If you had to come up with a way to measure the risk of holding a given stock, what would it be? If you had all the data in the world, what would you try to isolate to figure out how much risk a given company exposes you to? You might think that the amount a company's stock moves around—its variability—would be a great measure of risk. As seen in the box, "Value Creation or Value Destruction?" BP's stock price performance moves around a great deal and you can measure how much it moves around—its volatility. If a stock is highly volatile and therefore creating a lot of uncertainty, then you would demand a higher rate of return. This intuition seems correct but overlooks an important insight that leads to a completely different answer.

As discussed in chapter 2, diversification provides a powerful way to manage risks because as you diversify, you can maintain expected returns and reduce risk—the only free lunch in finance. If investors hold diversified portfolios, the volatility of any one given stock doesn't matter that much because much of that volatility gets washed away in the portfolio. As figure 4-4 shows, as you add more securities to a portfolio, the overall volatility of the portfolio decreases. But there is a level above which the gains from diversification diminish. Most important, there is some volatility you can never fully diversify away; it is called systematic risk or the risk of holding the market.

Because so much of a given stock's variability goes away within the context of a portfolio, we need only think about the

FIGURE 4-4

The power of diversification

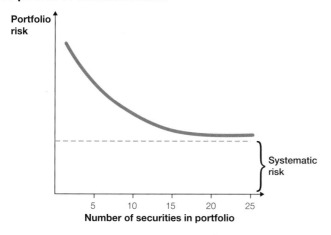

FIGURE 4-5

Sample beta graph

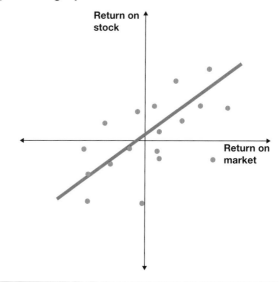

risk that doesn't disappear—the systematic risk. So every security's risk is not measured by how much it moves around in general but rather by how much each stock moves with the market, which represents the risk that will never be diversified away.

The measure of how a stock moves with the market is called a beta. More precisely, if a company has a beta of 1, it generally moves in sync with the market; if the market goes up by 10 percent, then the company's stock is likely to go up by 10 percent. If the company has a beta of 2 and the market goes up by 10 percent, then the company's stock goes up by 20 percent. If a company has a beta of negative 1 and the

market goes up by 10 percent, then the stock will go down by 10 percent. That's what a beta is meant to capture: If the market goes up or down, how will the stock do?

Calculating betas. A beta is surprisingly simple to calculate. Take a look at figure 4-5, which plots the monthly returns for a given company against the monthly returns for the market.

Every dot in the figure corresponds to a month and the associated returns for the market and the company during that month. Looking at the graph, where can you find the beta? Remember that a beta measures the correlation between a given company's returns and the market's returns. If you simply draw a line that best fits the data—also known as a regression—the slope of that line is going to capture what a beta is: literally how the company co-moves with the market.

Let's take two well-known companies—the insurance company AIG and food retailer Yum! Brands, discussed in chapter 1—and try to find betas for them. The data in figures 4-6 and 4-7 use monthly returns for both companies from January 2010 through July 2018, as compared to monthly returns for the S&P 500 during the same period.

AIG's equity beta is around 1.65, while Yum!'s is around 0.67. Why are the two betas so different? It helps to remember what beta is measuring—correlation with the overall market.

FIGURE 4-6

AIG's beta, December 2009–July 2018

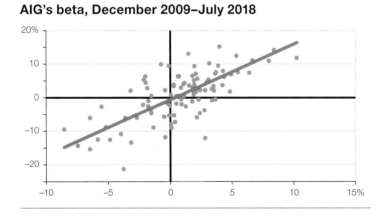

FIGURE 4-7

Yum! Brands' beta, December 2009–July 2018

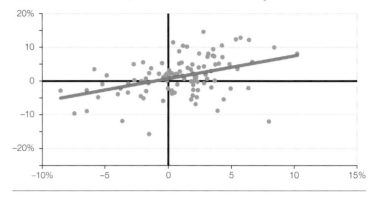

Yum!'s restaurants—KFC and Taco Bell—sell relatively inexpensive food. Even in the worst recession, people will likely still eat there, but they may be more cost-conscious and frugal. When things get better and people have more money, they may order more there, but they may also upgrade from fast food to casual dining. So Yum! is fairly insulated from the variability of the economy.

AIG, on the other hand, provides insurance to companies to help them manage their financial risks. When times are bad, it often has many claims it needs to pay out, reducing its profits. In good times, it receives premiums paired with fewer claims and does much better. AIG's investment of premiums paid performs better. As a result, AIG is more tightly bound to market performance.

Now that you have an idea of what a beta is and where it comes from, let's look at some industry-level betas. (See table 4-6.) Thinking about this at the industry level allows us to abstract from some of the variation at every given company.

Some of these industries have betas that are relatively high—higher than 1.0—which means that they move more than the market. Typically, cyclical industries look like this.

The intuition behind betas.

The central intuition behind betas relates to insurance. High-beta companies expose shareholders to larger amounts of systematic risk that they can't diversify away. Because of this, investors charge them a higher cost of equity. As a consequence, these firms have a higher weighted average cost of capital. And as a consequence of that, their values will be lower. That last step is the trickiest—if you apply high discount rates, what happens to present values? They become lower, so a high beta leads to a high cost of equity that leads to a high WACC that leads to lower values.

For a negative beta company, the costs of equity are going to be low. They might even be negative, which means that their WACC will be lower, which means their values will be higher. When the market goes up, this asset will perform poorly. When the market does poorly, this asset will do really well. Negative beta assets are special because when the world falls apart, they really deliver for you. As a consequence, you

TABLE 4-6

Betas for various industries

Industry	Industry beta
Food and staples retailing	0.6
Utilities	0.6
Household and personal products	0.7
Consumer staples	0.8
Food, beverage, and tobacco	0.8
Health care	0.8
Health care equipment and services	0.8
Transportation	0.9
Consumer services	0.9
Pharmaceuticals, biotechnology, and life sciences	0.9
Banks	0.9
Insurance	0.9
Telecommunication services	0.9
Industrials	1.0
Commercial and professional services	1.0
Consumer discretionary	1.0
Media	1.0
Financials	1.0
Real estate	1.0
Information technology	1.0
Software and services	1.0
Materials	1.1
Capital goods	1.1
Automobiles and components	1.1
Consumer durables and apparel	1.1
Technology hardware and equipment	1.1
Semiconductor and semiconductor equipment	1.1
Diversified financials	1.2
Energy	1.4

Source: Duff & Phelps, *2015 International Valuation Handbook: Industry Cost of Capital* (Hoboken, NJ: Wiley Business, 2015).

don't demand much of a return from them, and that leads to high values.

In this sense, much of the capital asset pricing model (CAPM) is about insurance. You love the assets that move against the market because they provide you with insurance. And, if you're risk averse, that's a valuable thing. Figure 4-8 plots the annual returns for gold compared to the annual returns for the S&P 500 stock index, from 1988 to 2015. Remember, the beta is the slope of the line. Notice how the slope of the line is negative, unlike the slope of the line for AIG and Yum! Part of the attraction of investing in gold is that when the world falls apart, the gold (hopefully) will be there for you, and that insurance is valuable and would lead you to ask for low or negative returns.

The price of risk. Now that we can measure the quantity of risk associated with a company by using a beta, we need to combine the quantity of risk with a price of risk to figure out the cost of equity. That price of risk is also known as a market risk premium.

People calculate this in different ways, but here's one calculation that shows how we can think about the price of risk. Let's consider the historic outperformance of equities versus a risk-free instrument like treasury bonds. As the table in the box "An Introduction to Risk and Return"

FIGURE 4-8

Comparison of annual returns for gold versus S&P 500, 1988–2015

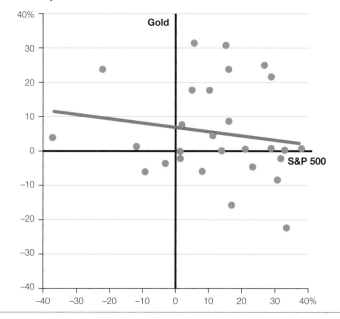

demonstrates, equities outperform safe securities like government treasuries by a fair margin.

If equities outperform risk-free instruments by 6 percent on average, that must be the compensation to investors for exposure to that risk of the market. In effect, that outperformance is the price of risk—the compensation people demand for bearing equity risk—also known as the market risk premium.

CAPM and the cost of equity

When we put together the ideas of the price of risk and the quantity of risk, we get an equation for the cost of equity.

Capital Asset Pricing Model

$$r_e = r_{\text{risk-free}} + \text{beta} \times \text{market risk premium}$$

where r_e = cost of equity and $r_{\text{risk-free}}$ = risk-free rate

What can we discern from the cost of equity equation? First, at a minimum, investors will demand at least the risk-free rate or the amount that you charge when you lend money to the government. Second, there has to be some notion of a risk adjustment that will be composed of the quantity of risk and the price of risk. To measure the quantity of risk, you do not use volatility, as you might think. Because of the power of diversification and the free lunch it provides, you're going to be concerned primarily with correlations, or betas. That, in combination with the price of risk, gives you the expected return for a given industry or company and, as a consequence, the cost of equity for those companies.

Let's generate the cost of equity for the two companies under discussion: AIG and Yum! We'll make some broad assumptions about the risk-free rate and the market risk pre-mium: specifically, that the risk-free rate is 4 percent and the market risk premium is 7 percent. In this case, AIG has a cost of equity of $4\% + 1.65 \times 7\% = 15.55\%$, while Yum! has a cost of equity of $4\% + 0.67 \times 7\% = 8.69\%$.

It's important to recall that these costs of equity are also the expected returns to the investors, which allows us to think about the essence of investment management. Figure 4-9 graphs the equation for expected returns of equity. As betas increase, expected returns increase. Note that zero beta assets have an expected return equal to the risk-free rate. Active investment management is all about pursuing assets that deviate from the line and deliver more than the expected return. This gap is called *alpha*. Alpha is the source of value creation, as isolating it means you're delivering greater-than-expected returns just as in the exercise at the beginning of chapter 1.

While the CAPM is a really powerful theory, it's also predicated on several assumptions that don't always hold. For example, it assumes no transaction costs and investors that are able to borrow and lend at relatively low rates, and many of these assumptions are inconsistent with reality. Most important, the theory relies on the idea that investors are highly rational—an assumption that has proven tenuous. Most concerning, it does not always appear that realized returns line up with betas as suggested by figure 4-9. While the capital asset

FIGURE 4-9

The security market line

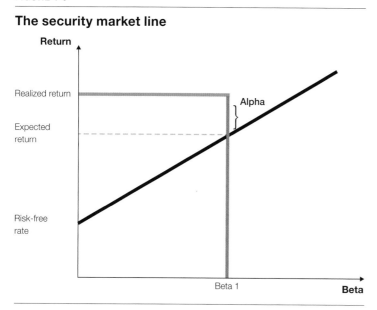

pricing model is hotly debated, it remains the cornerstone of the cost of equity and is a dominant framework for the investment management world.

Common Mistakes with WACC

Now that we have thought through the intuitions behind the weights, the tax term, and the costs of debt and equity, we can now use the WACC to value investments. In effect, the discount rate emphasized in chapter 2 will be the WACC as we move forward. The intuition for WACC is slippery, so it's useful to think through three common misconceptions about costs of capital in order to build our intuition further.

Using the same cost of capital for all investments

The first big mistake managers make is to use the same cost of capital for all the projects they invest in. The logic usually goes something like this: "Well, my capital providers have expected returns, so the cost of capital, *no matter what I invest in*, has to be the same for all my investment projects."

This logic is powerful, but it's wrong. Imagine a conglomerate that invests in different industries. Should it use the same cost of capital across those different industries? All those various industries and investments expose their capital providers to different risks, so every industry requires a different cost of capital. To see why, consider what would happen if a firm used the same cost of capital for all its divisions.

Imagine that a conglomerate invests in three different industries—aerospace, health-care, and media—with three different betas. If you use one cost of capital—let's say the average cost of capital—across multiple divisions with different betas, what mistakes will you make? Which divisions will you overinvest in and which industries will you underinvest in? (See figure 4-10.)

FIGURE 4-10

The cost of capital and betas in three industries

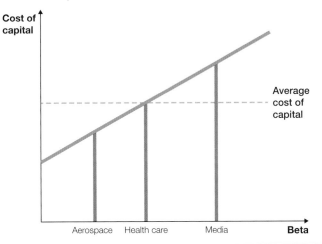

ital isn't a function of *who* is investing but rather a function of *what* you're investing in. Risk is embedded in the asset, not the investor.

Lowering your WACC by using more debt

Another appealing, but incorrect, intuition is that a company can lower its WACC by using more debt, given that debt has a lower cost than equity. The thinking usually goes like this: "Debt is typically cheaper, and with a tax advantage, even more so. So if I just use more debt, I'll reduce my WACC and, as a result, I'll end up having a higher value."

That's wrong. There is no free lunch here. If a company is at the optimal capital structure described above, it can't simply take on more debt because it's cheaper and think that's smart. Equity holders will demand a higher return for that risk, and that will actually offset any benefit from using more debt.

Figure 4-11—the most difficult figure in this book—will help you see that WACCs can't simply be lowered by taking on more debt. The figure shows what happens to betas on the vertical axis as the amount of debt used increases on the horizontal axis. One key difference from what we've seen previously is that there are three types of betas on the graph: equity betas, debt betas, and asset betas.

What mistakes will you make when investing in the media industry? In that situation, the correct cost of capital is actually higher than what you're using if you have the same one for all investments. As a consequence, you give too much credit to projects in that industry, so you end up overinvesting in those businesses. Similarly, for aerospace, the cost of capital you should use is lower than the one to use if you have the same one for all industries. As a consequence, you're penalizing those investment opportunities too much and end up underinvesting.

One final way to understand this intuition is "it's not about you"—the hardest lesson in life. The appropriate cost of cap-

FIGURE 4-11

Asset betas, debt betas, and equity betas as a function of leverage

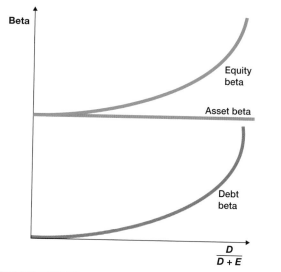

Remember that a beta is a measure of the correlation between an instrument's returns and the market's. First, let's think about the asset beta, which measures how the operating assets co-move with the market's returns. How does an asset beta change as you use more debt? The answer is that it doesn't change. The behavior of the assets relative to the market doesn't change as financing changes. This is similar to the intuition for the flat line in figure 4-3. What do you think happens to debt betas and equity betas as a company increases its reliance on debt? To think this through,

consider the extremes: What happens when the firm is fully equity-financed? What about when it uses very little equity? To consider this further, anchor your thinking in the beta of the business—the asset beta as well.

The orange curve represents what we think of as debt betas. When a company takes on that first dollar of debt, it's relatively risk-free, so debt betas are close to 0. As a company approaches complete debt financing, debt betas approach the level of asset betas as the company is entirely debt-financed. The final piece is, what do equity betas look like? When there's no debt or very little debt, equity betas look a lot like asset betas. And what happens as leverage increases? Equity betas shoot up as the equity has become more risky and therefore more expensive.

This is the core idea in figure 4-11. A company at its optimal capital structure can't simply switch from equity to debt and expect its cost of capital to go down. Why? Equity holders will penalize the company by raising their expected return, thereby undoing the benefits of using more debt.

Exporting WACC

The final mistake managers make is thinking that they can add value by buying another company and applying their WACC to its cash flows. Here's how their thinking works: "I'm bidding for an asset. Another company is also bidding

Real-World Perspectives

Corporate CFOs try to be very clear about what they consider their optimal capital structure and try to credibly return to it when circumstances change. Laurence Debroux, CFO of Heineken, commented:

At Heineken, we have promised ourselves and the rating agencies publicly that our net-debt-to-EBITDA ratio has to be 2.5, and whatever we do, we need to be able to bring it back to 2.5 in a short time. This has the merit of being clear, so when people invest in Heineken, they know what they're getting. They're not getting massive share buybacks and large debt. They also know that there is a margin and some room to maneuver in terms of acquisitions if something can actually be a good acquisition to increase the portfolio.

for an asset. I've got a lower cost of capital than they do because of my businesses. I'm going to be able to get this deal done and actually win the bid because I'll be using my cost of capital, which is lower than theirs."

The right cost of capital has nothing to do with the company or the alternative bidder. The right cost of capital has everything to do with the asset that the managers are buying, and that should be the same for the two buyers. There's no

way the company can export its cost of capital to that asset. The cost of capital is not about who you are. It's about what you're investing in.

As a consequence, it doesn't matter if you plan to use the cash on your balance sheet to make an acquisition or if you have a highly levered or all-equity balance sheet. What matters is using the right cost of capital for that investment, and that cost of capital should reflect the right capital structure for that investment.

IDEAS IN ACTION

Corning Glass and Return on Capital (ROC)

Corning was the leader in making display glass for electronics, and after examining the company's financials and what the future held, equity analyst Alberto Moel determined that the company was trading below book value. As we saw in chapter 2, the market at large thought that the company would not surpass its cost of capital with its returns.

For a company trading below its book value, like Corning, some might argue that it should shut down and sell its assets, especially if it can sell them for close to book value.

Why do you think Corning continued to run its business despite a ROC less than its cost of capital?

Corning likely believed, as Moel did, that the market was mispricing its future performance and that its future performance would be considerably better. Corning's market value was below its book value because it was facing pricing pressure in the market, which reduced its ROC. So the question is: Were these price pressures permanent or temporary?

This question returns us to core strategic business concerns. If Corning believes that its work adds value to its product and that it can protect its operations in a competitive environment, it should be confident that pricing pressures will be temporary. If the underlying conditions have changed, then it should analyze whether shutting down is the right decision for its shareholders.

Moel agreed that there was price pressure. However, when he looked at Corning's in-depth cost structure, he saw that the pricing pressure could be offset or even improved by its cost structure. In other words, its margins could remain flat or expand. The market didn't see this, so the expectations that Corning's margins would continue to compress were negatively affecting the stock price.

Therefore, Moel thought that the ROC of Corning was going to be better than the market thought and that in the future, Corning would trade above book value. In the end, he recommended "buy" to his investors.

Part of the reason Corning's market value was below its book value was that investors believed that their margins would continue to compress, which Moel disagreed with. Why do you think there is a tendency, in forecasting, to assume that current changes (reduced margins) will continue indefinitely into the future?

Forecasting the future is inherently difficult, and every decision the analyst makes carries the risk of being wrong. Faced with this difficulty, many analysts choose assumptions that extrapolate existing trends to determine future cash flows. Such reasoning may feel conservative but, in fact, is quite radical relative to thinking through the product or economic cycle.

Valuation is difficult because you have to consider everything about a company—its intellectual property, its strategy, its competitive landscape, and so on—and translate that into numbers and then forecast those numbers into the future. It's a thorough, complicated process that can take weeks. Then you have to write a convincing report. And, finally, you have to be right most of the time.

Biogen's Capital Structure

In 2015, due in part to low interest rates, Biogen took on $6 billion in debt in order to repurchase $5 billion of its own shares. This changed its capital structure; the net effect would be similar to not issuing those shares in the first place and taking on debt instead to purchase assets. The share repurchase was a way of returning cash to shareholders and providing them with more ownership after Biogen had grown significantly in recent years.

But what about the debt? According to Paul Clancy, Biogen's CFO at the time, taking on that much debt was rare for the pharma company. At the time, it had only $500 million dollars of debt on the balance sheet. However, like many other biotechnology companies, Biogen had cash trapped outside the United States that was inaccessible. So it had to take on some debt in order to execute the share repurchase. But it also took on more than it needed because interest rates were very favorable at the time. Since share repurchases or acquisitions were in the pipeline, it wanted to lock in a good interest rate before rates rose.

Why would low interest rates encourage companies to take on more debt?

The recent past has featured historically low interest rates. As such, firms may decide to lever up opportunistically in reaction to these conditions. The decision to time the issuance of equities or debt to market conditions is known as "market timing." In effect, firms are betting that they have the ability to time when the issuance of securities or share buybacks is most advantageous.

In order for the bet to pay off, Biogen's cash flows and pipeline products had to beat expectations. Of course, worrying about bets is the job of the CFO. Clancy commented: "If you're not worried about those types of bets, you're not being responsible to shareholders and to shareholder value creation."

When investors purchase a share of stock in a company, they are making a bet that the company will perform better than its cost of capital, and that the stock will increase in value by more than just its expected return. Here, Clancy is suggesting that a company buying back its own shares is making a similar bet. Why?

By spending cash to repurchase its own stock, the company is making an investment. As with any investment, that decision needs to have a positive net present value (NPV). Otherwise, Biogen should consider alternative uses of its capital, including simply distributing it as dividends. We'll discuss this broader capital allocation question in chapter 6.

One job of the CFO is to invest in the operating expenses that drive the business forward. This isn't always easy, especially in a big organization where people have different opinions and competing interests. The CFO's job is to get everyone on the same page. "When strategy gets focused," Clancy said, "it's actually easier all the way through an organization to discern the difference between what is really a good investment and what is not."

After the repurchase program and taking on more debt, Biogen had to execute a restructuring to ensure it was deploying its resources in the right way. This was a tough message to deliver to employees, especially since the company had just bought back $5 billion in shares.

Do you think it is appropriate for Biogen to restructure its company through layoffs while simultaneously announcing a $5 billion share repurchase? Why or why not?

On the one hand, these are independent decisions—one is about making sure you're operating as efficiently as possible and should be undertaken no matter what the financing decisions are. On the other hand, the coincidence of these occurrences will raise questions about why more capital expenditures (and the associated jobs) weren't a primary objec-

tive. Finance is at the crosshairs of these decisions, making Clancy's ability to speak to capital markets and to employees critical. CFOs increasingly play a central role because of the importance of the decisions and their own ability to address efficiency as well as capital allocation—the subject of chapter 6.

Heineken: Building a Mexican Brewery

In 2015, Heineken decided to invest $470 million in a new brewery in the Chihuahua region of Mexico, a key strategic move designed with a long-term view toward value creation. Let's look at the factors Heineken considered when making this decision.

According to Laurence Debroux, Heineken's CFO, the beverage giant first made inroads into Mexico in 2012 when it acquired the brewing operations of Femsa, a large Mexican conglomerate. At first glance, moving into Mexico might seem an odd choice for Heineken, which is based in the Netherlands, but it had many compelling strategic reasons to do so. Mexico is a large market, twice the size of Heineken's number-two market, and the country's GDP growth, in contrast to developed nations, was more promising.

Demographics were also promising. As many young people in Mexico reached legal drinking age, they became consumers. Mexican and craft beer in the United States was also growing, while the traditional beer market in the United States was stagnant. With the acquisition of Femsa, and its Mexican operation, Tecate, Heineken controlled Tecate Light and Dos Equis, two brands that were growing quickly in the United States and perhaps Europe in the future. For these reasons, Debroux and her colleagues invested in a new factory, which ended up being one of largest investments in Heineken's history.

Why do you think CFOs like Debroux tend to look at strategic concerns before they look at the NPV of a project? If value creation means choosing projects with a positive NPV, what does strategic analysis achieve?

Strategic analysis can help CFOs focus their attention on projects most likely to produce positive NPVs. Creating a forecast for projects requires understanding the overall strategic importance of a project and the interaction of that project with the rest of the organization.

Debroux had to determine the right capacity. How big should the factory be? You don't want to underinvest and miss out on revenues and sales. "Of course," as Debroux described, "it's a good problem—it's a problem that we want to have because if we ask ourselves in five years, should we build another one, that means that we're selling more and more in that country." But underestimating capacity can come at great cost.

When designing a new brewery, Debroux needed to balance future capacity with the current cost of construction. Thinking about costs of capital and the time value of money, what do you think her concerns were?

Heineken would incur the costs to build the brewery now, while it would gain the benefits from increased capacity in the future. Cash flows far into the future, when discounted, might not be worth the expense today. For this reason, Debroux constantly needs to balance the increased cash flows of future capacity with their cost today. As she commented, "When you look at a new brewery, you have the supply-chain employees in the driver's seat, and they have so much experience in a company like Heineken that they will tell you precisely how much the project is going to cost and how complicated it is going to be."

Since Heineken's supply-chain employees had a wealth of experience, they were usually accurate with their cost estimates and how long a project would take to build. From there, Debroux took those numbers, along with her assumptions about sales and productivity, and built a classical financial model, paying particular attention to NPV and the internal rate of return. When performing calculations like this, companies have rules and benchmarks. For example, depending on the project, if a company doesn't see itself recouping its initial investment in, say, five to seven years, then it may deem the project too risky. Projects often look good in isolation, but if the numbers look too good to be true and don't match up with similar projects, then it's possible the company is overlooking something. "But it is still a good question to ask yourself," said Lebroux. "If the project is all dependent on reaching a level of profitability or an EBITDA revenue that you don't see anywhere else in your company, you have to ask yourself, why would I reach it there, and I haven't reached it anywhere else?" That's an important conversation to have.

What if your forecasted cash flows are wrong? What if the brewery underperforms expectations? Think back to the lessons about sunk costs and the Sakai plant that Sharp built. What are the options?

If the brewery underperforms expectations, it may still have a positive present value. The costs to build the brewery are sunk costs, so they should have no relevance for the decision on what to do with the brewery once it is built. Every decision—whether to sell the brewery, modify its operations, and so on—is a new decision for which the company should construct a new NPV.

Quiz

Please note that some questions may have more than one answer.

1. **Which of the following can be a source of value creation? (Choose all that apply.)**
   A. Returns to capital that exceed costs of capital
   B. Reinvesting profits to grow
   C. Gross profits
   D. Earnings per share

2. **What is a beta?**
   A. A return on equity (ROE)
   B. A measure of how much a stock moves with the broader market
   C. A measure of how much taxes affect a company's weighted average cost of capital (WACC)
   D. A measure of how much ROE is higher than the cost of capital

3. Imagine a conglomerate with three divisions. Division A's assets have a beta of 0.5; division B's assets, a beta of 1.0; and division C's assets, a beta of 1.5. If the company uses the average, 1.0, when valuing projects for all its divisions, which division will the company overinvest in?

   A. Division A

   B. Division B

   C. Division C

   D. It will not overinvest.

4. How do you determine your cost of debt?

   A. Your lender can tell you what your current borrowing costs are.

   B. Multiply your current ratio by your credit rating and add the risk-free rate.

   C. Multiply your cost of equity by 1 minus the tax rate.

   D. Subtract your cost of equity from your WACC.

5. For a company with returns to capital of 5 percent and costs of capital of 10 percent, its market-to-book ratio will be:

   A. Greater than 1

   B. Less than 1

   C. Equal to 1

   D. I don't have enough information.

6. True or false: You can always increase company value by adding leverage.

   A. True

   B. False

7. How do you determine the cost of equity?

   A. Ask your stockholders or their representatives on the board of directors.

   B. Take the risk-free rate and add the product of your equity beta and the market risk premium.

   C. Multiply your cost of debt by 1 minus the tax rate.

   D. Subtract your cost of debt from your WACC.

8. Companies with higher betas have:

   A. Higher costs of equity

   B. Lower costs of equity

   C. Beta is irrelevant for cost of equity.

   D. It depends on their level of liquidity.

9. Why should companies invest in positive NPV projects?

   A. To shift their capital structures toward more equity and less debt

   B. Because all projects are positive NPV projects

C. Because they are riskier, they have higher returns

D. Because they create value by having returns greater than the cost of capital

10. **How can a company with sustainable returns to capital of 15 percent and a cost of capital of 12 percent maximize its value?**

    A. Reinvest as many of its profits as possible.

    B. Give out as much of its profits as possible in dividends.

    C. Liquidate the company as soon as possible.

    D. Offer dividends exactly equal to its cost of capital.

Chapter Summary

In this chapter, we developed a number of difficult but foundational ideas. First, we identified where value comes from and the specific recipe for value creation. Companies have to beat their cost of capital. They have to keep doing it, and they have to grow. The *sine qua non* of value creation is beating the cost of capital.

What does it mean to talk about a cost of capital? The first big idea is that costs of capital are associated with the expected returns of capital providers. And those expected returns are dictated by the risk investors bear. So a WACC says that for a given investment, you need to figure out what the debt and equity providers demand and average those costs of debt and equity by their weights. What are those weights? It depends on the industry. You tax-adjust them, because interest payments are tax deductible.

Next is the idea of the capital asset pricing model. The costs of equity aren't explicit. You need to rely on something to think rigorously about these costs. Because we live in a world with diversification opportunities, betas, rather than volatilities, of investments best measure the risk presented by an asset.

The final idea is that you have to use the WACC with care. It's not something that you can just export to other investments. And you can't use the same WACC for all investments. Finally, you can't simply increase firm value by taking on more debt than the optimal capital structure.

In the next chapter, we will first combine the WACC and the idea of free cash flows to create the foundation of valuation and then build upon that foundation to consider how to value assets in general.

5

The Art and Science of Valuation

How to value a home, an education, a project, or a company

Whether you're buying stock, acquiring a company, buying a house, or investing in education, you need to go through a process of valuation. Is the proposed investment justified? How much should you pay? These are all fundamentally questions of valuation, and finance has a rigorous set of tools for thinking about how to make those decisions. Consider the following examples:

In late 2012, Facebook reportedly made a $3 billion offer to purchase Snapchat. By 2016, Google had reportedly valued Snapchat at $30 billion. By mid-2018, the equity markets were valuing Snap at $17 billion. What were these wildly different numbers based on?

In mid-2018, Disney and Comcast were locked in a battle to acquire 21st Century Fox, with escalating prices. How did they know what to offer? Why were their bids so much higher than the valuation embedded in the stock price?

Is investing in an education worth it? Should I buy a home or rent? My buddy made a killing in Bitcoin; should I invest as well?

In previous chapters, we discussed how value is created and the relationship between risk and return. We also talked about the importance of cash. In this chapter, we'll bring those two pieces together to build a method for valuation.

While the methods are rigorous, it's critical to remember that valuation is an art, not a science. More accurately, it's an art *informed* by science. Valuation is subjective, prone to error, and leads to ambiguous answers. While you might find that unsatisfying, there simply is no other way to make these important decisions wisely. Although ambiguous, the process of valuation is as important as the end point. Only by evaluating different scenarios, probabilities, and models can you fully understand a business. So even if it's flawed and problematic, valuation is critical to sound managerial decision making.

In the first half of the chapter, we'll focus more on the science and clarify the underlying methods. In the second half, we'll turn to the art—the most subjective elements and the areas where the most games are played.

Two Alternative Valuation Methods

Given the imprecision of valuation, it's useful to rely on alternative methods to ensure an accurate outcome. There is no magical way to figure out value; there are just multiple methods that help you triangulate around reality. The two most important valuation methods are multiples and discounted cash flows. Let's start with multiples. Though you may not realize it, you've probably used them in your own life. Once you understand their weaknesses, we'll move on to the gold standard—discounted cash flows.

Multiples

A multiple is a ratio that compares the value of an asset to an operating metric associated with that asset. Beyond that fundamental structure, there is no other rule for creating multiples, and therefore there are numerous variants. A common multiple used in valuations is the price-to-earnings, or P/E, ratio, which divides a company's stock price by its earnings per share. Alternatively, it's the value of a company's equity divided by its net profit. That ratio, for example, might be 15 times, or "15X." This means that you're willing to pay $15 for every dollar of earnings that a company generates. This quick, back-of-a-napkin calculation is easily communicated and provides an easy method to compare companies.

A P/E multiple of 15X might seem puzzling. Why would you be willing to pay $15 for $1 of earnings? In short, that 15X, like everything in finance, reflects expectations of the future. So you're not just paying for $1 of earnings; you're paying for a stream of future earnings that is expected to grow. Does this imply that all multiples should be the same within an industry? Because firms may grow earnings at very different rates and because companies might be judged to have earnings that vary in quality, the P/E ratio can vary across companies within an industry. Differences in P/E ratios should occasion a question: Why would $1 of a company's earnings be worth so much more than another? Is it that much better operationally or is it overvalued?

As we saw in chapter 2, earnings are a problematic measure, and we can use other measures of cash—earnings before interest, taxes, depreciation, and amortization (EBITDA); operating cash flow; or free cash flow—to construct multiples as well. As we saw in chapter 4, there is another important capital provider—a lender who provides debt—so the multiples should reflect the fact that companies can use that type of capital as well. These two lessons are reflected in the use of enterprise value (EV) to EBITDA multiples (EV/EBITDA), where EV is the sum of the market value of debt and equity, or the value of the business. The EV/EBITDA multiple helps us compare companies of varying capital structures.

How can you use multiples? Table 5-1 shows three major companies in the cosmetics industry and their enterprise value/EBITDA multiples at year-end 2016.

Using this information, how would you value Procter & Gamble (P&G), a fourth company in the same industry, that generated an EBITDA of $17.4 billion for fiscal year 2016. Using the average of the multiples above—12.5—you would multiply P&G's EBITDA by 12.5 to arrive at an estimate of its enterprise value, which would be $217.67 billion.

TABLE 5-1

EBITDA multiples for three cosmetics companies, 2016

Company	Ratio of enterprise value to EBITDA
Avon Products	8.91
L'Oreal	17.42
Shiseido	11.20

What do you make of this exercise? It raises the following questions: (1) Is P&G only a cosmetics company? (2) Do all these companies serve the same geographic markets and the same customer segments? (3) Do these companies distribute their products in the same way? The enterprise value of P&G at year-end 2016 was $242.1 billion. In other words, P&G trades at a 13.9X EV/EBITDA multiple.

Like much of finance, using multiples is a method that initially seems odd but is something that you may already understand. You may have used a multiple in the most important financial decision you've ever made—buying a home. Specifically, most of us figure out if a home is a good investment by looking at "price per square foot (or meter)," which is nothing more than a multiple. You derive prices per square foot by dividing house prices by total square footage—a measure of value divided by an operating metric. It can be a useful way to talk about transactions in your neighborhood

Twitter versus Facebook

Multiples are a pliable method and can use any operating metric. Consider Twitter's initial public offering (IPO). How would you value Twitter at the time it went public? It didn't have profits or EBITDA or, for that matter, much revenue. But surely it was worth something. At the time, market participants emphasized its valuable user base and looked for companies with comparable revenue models within social media.

They turned to Facebook and calculated how much every user of Facebook was worth and used that multiple to value Twitter.

For example, each Facebook user was worth slightly more than $98 (taking its total stock market capitalization divided by its number of active users [$117 billion divided by 1.19 billion active users]); LinkedIn users were worth about $93 each ($24 billion divided by 259 million

active users). A few hours after its IPO launched, Twitter was trading at a valuation that indicated the market valued each of its 232 million active users around $110. The graph shows Twitter's and Facebook's relative stock performance from November 2013 to late 2018.

Clearly, comparing the value of Facebook and Twitter users was faulty. Why? There are many reasons, including:

- Varying levels of engagement with the platform

- Different demographics of the user base

- Different possibilities for monetizing their users for the two platforms

This example demonstrates the plasticity of the multiples method and also its great dangers. Faulty comparisons and assumptions can lead to significant misvaluations.

Twitter versus Facebook, 2013–2018

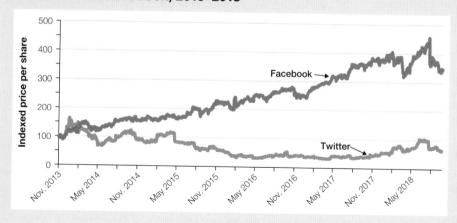

(e.g., "Honey, did you see that the house down the street sold for $600 per square foot—we're rich!"), and whether or not you should pay so much for a home (e.g., "The house down the street sold for only $300 per square foot—why should we pay $400?"). These sentiments are no more or less sophisticated than an experienced private equity investor saying, "We bought that company at an EBITDA multiple of 8X."

The pros and cons of multiples

This discussion of multiples highlights their many strengths. They are simple to calculate and communicate. Multiples also can be powerful because they are based on current market prices, and that means *someone* actually valued a company and put their money where their mouth is—it's not some imaginary value conjured by a spreadsheet. Finally, its ease of use makes comparisons between companies (and houses) seemingly quick and straightforward. The key word there is "seemingly."

Although multiples provide quick, easy ways to compare companies, they have many flaws. The attributes that make multiples popular—the ease of comparability, their market-based logic—are also what led people into trouble. First, and foremost, comparability is not always so

straightforward. Think back to the house example. Price per square foot ignores many factors. Does one home have a better view, while the other looks at a parking lot? Does one have shag carpeting, while the other has original hardwood floors from the 1800s? There are many factors that make a square foot in one home not the same as a square foot in another.

But surely a dollar of earnings is simply a dollar of earnings? Let's say you were looking to invest in eBay and began your valuation process by comparing it to Apple. For the year ending December 31, 2015, eBay generated earnings per share (EPS) of $1.60. On that same date, Apple's share price was 12.7 times its EPS. Using Apple's 12.7 × P/E ratio to value eBay would value eBay's stock at $20.32.

eBay finished trading on that day at $27.48—$7 more than expected. This simple comparison—and discrepancy—would lead you to believe that eBay is either overvalued or doing something truly exceptional, or Apple is undervalued.

But does it make sense to compare Apple with eBay? Probably not. Apple sells products and eBay is an online marketplace that connects sellers to buyers. Is it Amazon? Is it Facebook? Not really. It's hard to come up with a company that is really comparable with eBay's business and revenue models. Yet using a multiple may trick you into thinking that there is.

Shake Shack's Valuation

After Shake Shack, a fast-rising fast-food chain, went public in 2014, its stock price soared from its original price of $21 to between $47 and $90. But how did the chain compare to others in the industry? By using a multiple—in this case, dividing a chain's valuation by the number of stores it operates (a key operating metric in retail)—you can more accurately compare Shake Shack to other well-established chains, which have more stores (see the bar graph).

Shake Shack's per-store valuation was much higher than its competitors. In this case, the use of a multiple may sweeten your view of Shake Shack's valuation because it reflects a very different growth trajectory—or perhaps it makes you think that it's overvalued: What exactly is it doing that's so different from McDonald's? The line graph shows the subsequent stock price performance.

Comparison of top chain restaurant valuations, 2014

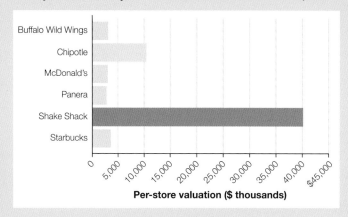

Per-store valuation ($ thousands)

Shake Shack's stock performance, January 2015–July 2018

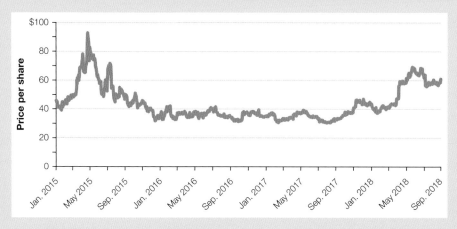

Source: Whitney Filloon, "How Does Shake Shack's Valuation Compare to Other Publicly-Traded Chains?" Eater.com, May 5, 2015.

Even when a within-industry comparison is more straight-forward, it's not clear a dollar is a dollar for undertaking multiples analysis. The earnings stream in one company may grow substantially faster than another, making the implicit assumptions of a multiples analysis faulty. And because many decisions associated with calculating earnings might differ across companies, they can be incomparable for multiples purposes. Investors sometimes talk about the "quality" of earnings, implying that some companies have more sustainable earnings than others. By taking a multiple from one company and slapping it on the other, you're assuming the growth trajectories and quality of earnings are fundamentally similar, and that could be a mistake.

Although market-based logic can be a virtue, it can also be a vice. Just because your neighbor paid an exorbitant $500 per square foot, that's no reason for you to make that same mistake. That is precisely what happened in the real estate bubble. If the "masses are asses," you're going to have a serious problem. As a consequence, we need a better way to think about valuation.

Problematic Methods for Assessing Value

Let's look at two more problematic methods of valuation before exploring the gold standard method.

Payback periods

The first method assesses projects based on the amount of time it would take for investors to get their money back—the payback period. You simply compare the initial outflow of funds with subsequent inflows and ask: In what year do I get my money back? That's a very appealing way to think about whether an investment is attractive or not. Inherently, it feels good to get paid back quickly.

To see this method and its problems in action, choose between two projects, each of which requires a $900,000 investment. You can choose only one and use payback period as your criterion. Table 5-2 shows the projected cash flows for each project.

Which project would you choose? Project A has a payback period of less than two years, and project B has a payback period of three years. If payback period is your decision-making criterion, you should choose project A.

TABLE 5-2

The problems with payback and IRR analysis

	Project A	Project B
Year 0	−$900,000	−$900,000
Year 1	500,000	0
Year 2	500,000	0
Year 3	300,000	1,670,000

Worldwide Housing Prices per Square Foot

The table shows the average price per square foot for housing in twenty-five cities worldwide. As you can see, there is tremendous variation—from $77.20 per square foot in Cairo to $2,654.22 per square foot in Hong Kong. What accounts for this disparity? In some cases, prices reflect demand—prices are correlated with average income levels. But cities such as Hong Kong, London, and New York effectively enjoy worldwide demand because they are global commercial centers. Supply can play an important role as well—Hong Kong is a small area that can only accommodate so many units of real estate. Alternatively, local government policies can reduce the amount of building allowed and thus available housing (one reason that San Francisco is so expensive).

Average price per square foot for housing in selected cities

Ranking	City	Price per square foot
1	Cairo, Egypt	$77.20
2	Mexico City, Mexico	172.05
3	Brussels, Belgium	348.29
4	Bangkok, Thailand	367.15
5	São Paulo, Brazil	405.98
6	Copenhagen, Denmark	492.94
7	Madrid, Spain	504.83
8	Istanbul, Turkey	527.68
9	Dubai, UAE	549.80
10	Berlin, Germany	680.51
11	Amsterdam, Netherlands	795.06
12	Stockholm, Sweden	805.37
13	Rome, Italy	972.13
14	Toronto, Canada	990.06
15	Sydney, Australia	995.08
16	Shanghai, China	1,098.94
17	Singapore	1,277.22
18	Geneva, Switzerland	1,322.00
19	Vienna, Austria	1,331.57
20	Moscow, Russia	1,366.96
21	Paris, France	1,474.08
22	Tokyo, Japan	1,516.35
23	New York, US	1,597.08
24	London, UK	2,325.90
25	Hong Kong	2,654.22

Source: Global Property Guide, globalpropertyguide.com.

As this example illustrates, the payback period method has some significant problems. By comparing these flows over time in this way, the time value of money is ignored. The second—and even worse—problem is that the answer to a payback period analysis is a simple number of years. But that's actually not what we're interested in; we're interested in creating value. The payback method could lead you to choose an investment because you get your money back faster, but turn away from an investment that creates much more value.

Using a discount rate of 10 percent, project A has a net present value of $193,160, and project B has a net present value of $354,700. By using payback period, you selected the project with a considerably lower net present value, which leads to much less value creation. That comparison reflects why payback analysis is so problematic.

Internal rates of return

Using internal rates of return (IRR) to assess projects is another very common valuation method. This method is not as problematic as payback analysis, partially because it is closely linked to discounted cash flows. But it still has problems. When we introduced the idea of discounting, we used forecasted cash flows and a discount rate to find a present value.

IRR flips that analysis. IRR analysis takes forecasted future cash flows and finds the discount rate that makes the present value zero. Here is the formula for calculating an IRR:

$$0 = \text{Cash flow}_0 + \frac{\text{cash flow}_1}{(1 + \text{IRR})} + \frac{\text{cash flow}_2}{(1 + \text{IRR})^2}$$
$$+ \frac{\text{cash flow}_3}{(1 + \text{IRR})^3} \ldots$$

In other words, IRR analysis captures the rate of return that will be experienced if the forecast is realized for a project. What could possibly be wrong with that? Why not analyze investments by just looking at their IRR? The idea of a rate of return is very powerful and accounts for IRRs' pervasiveness. Once you have an IRR, you can compare it to the weighted average cost of capital or discount rate. That's a little bit like the value creation exercise from chapter 4.

While this is an appealing way to think about the world, IRRs are problematic for two reasons. First, IRRs can give you the wrong answer because they're focused on returns and not value creation. You can compare two projects, and the higher IRR project might actually lead to less value creation. Again, you're interested in value creation, not in rate of return maximization.

Second, if cash flows are characterized by outflows, and then inflows and outflows again, and then inflows (as opposed to a simpler version using just outflows and then inflows), IRRs can give you wrong answers. Moreover, IRRs incur these risks and don't actually save any effort. Calculated IRRs must be compared to a weighted average cost of capital using forecasted cash flows. So we need the same information as we did to do the discounting in chapter 2.

Let's return to the earlier example to see the first problem. (See table 5-2.) The net present value (NPV) of project A was $193,160, and the NPV of project B was $354,700. Now that you understand IRR, you can calculate the two IRRs. The IRR of project A is 22.9 percent, and the IRR of project B is 22.9 percent. Ignoring NPV and focusing on IRR would have made you indifferent to the two projects. There is a clearly dominant project choice that IRR analysis obscures. This difficulty occurs, in part, because, as managers, we are not interested in increasing returns; instead, we should prioritize creating value.

Discounted Cash Flows

The discounted cash flow method is the gold standard of valuation. Fortunately, it does nothing more than combine the key lessons from chapters 2, 3, and 4. From chapter 2, we know that assets derive their value from their ability to generate future cash flows, and those cash flows aren't all created equal—they require discounting to translate them to today's numbers. From chapter 4, we know that the appropriate discount rate is a function of an investor's expected returns as they translate into a manager's cost of capital. Finally, from chapter 3, we know that ascertaining the information to do this valuation will be a tricky process.

Let's begin by providing a slightly modified version of the basic present value formula from chapter 2:

$$\text{Present value}_0 = \frac{\text{cash flow}_1}{(1 + r)} + \frac{\text{cash flow}_2}{(1 + r)^2}$$

$$+ \frac{\text{cash flow}_3}{(1 + r)^3} + \frac{\text{cash flow}_4}{(1 + r)^4} \ldots .$$

$$+ \text{terminal value}$$

There's one new term (i.e., the terminal value) at the end of the formula—we'll return to that soon. But the basic logic is still the same. All value today is derived from the expectation of future cash flows. We need to figure out how to forecast those cash flows and to decide which definition of cash and what discount rate to use.

Buying a Home Using Discounted Cash Flow Analysis

One way to appreciate the importance of discounted cash flow analysis relative to multiples is to revisit housing decisions. Rather than using multiples when buying a home, how could you use discounted cash flow analysis?

With multiples, your analysis is limited to looking at your neighbors and deriving the average price per square foot that they paid. To do a discounted cash flow analysis, ask instead: What are the cash flows from owning a home? Some flows are obvious. On an ongoing basis, you might have to invest in a new roof. That would be the capital expenditures from your free cash flow analysis. Similarly, there may be some tax effects. But the primary cash flow associated with buying a home is the cash flow that you *don't* spend on rent. Any project's cash flows are the incremental cash flows generated by that project, and buying a house means you don't have cash outflows of rent. So the value of a house is primarily associated with the rent payments you don't have to make once you buy a home.

This way to think about buying real estate can help you avoid overpaying. The key metric that revealed that a housing bubble had been created in the mid-2000s was the rental yield ratio—a comparison of renting versus buying. If you do a discounted cash flow analysis, you may find that it really doesn't make sense to buy and instead you should be renting. Multiples obscure a lot of hidden assumptions about what's going on when you use them. Discounted cash flow analysis makes things explicit. In this particular case, the analysis makes explicit the trade-off between renting and owning, which is precisely what was ignored during the housing bubble.

Free cash flows

Free cash flows, as you might remember, are flows that assets generate that are truly free and truly cash. They are available to capital providers after accounting for costs and expenses. Free cash flows can be deployed for new investments, or they can be distributed to capital providers.

Just to recall the basic formula: (1) start with projected EBIT, or earnings before interest and taxes, that is generated by the operating assets, (2) subtract taxes to get EBIAT, or earnings before interest and after taxes, (3) add back noncash expenses like depreciation and amortization because they should never have been taken out, and (4) accommodate the capital intensity of the business by penalizing it for investments in its working capital and fixed assets.

Step 1: Forecast future cash flows. Imagine that your company is considering investing in a new laboratory.

- The lab will require an initial capital expenditure of $2.5 million in year 0.

- The expected EBIT in year 1—the first year of operations—will be $1 million.

- This EBIT of $1 million is expected to increase by 5 percent every year thereafter. At the end of year 5, operations will end and the assets will be sold for their salvage value of $1 million.

- During the life of the project, the assets will be depreciated and ongoing capital expenditures will be made to maintain the assets. The net effects will be a $300,000 depreciation expense and $300,000 in capital expenditures for years 1 to 5 to maintain the equipment.

- Working capital is required for the project and is assumed to equal 10 percent of EBIT. In other words, in year 1, when EBIT goes from $0 to $1 million, the company will need to invest $100,000 in working capital. In year 2, when EBIT goes from $1 million to $1.05 million, the company will need to invest $5,000 more in working capital. For simplicity, let's assume that all working capital associated with the project expires worthless at the end of the five years.

- The company's tax rate is 30 percent and there are no tax consequences to selling the asset in year 5.

Creating your own spreadsheet with this information is a great exercise. The spreadsheet in table 5-3 provides the free cash flows for this project. You can try to match it. To build such a spreadsheet, I always find it useful to begin with a section at the top that lists the relevant assumptions. Once I have gathered my assumptions, I begin filling out the spreadsheet by taking the initial EBIT, growing the EBIT at the prescribed growth rate, and adjusting for tax payments, which gets me to the EBIAT. Then I can follow the formula for free cash flows.

There are a few tricky steps here. First, following the timing of the project is critical. Second, the working capital calculation is not the *level* of working capital but rather the *change* in the level of working capital. Third, I've lumped together capital expenditures with the asset disposal in the final year, which creates a positive cash flow in that year. And, finally, it's important to settle on a system of keeping track of what the inflows and outflows are. In this spread-

TABLE 5-3

Valuing the laboratory investment

Laboratory project assumptions

EBIT growth rate	5%					
Tax rate	30%					
Working capital as percent of EBIT	10%					
Year	**0**	**1**	**2**	**3**	**4**	**5**
EBIT		$1,000.00	$1,050.00	$1,102.50	$1,157.63	$1,215.51
– taxes		–300.00	–315.00	–330.75	–347.29	–364.65
= EBIAT		700.00	735.00	771.75	810.34	850.85
+ depreciation and amortization		300.00	300.00	300.00	300.00	300.00
– change in working capital		–100.00	–5.00	–5.25	–5.51	–5.79
– capital expenditures	–$2,500.00	–300.00	–300.00	–300.00	–300.00	700.00
= **free cash flow**	**–$2,500.00**	**$600.00**	**$730.00**	**$766.50**	**$804.83**	**$1,845.07**

sheet, all outflows are negative. Then the totals for the free cash flows are just sums of the figures.

Step 2: Apply the WACC.

The free cash flows this business generates are free to the capital providers, so their expected returns translate into the cost of capital used to discount future cash flows—via the weighted average cost of capital (WACC). To briefly summarize, the WACC calculates the costs of both debt and equity, weighs these costs by their relative importance in the financing of the investment, and includes a tax effect that captures the deductibility of interest. The capital asset pricing model helps us understand where costs of equity come from, and betas capture the measure of risk by considering the perspective of a diversified investor.

To figure out the relevant WACC for the investment in this lab, consider these facts:

- The optimal capital structure for such investments is 35 percent debt and 65 percent equity.

- The risk-free rate is 4 percent.

- The lender will charge 7 percent interest on the new project.

- The market risk premium is 6 percent.

Now you have everything needed to generate a cost of equity and figure out the WACC—except the beta. To do that, plot the monthly returns for companies that capture the risk of

Real-World Perspectives

Although multiples have their flaws, they can often double-check discounted cash flow assumptions, so many companies use them as part of a multipronged valuation effort. Alan Jones, global head of private equity at Morgan Stanley, commented:

The multiple of EBITDA is meant to be a quick, short-term proxy, because it is linked to a cash flow measure. Heuristic measures have evolved in which people talk about valuations in terms of multiples of EBITDA. We also tend to look a lot at multiples of free cash flow because we want to know what our capital expenditures are and what our investments in working capital are, but that's a very frequent multiple for us to look at as well.

So when we're looking at the valuation of the business, we're typically triangulating a number of different metrics. We do a discounted cash flow analysis first and foremost; that's really the anchor of a valuation approach. It's particularly important because we can determine what changes we can make to the business that will affect the discounted cash flow. But we also look at where comparable companies trade in the public market; that's typically a multiple of, again, EBITDA or net profit in the business. We look at EBITDA multiples and then comparable acquisition multiples, where have people recently purchased companies, and what they are paying for businesses like ours.

When we're looking at a valuation opportunity, we ask: What is the discounted cash flow analysis telling us, what are comparably traded companies telling us, and what are comparable acquisition multiples telling us? Then we gauge which is most important in the business we're looking at. Is one an outlier for a particular reason? We apply some real thoughtfulness to triangulating among those three measures of value. But at the end of the day, it's all about generating cash and our ability to purchase what's ultimately a stream of cash flows over time.

the project, plot them against the market return, and then plot the regression line (see figure 5-1).

The slope of the line in the figure is 1.1; therefore, the beta is 1.1. Now, use the capital asset pricing model to determine the cost of equity and then the WACC using the formulas from chapter 4. (See table 5-4.)

The final step is to return to the forecasted free cash flows and determine net present values. Discount factors are simply

FIGURE 5-1

Beta graph

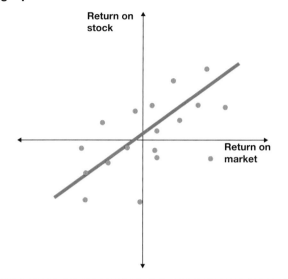

TABLE 5-4

Calculation for the weighted average cost of capital

Percent debt	35%	
Percent equity	65%	
Tax rate	30%	
Cost of debt	7%	
Risk-free rate	4%	
Market risk premium	6%	
Beta	1.1	
Cost of equity	10.6%	◄—— Cost of equity = risk-free rate + beta × market risk premium
WACC	8.61%	◄—— WACC = tax-adjusted cost of debt × debt share of capital + cost of equity × equity share of capital

1 divided by 1 plus the WACC. Finally, multiply all of the free cash flows by the discount factors and sum them to determine the net present value. (See table 5-5.)

The net present value of this investment is $1.069 million. Because the NPV is positive, the lab project will create value for the company, and you should go forward with it. Alternatively, if you were to measure the present value of the cash flows, it would be $3.569 million.

Step 3: Calculate terminal values. Most companies and many investments are expected to continue indefinitely. In these situations, it's typical to settle on a year when you expect the company's growth to stabilize and then summarize the value in all future cash flows through a simple set of calculations. This is called a "terminal value"; it summarizes the value of the investment at the end of the forecasted cash flows.

There are two ways to get terminal values. The first is via multiples. When you've reached an end point, say, five years into an investment, you could say that the company has reached a valuation of, for example, ten times free cash flow.

The other, and preferred, way to think about terminal values is to deploy a "perpetuity formula"—a neat trick that effectively calculates today's value for a stable set of cash flows. If you want to get the present value of a stream of

TABLE 5-5

Valuing the laboratory investment

Laboratory project assumptions

EBIT growth rate	5%					
Tax rate	30%					
Working capital as percent of EBIT	10%					

Year	0	1	2	3	4	5
EBIT		$1,000.00	$1,050.00	$1,102.50	$1,157.63	$1,215.51
− taxes		−300.00	−315.00	−330.75	−347.29	−364.65
= EBIAT		700.00	735.00	771.75	810.34	850.85
+ depreciation and amortization		300.00	300.00	300.00	300.00	300.00
− change in working capital		−100.00	−5.00	−5.25	−5.51	−5.79
− capital expenditures	−2,500.00	−300.00	−300.00	−300.00	−300.00	700.00
= free cash flow	−$2,500.00	$600.00	$730.00	$766.50	$804.83	$1,845.07
WACC	8.61%					
Discount factor	1.00	0.92	0.85	0.78	0.72	0.66
Present value	−$2,500.00	$552.46	$618.90	$598.36	$578.50	$1,221.13
Net present value	**$1,069.35**					

cash flows that doesn't grow over time, you can just divide that cash flow by the discount rate.

Perpetuity Formula

$$\frac{\text{Cash flow}_1}{\text{discount rate}}$$

Of course, many perpetuities, including companies, continue to grow. In particular, if somebody promises you a growing perpetuity—for example, $100 every year forever that grows at 3 percent—that also collapses into a very convenient

formula. The present value of that growing perpetuity is nothing more than the initial cash flow divided by the discount rate less the growth rate. It almost seems like magic.

Growing Perpetuity Formula

$$\frac{\text{Cash flow}_1}{\text{discount rate} - \text{growth rate}}$$

When you use this as part of a discounted cash flow analysis, the present values these formulas provide are the present value as of the year before the initial cash flow. For example, if the numerator of the equation is the cash flow in year 6, the formula will produce the present value in year 5. That means you will need to discount this value again in order to get the present value today.

If these formulas are so convenient, why don't we just use them rather than the spreadsheet mechanics discussed? In short, there are many short-run dynamics that can be very important to model explicitly—new factories, sales trajectories, cost reductions, and so on—and those dynamics can have a large impact on value. You can only use these formulas when things settle into a steady state.

Of course, there's a danger in this step of the valuation process, especially in the assumption of the growth rate. For example, if the company is in an economy that's growing at 3 percent and uses a terminal growth rate of 7 percent, that's an untenable assumption. It means that ultimately the company will take over the world, which we don't really believe will happen. As a consequence, in the long run, overall economic growth rates are a useful way to think about what growth rates should be in a terminal value calculation.

Step 4: Compare enterprise values versus market values.

Now that you have the value of a given enterprise (the lab project), you can just divide that figure by the number of shares and compare it to the existing stock price, right?

Not quite. Through the valuation, you have determined the *value* of the business, not its equity. The value of the business is often called enterprise value. If you think back to the diagram of free cash flows seen in chapter 2, you have valued the cash flows to the capital providers—both debt and equity—that the enterprise generates.

Sometimes, enterprise values will be much more than the market value of equity. For example, if the enterprise value is $100, and the company holds $40 of debt, the equity value is only $60. This can go the other way, especially if the company holds a great deal of cash, in which case, the company's market value can be greater than its enterprise value.

If you take a look at Apple in 2013 or 2014, you'll see that its market value was $500 billion, but it held more than $100 billion in excess cash that it didn't require for its operations. As a consequence, the actual implicit value of the enterprise was lower than the market value. The important lesson here is that to get to the value of a company's equity from the enterprise value, you need to think about how much debt and cash there is.

Figure 5-2 shows Apple's enterprise value and cash versus the market value of its debt and equity from 2012 to 2016. In the figure, market values are used along with cash and debt levels to arrive at *implied* enterprise values. When conducting a valuation of Apple's business, you should compare the

Multiples and Perpetuities

One opportunity the growing perpetuity formula provides is that it allows us to work backward from existing valuations to determine the underlying assumptions.

Let's look at three major retailers and see what the market thinks about their implied discount rates and growth rates. The three retailers are Walmart (a discount retail chain), Costco (a wholesale bulk consumer retailer), and Amazon (an online retailer). We'll compare their enterprise value (EV), a measure of the total market value of their debt and equity, to their EBITDA using the data in the table.

Assuming that all three companies are growing at steady rates, what do these multiples imply for how the market feels about the implied discount rates and growth rates for these companies?

Look more closely at Walmart. We can use some algebra to convert the enterprise-value-to-EBITDA multiple into a growing perpetuity formula. In short, a 10X multiple must correspond to a ten percentage point difference between discount rates and growth rates. For example, it might indicate a discount rate (r) of 15 percent and a growth rate (g)

Comparison of retailers' EBITDA multiples

Retailer	Ratio of enterprise value to EBITDA
Walmart	7.97
Costco Wholesale	13.57
Amazon	46.42

of 5 percent ($r - g = 10$ percent). A 7.97X multiple might represent a growing perpetuity formula in which the denominator ($r - g$) equals 1/7.97, or 12.5 percent. That might represent a discount rate of 18 percent and a growth rate of 5.5 percent, or it might represent a discount rate

valuation to the implied enterprise value rather than to the market value because those values can differ by more than 30 percent.

Step 5: Analyze scenarios, expected values, and bidding strategies.

Once you've created the machinery and arrived at a value for one scenario, you might think you're done. In reality, this is where the fun begins. To really understand the investment and to arrive at a value of the asset, you have to think through the "expected value" of the asset. You just valued the asset under a certain set of assumptions. What if you're wrong? In some sense, you're sure to be wrong—the likelihood of the world lining up with your assumptions precisely is close to zero.

The appropriate way to arrive at the correct expected value is to consider alternative scenarios such as a worst-case scenario, of 15 percent and a growth rate of 2.5 percent.

For Costco, this same calculation would yield an $r - g$ in the denominator of 1/13.57, or 7.4 percent. This may reflect a discount rate of 12.9 percent and a growth rate of 5.5 percent, or it might mean a discount rate of 15 percent and a growth rate of 7.6 percent.

Amazon has an EV/EBITDA ratio of 46.42. This yields an $r - g$ of 1/46.42, or 2.1 percent in the denominator. This might reflect a discount rate of 7.6 percent and a growth rate of 5.5 percent, or a discount rate of 15 percent and a growth rate of 12.9 percent.

We can compare these companies' values and implied growth rates. The market may believe that Amazon has a higher growth rate than Costco, which has a higher growth rate than Walmart. Alternatively, it may believe that Amazon is a less risky business and has a lower discount rate than Costco, which has a lower discount rate than Walmart. Or it could be a combination of the two. Given the similarity of the companies, it's likely that the discount rates are the same and that all the variation reflects differential expected growth rates.

One key difference to be aware of in this example, and generally, is that mapping multiples to discounted cash flow (DCF) analysis works best when the multiples are of free cash flow (FCF) rather than earnings or EBITDA. In short, value corresponds to discounted FCFs, so using EBITDAs is imprecise. In particular, if there are large future capital expenditures, future EBITDAs might be considerably higher than future FCFs.

a best-case scenario, and a base case and attach probabilities to them. Creating these scenarios and attaching probabilities to them is one of the most important steps for an analyst—it forces you to really think through the nature of the business and its potential outcomes. For example, if there's a 10 percent chance that the value is $120 (best case), a 70 percent chance the value is $100 (base case), and a 20 percent chance of a $10 value (worst-case or fraud scenario), what is the expected value? $120, $100, or $10? In fact, it's none of those. The expected value must be calculated by probability-weighting scenarios.

The expected value formula is fairly simple:

$$\text{Expected value} = 10\% \text{ PV (best case)}$$
$$+ 70\% \text{ PV (base case)}$$
$$+ 20\% \text{ PV (worst case)}$$

So, in this case, the expected value is $84.

FIGURE 5-2

Apple's market value balance sheets, 2012–2016

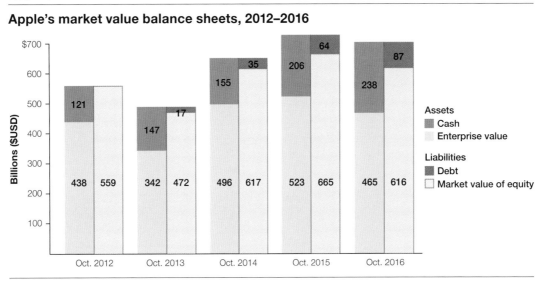

Once you get the expected present value and know it's associated with an enterprise value, how would this inform your bidding strategy if you're buying a company? Let's say you come up with the underlying expected value of $84. Is that your opening bid? Or is it the most you're willing to pay? Are you willing to go as high as the best-case scenario of $120? Maybe the maximum bid should be the value associated with the worst-case scenario?

The expected value should be the final offer. If you pay that price, your investment will have a net present value of 0. There's nothing wrong with that, per se, but you haven't actually created any value for yourself. It should be your final and ultimate bid. Your opening bid should be something considerably lower. If you end up paying $75 for that asset, you've actually created $9 in value and unless you pay less than the expected value, your purchase is not actually creating any value in expectation. And if you pay up to the best-case scenario of $120, for example, in the first two scenarios, you have transferred value to the seller and created no value in the best case. In expectation, you are destroying value for your capital providers.

Valuing an Education

Valuation is everywhere, including the most important investment of all: how you should invest in yourself. Is paying for an education worth the money? In a September 2016 memorandum on higher education that the US Council of Economic Advisers produced for the Obama administration, it was determined that workers with bachelor's degrees earn nearly $1 million more over the course of their careers than similar workers with only a high school diploma. Individuals with an associate's degree earn $330,000 more than those with only high school diplomas.

As we know, pure cash flow values cannot just be added up. Instead, we need to discount them and then find the present value. The present value of these cash flows is $510,000 for bachelor's degrees and $160,000 for associate's degrees. If prospective students took this valuation, subtracted the cost of education, and applied the NPV rule (invest whenever NPV is positive), they would pursue a bachelor's degree whenever the costs of that degree were less than $510,000. Given that this calculation will often be positive, does it mean that every college education will be worthwhile in terms of incremental wages? No—it simply means that education is worth the investment on *average*, not that *every* education is worth the cost.

Valuation Mistakes

Now let's turn to the mistakes that are often made when doing a valuation. This is an art and not a science, so there are a variety of judgment calls involved. After the announcement of an acquisition, it's fairly common for the stock of the acquirer to fall, indicating that it likely overpaid and transferred value from itself to the target.

That begs the question: Why are firms systematically overpaying? The answer is that they must be doing something wrong during the valuation process. Here, I highlight three major mistakes and consider more in the next chapter.

Ignoring Incentives

The first, and most pervasive, mistake is that it is easy to ignore the incentives of the people involved in an acquisition. Certainly, sellers of assets want acquirers to overpay. And sellers control important sources of information, including historic financial information. This problem is reminiscent of the asymmetric information problem from chapter 3. What do you think the seller has been doing as it prepares for a sale? The seller might make itself look particularly good by accelerating sales, deferring costs, and underinvesting. This circumstance makes due diligence a critical part of any acquisition process.

The problem doesn't stop with the seller. Typically, investment bankers get paid only on completion, so they want you to make the deal. Even people within your company who have analyzed the transaction have perverse incentives. They may well anticipate getting a promotion to run the new division just acquired. Everyone involved in the transaction wants the transaction to happen and may subtly change assumptions or forecasts to help make that outcome a reality. As a result, this sea of unbalanced information leads to overpayment and overconfidence.

Exaggerating Synergies and Ignoring Integration Costs

Synergy is the idea that once merged, the value of two companies will be greater than the sum of the values of each individual company. On the surface, the idea of synergies isn't unreasonable. For example, if you bring two sales forces together and rationalize them, this should result in cost savings. If you bring two companies together, you could control more capacity within an industry and gain more pricing power.

Imagine if Amazon wanted to merge with eBay. The ability to use both sets of customer lists or both sets of vendors in the combined entity might be powerful. Alternatively, there might be a number of back-office and computing expenses that could be reduced by combining the two companies. Both cases are examples of synergy. The combined company could access customers the companies couldn't have otherwise or it could cut costs in a way that it wouldn't be able to separately.

The problem with synergies is that people tend to overestimate how quickly those synergies will work and overestimate the magnitude of their effects. They ignore the fact that mergers are complicated and that changing cultures and changing workforces takes time. The second, related problem is that, even if the synergies are legitimate, people will often incorporate all those synergies into the price they pay for a company. That too can lead to overpayment since the rewards from the value creation of synergies are transferred to the acquired company's shareholders instead of being part of the value creation the merger brings to the acquiring company.

Underestimating Capital Intensity

One final error that eager bidders make is to understate the capital intensity of the business. Ongoing growth in EBIT or free cash flows typically requires increasing the asset base through capital expenditures. But those capital expenditures reduce free cash flows dollar-for-dollar—and are conveniently ignored by people anxious to do deals. For example,

Real-World Perspectives

Alan Jones, global head of private equity at Morgan Stanley, commented that he often tries to consider the ratio of the terminal values to total values to better understand a transaction:

One of the chief problems with discounted cash flow analysis is that so much of it depends on the terminal value, the value for which you ultimately sell the business; we focus very heavily on that. So whenever we generate a discounted cash flow analysis, we literally print out what percent of the overall valuation is as a result of the sale of the business because then we're not really thinking about the cash flow generation in the business—we're really making a bet on where we'll be able to sell that business ultimately.

terminal values will assume perpetual growth rates but in the final year you are modeling (which serves as the basis of the terminal value), capital expenditures will just equal depreciation, indicating no growth in assets. In effect, understating capital intensity inflates values.

Recall the example of Netflix from chapter 2. The key question for Netflix is how content acquisition costs will grow over time to sustain its growth. If you assumed tremendous growth in Netflix's subscribers, you would also want to carefully project the capital intensity of the underlying business. Similarly, the valuation of a company such as Tesla hinges not just on customer growth—it must build factories to satisfy that demand—so understating capital intensity can lead to incorrect valuations.

IDEAS IN ACTION

Investing in Spirit Aero Systems

In 2012, Scopia Capital invested in Spirit AeroSystems, an airplane parts manufacturer, which it thought the market was mispricing. Boeing formerly owned Spirit and made up an outsized portion—over 80 percent—of its business. Rather than exclusively focus on Boeing's 737, Spirit began working on airplanes for Airbus and Gulfstream, as well as a new project from Boeing—building a new fuel-efficient 787 called the Dreamliner.

A lot of excitement surrounded Spirit, but as it moved further along in the investment cycles for the Airbus and Gulfstream platforms, its earnings per share dropped from $2 to below $1. One problem was that Spirit's operating assumptions about the profitability of these investments had been incorrect, and because its projects have extremely long time horizons (ten to twenty years), it had to account for those charges up front, which hit its income statement. The stock, as a consequence, dropped.

Investors were valuing Spirit based on its price-to-earnings multiple, and its earnings had dropped significantly. What are the problems with using a P/E multiple–based valuation that may be relevant here?

There are two major problems with using a price-to-earnings multiple to value Spirit. First, earnings, as represented by net profit, are a problematic measure of economic performance, as discussed in chapter 2. Second, Spirit's earnings were temporarily diminished due to up-front investments and the unique nature of its accounting system—a price-to-earnings multiple assumes that these temporary fluctuations will continue forever.

Scopia was in a prime position to evaluate Spirit because Spirit was a leader in a niche business—creating airplane fuselages and wing assemblies—that Scopia understood. Because of this familiarity, Scopia was able to take a deeper look at Spirit's business and determine if the problems that the market was detecting were truly warning signs. For example, as Spirit built its 787 business with Boeing, the company's cash flows took a dive because Boeing was still in the design stage and therefore had delayed the manufacturing process. In the meantime, Spirit was sitting on a huge inventory of parts. For investors, these circumstances were troubling. In most cases, this scenario would have been a great shorting opportunity.

On closer inspection, Scopia didn't see these developments as problems at all. Although Spirit's cash flows were negative, this was only temporary. Once its projects went into production, things would turn around. And those one-time charges to its balance sheet would disappear. Its contracts with Boeing, Airbus, and Gulfstream were long-term contracts that covered the life of the platform; in other words, as long as those companies were working on those platforms, Spirit would be the builder.

What are some of the risks associated with stockpiling inventory for a future project? Think about discounting and the time value of money, as well as the nature of risk.

There are two main issues here. First, Spirit is paying now for uncertain future cash flows that it may or may not realize. Second, Spirit is betting that its stockpiled inventories will not become obsolete and worthless. The first concern is a generic one for all investments, while the second concern is particularly acute for inventory.

Scopia's investment in Spirit wasn't all smooth sailing. It was confident that Spirit's price per earnings could rise to $3.50

a share and its stock price could rise above $40. But early on in Scopia's investment, Spirit had to take on another big charge, and the stock, which had hovered in the twenties, dropped to the midteens. At that point, Scopia had to decide if it should add more stock or exit the investment. Some investors see stock dips as opportunities to buy more stock. The market is ill-informed, the thinking goes, so why not double down at a cheaper price?

The team at Scopia took a step back, looked at its initial valuations, and examined the new situation. Ultimately, Scopia decided to invest more in Spirit—those charges, again, were one-offs. Once the drags on its business went away, and when its airplane projects went into production, Spirit began to follow the trajectory that Scopia had anticipated. Figure 5-3 provides Spirit's stock price movements from 2010 to 2017.

Lessons from Dell

On September 13, 2013, one of the most iconic technology companies, Dell Computer, was taken private through a buyout undertaken by current management. The founder and CEO of Dell, Michael Dell, was working with the private equity firm Silver Lake to purchase Dell.

Since the February 2013 announcement of the proposed transaction, shareholders had been fighting the buyout. Ac-

FIGURE 5-3

Spirit Aero Systems's stock performance, 2010–2017

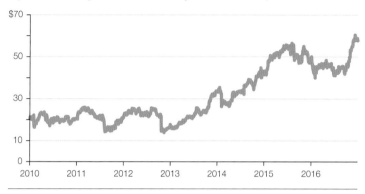

cusations were levied against Michael Dell for his role in the process, and ultimately the case went to court for resolution. Walking through the conditions that led to the management buyout, the bidding process, and the subsequent court case that attempted to determine an accurate valuation for Dell can reinforce a number of lessons we've seen throughout the last few chapters.

In 1983, Michael Dell founded Dell in his freshman dorm room at the University of Texas. By 2012, it had grown into a global technology company that was selling PCs, servers, and storage devices. More recently, Dell had become convinced that to transform the company, he would have to branch out into software and services, as many of his competitors had done. Many analysts disagreed with the approach, and revenues were flat and earnings were declining. In many ways, Dell felt that the market just didn't understand what he was trying to do. During the first half of 2012, the stock decreased from $18 to $12, while the market was up nearly 25 percent. Feeling quite misunderstood, Dell began to explore the possibility of taking the company private via a management buyout. By taking it private, he would be able to rebuild the company, transform it into his vision, and do so without the scrutiny of public capital markets.

Given that Michael Dell was one of the potential buyers, the board formed a committee to review the management buyout proposal. Various valuations were done for the board and for different buyers, including private equity firms Silver Lake and KKR. By the time the bids were evaluated, the market had driven the stock price down to nearly $9.35, and in late 2012, Dell reported that revenue was down 11 percent and earnings were down 28 percent. (See figure 5-4.)

To consider the buyout, Dell's board needed two things—a sense of the value of the cost-saving measures Michael Dell was proposing, and an idea of how private equity firms would value the company—to set prices at which the board would consider bids.

Dell management had identified $3.3 billion in potential cost savings. At the request of the Dell board, on January 3, 2013, Silver Lake had brought in the Boston Consulting

FIGURE 5-4

Dell's stock performance, January 2011–January 2013

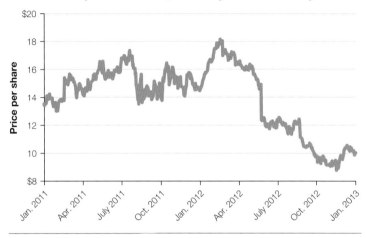

Group (BCG) to help with the valuation; it created three scenarios for the potential cost savings:

- A base case, where no savings were realized

- The BCG 25 percent case, where 25 percent of the savings were realized

- The BCG 75 percent case, where 75 percent of the savings were realized

BCG believed that the 25 percent case was attainable, but doubted that the 75 percent case was very likely, as it would require Dell to achieve margins higher than it or any of its competitors had ever achieved. That provided the Dell board with a sense of the cash flows. Next, it needed an idea of how private equity firms would value Dell.

The assumption was that Dell would be held private for 4.5 years before a public offering returned the shares to the public. Using the scenarios to determine the amount of cost savings, along with other forecasted assumptions, a future price of the stock in 4.5 years was determined: $32.49, $35.24, and $40.65, depending on the cost-saving scenario.

With these scenarios and future prices in hand, JP Morgan, on behalf of the Dell board, attempted to work out a price that an acquirer would pay for the company. For private equity, it is not unusual to work backward—determine the future price you expect to sell the company for, determine the rate of return you would like to earn, and then discount the price at that rate of return to determine the price you would pay today. Table 5-6 summarizes the stock prices an acquirer would pay to achieve a 20 percent, 25 percent, or 30 percent return, assuming specific scenarios and future stock prices.

How is this method similar to or different from the discounted cash flow method?

In this situation, the investor is determining the required rate of return—not as a function of the asset's risk, but just as a

TABLE 5-6

Boston Consulting Group's stock prices for various scenarios

Internal rate of return	Base case, no savings realized	25% of the savings realized	75% of the savings realized
20%	$13.23	$14.52	$17.08
25	12.67	13.75	15.88
30	12.23	13.13	14.92

function of what it would like to earn—and determining a current value it would pay to achieve it, by discounting the future expected cash flows. A discounted cash flow analysis attempts to find an appropriate discount rate and determine the current value of an asset. In contrast, the method described determines the return desired in a vacuum and the price that would yield that return. It may look very similar to a DCF analysis; it still takes the cash flows and discounts them back to find a value, but this method does not seek to arrive at an assessment of value. It seeks to find a price at which a return will be achieved.

On January 15, 2013, Silver Lake and Michael Dell offered to buy out the company for $12.90 per share. Three days later, the Dell board of directors rejected the offer and decided to set a minimum sale price before agreeing to any deal.

What do you think is a good minimum price for the board to set, and why? Remember that Dell's board wants to entice investors to bid on its company but also not give away too much value. Consider also the likelihood of the various scenarios occurring (make up percentages you think are reasonable). There's no right or wrong answer, since any answer will be based on your own assumptions and beliefs.

Based on these projections, the Dell board decided on a minimum price of $13.60 per share before beginning the bidding process. This minimum price was distributed to all potential bidders.

The Winner's Curse

The board invited bids. Ultimately, Dell and Silver Lake submitted the winning bid, and the company was sold for nearly $14 a share. While the winning bid was 40 percent higher than the low stock price of $9.35, many shareholders were suspicious of the transaction. They thought that the value was actually quite a bit higher. They were particularly worried that the nature of this transaction compromised the bidding process and emphasized two problems. First, in many ways, Michael Dell was functioning as a seller on behalf of the company and its shareholders, and as a buyer in tandem with Silver Lake, the private equity firm. Because he was both a buyer and seller, the shareholders argued there was an inherent conflict of interest for Dell. More importantly, because Michael Dell was a potential buyer and had all the information as the CEO of Dell, that created an informational problem. Dell had the most information about the company and knew the best value. Upon completion of the auction, anyone who had bid higher than Dell and won the auction would feel quite regretful, given that the person with the most information had a lower bid. That's a version of the winner's curse that can help undercut a competitive process.

The Process

Let's look at how the deal actually played out. First, on February 3, 2013, Michael Dell and Silver Lake proposed a purchase price of $13.65 per share. Shareholders were immediately upset. On March 5, Carl Icahn and Icahn Enterprises proposed that Dell should instead perform a leveraged recapitalization worth $22.81 per share (through a $9 dividend and a $13.81 purchase price; for more on leveraged recapitalizations, see chapter 6). On March 22, the investment firm Blackstone floated a transaction at $14.25 per share, but decided against pursuing it without "a more level playing field." On June 19, Icahn submitted a proposal to the Dell shareholders to elect an alternative slate of board members who would stop the merger.

In response, on July 31, Michael Dell and Silver Lake raised their offer to $13.96 per share and proposed a modified voting process, in which fewer shareholders would need to approve the deal. The board approved these conditions on August 2, and at a special meeting on September 12, 2013, shareholders holding 57 percent of Dell's shares voted in favor of the merger.

Many shareholders, nevertheless, remained upset. Some investors disagreed with Dell's explanations for the recent poor performance of Dell's stock, claiming instead that he had driven down the stock price of the company in order to decrease the price he would have to pay to take control of the company. Sometimes management might manipulate operations or accounting values to make the company look better (see chapter 3); in this case, the shareholders claimed Dell had used his power as a manager to make Dell look worse to gain a bargain price for himself during the buyout.

Dell's largest shareholder, Southeastern Asset Management, characterized its concerns by saying the current deal "falls significantly short," adding that it "appears to be an effort to acquire Dell at a substantial discount to intrinsic value at the expense of public shareholders."[1]

Take a look again at Dell's performance from 2011 to 2012 (see figure 5-4). Dell's price had suffered after poor results throughout 2012, but it dipped further following a change in guidance released on August 16. That day, Dell reported that its revenue growth estimates had been revised down from 5 to 9 percent to from 1 to 5 percent. Michael Dell was the CEO of Dell at this point and had decided on August 14 that he wanted to take the company private.

The stockholders further disagreed with the way they felt the board had handled the buyout. In a particularly frustrated moment, Icahn characterized the Dell board in this fashion: "We jokingly ask, 'What's the difference between Dell and a dictatorship?' The answer: Most functioning dictatorships only need to postpone the vote once to win . . . The Dell board, like so many boards in this country, reminds me of Clark Gable's last words in *Gone with the Wind*—they simply 'don't give a damn.'"[2]

Finally, the shareholders objected to the manner in which the bidding process had been conducted; since Dell had full knowledge of the company's internal forecast, who would bid against his stated valuation? In the ensuing legal case, the judge characterized the problem of the winner's curse in this way: "You don't bid on the contents of someone else's wallet when they know how much money is in it."[3]

With all these concerns, it might seem impossible to conduct a fair bidding process. If you were Michael Dell, what might you have done to create a level playing field?

While full transparency with all documents seems like a good solution, it likely wouldn't have left Michael Dell in a good negotiating position to place a competitive bid. Perhaps the best solution would have been to recuse himself entirely from the process, both as a bidder and as the CEO of Dell. As it was, the information concerns were impossible to ignore. Wall Street analyst Leon Cooperman characterized the deal as "a giant case of insider trading by management against shareholders."[4] The result of these concerns was litigation. The shareholders asked the court for an appraisal to see if the value of $14 a share was fair.

In these types of litigations, both sides commonly employ expert witnesses who try to value the company and help the judge figure out the correct value. The two experts here came to quite different numbers that reinforced their sides' perspective. In particular, the expert for Silver Lake and Dell came up with a value of the company of less than $13 a share, suggesting that the $14 price was more than fair. In contrast, the expert for the shareholders who had felt cheated by the process valued the company at twice the value of the $14 bid, nearly $29.

So, ultimately, the two experts had valuations ranging from $13 to $29—a difference of nearly $28 billion! How could two experts come up with such different valuations? The valuation processes that the two experts undertook formed part of the record in this trial and provide a great opportunity to reinforce a number of lessons about valuation.

Why and how did the experts come up with very different valuations?

First and perhaps most important, they used BCG's scenario analysis in very different ways. The expert for the shareholders used scenarios that included quite optimistic situations for those underlying cost savings, while the expert for Dell and Silver Lake used relatively pessimistic assumptions about what would happen with those cost savings.

In addition to this difference in scenario analysis, they used a variety of other, different inputs to their models. In particular, the two experts used different growth rates of 1 percent and 2 percent for their terminal values. In addition, the expert for the shareholders used a tax rate of 21 percent, while the expert for Dell and Silver Lake used an 18 percent tax rate but then raised it to 36 percent for the terminal period. They disagreed on the right capital structure for the company, on the correct beta for the company, and interestingly, on the appropriate market risk premium. The expert for the shareholders used a smaller market risk premium of 5.5 percent, while the one for Silver Lake and Dell used an market risk premium of almost a point higher at 6.4 percent. Finally, the two experts differed on the amount of cash that the business actually needed and how much net cash was in the business.

Ultimately, the court decided that the fair value of Dell was not the $14 per share that had been agreed on at the time of the sale, but $18 a share. The court concluded that the company was sold 25 percent cheaper than it should have been. The conclusion to the case resulted in Dell and Silver Lake paying the additional $4 to the shareholders.

The Future

This decision was controversial. Shareholder advocates cheered it, but others wondered about the precedent this decision created. The *New York Times* expressed concern that it could "lead to a spate of lawsuits and second-guessing over the price of the next big merger."[5]

Interestingly, the judge explicitly stated in the case that he believed Michael Dell and Dell management had acted ethically; yet, the price was not fair. The judge said, "It bears emphasizing that unlike other situations that this court has confronted, there is no evidence that Mr. Dell or

his management team sought to create the valuation disconnect. To the contrary they tried to convince the market that the Company was worth more," yet "the foregoing evidence, along with other evidence in the record, establishes the existence of a significant valuation gap between the market price of the Company's common stock and the intrinsic value of the Company."[6]

Finally, what does this case suggest about valuation in general? Once you've completed a valuation, what should you do with it?

This story reflects a number of lessons from chapter 3 on the importance of incentives and information that are clearly present in the Dell management buyout. First, Michael Dell's incentives as both a seller and a buyer were not exactly clear; that conflict of interest is the foundation of this case. Second, the company, the seller, was also the buyer in the form of Michael Dell. That's what led to the winner's curse setting where nobody wanted to bid higher than Michael Dell and Silver Lake.

The example also highlights a number of lessons about valuation. First, it points out the importance of scenario analysis and thinking about expected cash flows. Second, it shows how all the different assumptions in a valuation matter when figuring out current value. Finally, and perhaps most importantly, the story reflects the idea that valuation is an art and not a science. Two well-respected experts came up with extremely different values based on different assumptions.

Quiz

Please note that some questions may have more than one answer.

1. You work for an industrial conglomerate interested in the acquisition of a steel company. Having run your valuation model through several scenarios, you come up with three outcomes. First, the worst-case scenario has a probability of 25 percent, and the company is worth $50 billion. The base-case scenario has a 50 percent chance of happening, and the company is worth $100 billion. Finally, the best-case scenario has a 25 percent chance of happening, and the company is worth $200 billion. What is the highest amount you would bid for the company?
   A. $50 billion
   B. $100 billion
   C. $112.5 billion
   D. $200 billion

2. You work for a paper mill wanting to acquire a lumber company to reduce costs. You estimate that the present value of the lumber mill as it currently operates is $500 million, based on the DCF analysis. By purchasing the lumber company, you believe you could create synergies with a present value of $50 million, in the form of reduced costs and vertical integration. The lumber mill is publicly traded, so you're able to see that the market is valuing the company at $400 million (considering the stock price, the number of shares, and accounting for debt and cash). If you want to retain all the synergy value creation for the paper mill, what is your highest bid for the company?
   A. $50 million
   B. $400 million
   C. $500 million
   D. $550 million

3. Table 5-7 shows sample P/E ratios of three fast-food companies on August 1, 2016: McDonald's, The Wendy's Company, and Yum! Brands. Which of the following is a possible explanation for the differences in P/E ratios?

TABLE 5-7

Price-to-earnings ratios for three fast-food companies

Company	Price-to-earnings ratio
McDonald's	22.0
Wendy's	20.7
Yum!	27.4

A. The market believes that Yum! Brands has more growth opportunities than Wendy's or McDonald's.

B. McDonald's has a higher discount rate than Wendy's.

C. Wendy's has a lower discount rate than Yum! Brands.

D. McDonald's has higher earnings than either Yum! Brands or Wendy's.

4. The company you work for just acquired one of your competitors. Immediately after the announcement, your company's stock dropped by 10 percent, resulting in the loss of $50 million in market capitalization. The target company's stock jumped by 15 percent, resulting in a gain of $25 million in market capitalization. Which of the following has occurred as part of the acquisition?

A. Value creation and transfer of value from acquirer to target

B. Value creation and transfer of value from target to acquirer

C. Value destruction and transfer of wealth from acquirer to target

D. Value destruction and transfer of wealth from target to acquirer

5. Which of the following is *not* an example of a valuation multiple?

A. Price to earnings

B. Enterprise value to EBITDA

C. Current assets to current liabilities

D. Market capitalization to EBITDA

6. On December 31, 2016, Goodyear Tire and Rubber Company had a multiple of enterprise value to free cash flow of 16.1. Which of the following implied assumptions were likely to be true?

A. A discount rate of 5 percent and 4 percent growth

B. A discount rate of 12 percent and no growth

C. A discount rate of 9 percent and 3 percent growth

D. A discount rate of 20 percent and 5 percent growth

7. In an attempt to figure out how much you should pay for an educational program, you perform a valuation. You estimate that the program will increase your annual earnings by **$1,000** each year, which will grow along with your salary at 3 percent each year. Considering other similarly risky investments, you calculate a discount rate of 13 percent. For the sake of convenience, assume you will live forever (there's typically not much difference between this and twenty to thirty years of cash flows). What is the maximum you are willing to pay for this educational program?

   A. $1,000

   B. $3,000

   C. $5,000

   D. $10,000

8. You are considering two projects and can choose only one: the first has an **IRR of 15 percent**, and the other, an **IRR of 25 percent. The WACC is 12 percent.** Which project should you choose?

   A. The project with the IRR of 15 percent

   B. The project with the IRR of 25 percent

   C. Neither—both projects are value destroying

   D. The project with an IRR of 25 percent is probably preferable, but you should conduct a DCF analysis.

9. You are on the acquisition team valuing a candy factory, trying to find opportunities better than the 2 to 4 percent growth rate in the overall economy. Your assistant has prepared the preliminary valuation that you are reviewing. You can see that he assumed a 6 percent growth rate for the first two years, based on the average growth rate of the industry, and then used that 6 percent growth rate as part of the growing perpetuity in the terminal value, whose present value, you notice, makes up 80 percent of the total valuation of the business. Based on these numbers, he estimated the enterprise value of the company to be **$100** million. Furthermore, he estimated that the present value of synergies is **$20** million. The company currently has **$50** million in debt and **$10** million in cash on hand. Your assistant recommends paying **$120** million for the equity of the company, which he explains is the sum of the company's valuation plus its synergies. Which of the following is a mistake your assistant may have made? (Choose all that apply.)

   A. Too high a growth rate in the terminal value

   B. Basing his growth rate on the industry

   C. Basing a purchase price on the company's value, not the equity value

   D. Paying for synergies

10. **Which of the following projects will surely create value for your business?**

    A. A project with an NPV of $100 million

    B. A project with a payback period of two years

    C. A project with an IRR of 15 percent

    D. A project with a present value (PV) of $200 million

Chapter Summary

Valuation is central to finance and management. Some methods discussed, like multiples, are simply shortcut methods. Others, like IRR, can be useful but can go wrong. Fortunately, there is a gold standard—discounted cash flow analysis—that provides a way to understand the value of a business as the present value of all future cash flows.

The exercise of forecasting, though, returns us to one of the most important lessons of this chapter—valuation is an art informed by science. There is some science involved, but fundamentally valuation is subjective and laden with judgment. We have to make sure that we don't make mistakes systematically, like overestimating synergies or underestimating the capital intensity of a business. The final lesson about valuation is that if you really want to understand a business, do a valuation of it. Only by thinking about the future, the cash flows, the capital intensity of a business, and the risk of the business can you truly understand that business.

Now that we've discussed value as a function of free cash flows and discount rates, there is one final question to tackle. What should companies do with all those free cash flows? How should they give it back to capital providers? Or should they invest in new things? How should they allocate all those free cash flows across the businesses and capital providers? Those questions are the subjects of the next chapter.

6

Capital Allocation

How to make the most important decisions facing CEOs and CFOs

n 2013, Apple shareholders mounted a revolt against Tim Cook because they didn't approve of Apple's growing cash piles and wanted Cook to distribute the cash to shareholders. Why would it matter if the cash was on Apple's balance sheet or in shareholders' pockets? Since then, Apple has distributed more than $280 billion to shareholders, largely by buying back shares. Was that wise?

At the time of the revolt, Alphabet (aka Google) changed its shareholding structure to ensure that it would never face such a challenge by increasing the voting rights of key shareholders. Since then, Alphabet has generated mountains of cash but has distributed very little, choosing instead to reinvest the cash in its varied businesses. Was that wise?

In previous chapters, we saw how generating free cash flows is critical for thinking about how, and if, companies create value. But that leads to another question: Once a company is generating free cash flows, what should management do with that cash? Should managers invest that cash in new projects? Should they acquire companies? Or should they distribute the cash to their shareholders? In recent years, we've seen a large increase in share buybacks, sometimes called repurchases. Why are companies undertaking repurchases?

Every CEO and CFO must answer these central questions. Together, these questions determine the capital allocation process. With corporate profits and cash levels at historic highs, the question of how to allocate capital is increasingly salient, and shareholders are less and less tolerant of mistakes. The capital allocation problem is another way of framing the problem we introduced in chapter 3: capital providers entrust managers with their capital and consider the fulfillment of the related obligation as a central indicator of how well management is doing their job.

A Decision Tree for Capital Allocation

The capital allocation problem is best understood as a nested series of decisions, as seen in figure 6-1. The first question a manager has to address involves the availability of positive net present value (NPV) projects to spend money on. Creating value is central to a manager's task, and that process involves beating the cost of capital, year over year, and growing, as we saw in chapter 4.

If positive NPV projects are available to you, then you should undertake them. Those projects may involve organic growth—say, introducing new products or buying new property, plant, and equipment—or inorganic growth via mergers and acquisitions. If there aren't value-creating opportunities—that is, projects with positive NPVs—then a manager should distribute the cash to shareholders through dividends or share buybacks. If you choose dividends, you'll

FIGURE 6-1

The capital allocation decision tree

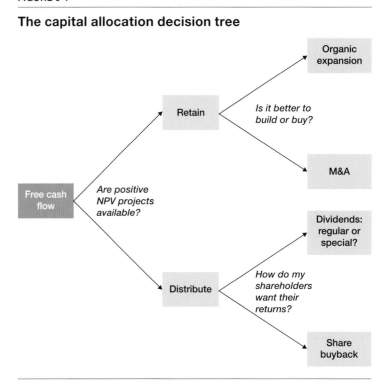

need to decide if you will create a regular dividend or issue a special one-time dividend.

While this decision tree in figure 6-1 seems simple, there are innumerable hazards and fallacies that can trip up management as they choose what action to take. In this chapter, we'll work through the entire decision tree and figure out how to make each trade-off and what mistakes to avoid.

Capital Allocation in the Pharmaceutical Industry

The figure shows R&D and cash distributions (dividends and stock repurchases) as a percentage of sales for Amgen, one of the largest biotechnology and pharmaceutical companies.

Amgen's R&D and cash distributions as a percentage of sales

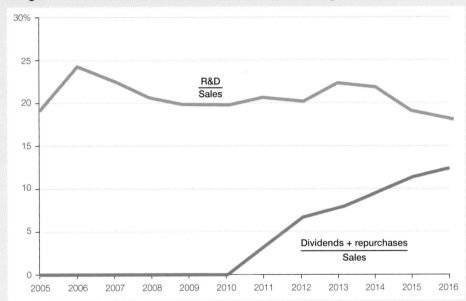

What does the figure tell you about how Amgen and the pharmaceutical industry are approaching capital allocation? Why do you think the approach is changing? The level of R&D has stayed the same or decreased during this period, while distributions—previously not done at all—have become a major element of its capital allocation process. This suggests that Amgen simply can't find enough investment opportunities given the cash flows it is generating. If Amgen is allocating capital well, shareholders are better off than if managers had invested in products or research that wouldn't yield sufficient returns. If Amgen isn't allocating capital well, it may be underinvesting in R&D to satisfy impatient shareholders.

Retaining Cash

If you're in a position to make investments, there are some basic criteria to use to make that decision. First, you need to calculate the net present values of a number of options in order to identify the best value-creation opportunities. They could be organic or inorganic, and although the simple rule is to pursue the option with the highest net present values, there are a number of trade-offs to consider.

Real-World Perspectives

Paul Clancy, former CFO of Biogen, commented:

I define capital allocation as what to do with the excess cash flow generation of the company. If a company is spending a lot of money over a long time on R&D, then that should be included in the definition as well. There are strategic deployments of capital, and then there is cap- ital deployment in the form of returning cash to shareholders. Strategic deployment is investing in plants and in capital expenditures that don't hit the P&L in the near term but are designed to improve the business over a long time. Acquisitions certainly are a big piece of it for a company that has tremendous cash flow generation and R&D. A majority of the annual R&D expenditures are also capital allocation decisions. It's deploying capital that otherwise could be freed up for shareholders.

For example, as we learned in the previous chapter, there are many problems to consider when undergoing mergers and acquisitions, which can complicate present value assessments.

The Perils of Inorganic Growth

The lure of mergers and acquisitions as opposed to organic investment is often the apparent speed of buying existing assets instead of taking the time to build those assets. Moreover, the M&A logic also implies that buying assets, as opposed to building them, is also safer, as the risk of completion has been resolved. While many people think mergers are faster and safer ways of achieving growth, there are many complications that companies must contend with before and after a transaction is completed.

Before the merger

When you buy preexisting assets, the seller has much more information about the asset than the buyer, and the buyer can only make educated guesses (as in the discussion in chapter 3). That's why due diligence is such an important part of the M&A process. Buyers need to understand the assets they're acquiring. But, in the end, they have to remember that the seller has a large informational advantage.

What might sellers do in approaching a sale? They might underinvest in assets to understate the capital intensity of the business. They might accelerate revenues and delay costs. And they might bury problems such as bankrupt customers who owe them by declaring those receivables still open.

Intermediaries, like consultants and investment banks, can help buyers with these problems, and the buyer's own deal teams can find out where the bodies are buried.

Unfortunately, everyone involved, from the seller to the intermediaries to the people within the buyer's organization

Hewlett-Packard's Acquisition of Autonomy

On August 18, 2011, Hewlett-Packard, a computer hardware manufacturer, announced that it would purchase Autonomy, a search and data analysis company. HP paid $11.1 billion for the acquisition, corresponding to a 12.6 times EBITDA multiple. This price was considered quite rich; Oracle's valuation of Autonomy determined that $6 billion would be the highest it would be willing to pay. Even HP's CFO Cathie Lesjak had reportedly spoken out against the deal.

The market's reaction to the announcement was harsh. HP's stock fell from $29.51 to $23.60 on the day of the announcement (reflecting a $5 billion drop in market capitalization). Ray Lane, chairman

of HP's board, was asked about the discounted cash flow (DCF) model used to analyze the valuation and the underlying assumptions. In response, he claimed he was not familiar with the DCF model and instead emphasized HP's strategic vision. Less than a month after the announcement, HP's chief executive was removed.

One year later, HP wrote down the value of Autonomy by $8.8 billion (in other words, it reduced the goodwill asset on its balance sheet and recorded the loss as a onetime expense), including $5 billion in what HP claimed were "accounting irregularities" that it blamed on Autonomy's management. HP claimed that Autonomy managers had inflated financial metrics in

order to mislead potential buyers. By August 2012, HP's market capitalization had fallen 43 percent from the time of the acquisition announcement.

What mistakes did HP make in its Autonomy acquisition?

HP's mistakes include, but are not limited to:

- Poor due diligence

- Insufficient investigation of accounting practices

- Lack of adherence to traditional valuation models

- Inadequate assessment of organic possibilities versus inorganic possibilities who are on those deal teams, are incentivized to complete a transaction. If you're not careful, it's easy to be swayed by their enthusiasm and end up paying too much. So the notion that M&A is safer than organic investment is far from well-grounded, and the data on the failure rates of mergers directly contradicts their supposed safety.

After the merger

Although the rationale of synergies can be tantalizing when assessing a merger, *realizing* those synergies is no trivial task. At the time of a merger, it's common to overestimate synergies, underestimate the time to realize them, and underestimate the onetime costs to realizing the synergies. Even worse, the acquirer can end up retaining two separate capacities for various functions for a long time, resulting in significantly higher costs than it had anticipated. The time it takes to realize the synergies can have a massive impact on the value creation of the merger.

Finally, and perhaps most important, cultural issues in bringing two organizations together must be considered. While the difficulty of cultural integration is easy to ignore on a spreadsheet, the issues raised by cultural differences are paramount and have significant financial consequences. It's all too easy to forget that those assumptions in the cells in spreadsheets are contingent on human actions, so ignoring them can

be fatal. These issues also signal why the seeming speed and safety of mergers and acquisitions versus organic growth can be illusory.

Conglomerates

Aggressive M&A strategies can also lead to conglomerates, or multidivisional companies with broadly diversified holdings with little shared between the holdings. For example, in the 1960s, the ITT Corporation (a telecommunications company) attempted to purchase ABC Television until federal antitrust regulators halted the deal. Seeking to avoid antitrust laws and still expand, it purchased such dissimilar companies as Sheraton Hotels, Avis Rent a Car, and the bakery that makes Wonder Bread. Ultimately, ITT purchased over three hundred companies. Conglomerates, still popular in some parts of the world, are an opportunity to revisit some important finance intuitions.

There are two finance justifications for becoming a conglomerate. The first is a cost-of-capital argument. The thinking goes like this: "By doing the diversifying acquisition, I will bring my cost of capital to that target. For example, we have a 10 percent discount rate or cost of capital and look at that target company with a cost of capital closer to 15 percent. Well, if I can buy that company and put it inside my company, it will

Merger of AOL and Time Warner

In late 2000, AOL and Time Warner announced one of the biggest mergers of the dot-com era—a deal valued at $350 billion. Before the merger, there were high expectations on how the two companies would fit together. At the time, AOL had a dominant dial-up internet business, and Time Warner owned content but didn't understand the internet. The synergies seemed clear and easy to access. The deal was pitched as a "merger of equals," but AOL was dominant at the time of the merger.

Shortly after the merger, trouble emerged. AOL's culture was aggressive and sales-driven, while Time Warner was a more traditional company. Time Warner also discovered accounting irregularities at AOL that undercut its purported performance. As frictions increased, Time Warner began to push back on AOL initiatives and found other partners for distributing its content online. When the bloom came off the internet rose in early 2001, the balance of power shifted away from AOL and toward Time Warner.

The merger collapsed, and the combined value of both companies today is a fraction of what it was before the merger. In March 2009, Time Warner spun off Time Warner Cable, and in December 2009, AOL and Time Warner completely demerged. AOL was purchased by Verizon in 2015, and AT&T reached a deal to buy Time Warner on October 22, 2016. AOL CEO Steve Case concluded, " 'Vision without execution is hallucination' pretty much sums up AOL/TW."[1]

get revalued higher because of my 10 percent cost of capital—and that can be powerful and value-creating." This reasoning is flawed, as the correct cost of capital to use is a function of that business. You can't export your cost of capital.

The second finance rationale for diversifying is to manage risk. By owning different types of companies in different industries, shareholders are thought to benefit from diversification. The thinking equates acquisitions to stock portfolios: if one company goes south, then the other companies in

your portfolio will prop it up. This line of inquiry, though, is faulty and ignores the fact that managers are undertaking diversification, while shareholders could arguably achieve that risk management themselves. The logic of finance is that you shouldn't do something for your shareholders that they can do for themselves. And diversification at the corporate level is exactly that.

Indeed, conglomerates appear to destroy value rather than create it. Conglomerates often trade at a discount, which

Jaguar Land Rover Acquisition

In late March 2008, Indian carmaker Tata Motors purchased Jaguar Land Rover (JLR) from Ford Motor Company, paying $2.3 billion for the acquisition (Ford had paid $5.4 billion for the two brands: $2.5 billion for Jaguar in 1989, and $2.9 billion for Land Rover in 2000). The market wasn't impressed, and Tata Motor's stock fell during 2008 as a result (from a market capitalization of $6.93 billion the day before the announcement to $1.72 billion at the end of the year, a 75 percent drop in a period when the broader market fell 33 percent).

After the merger, Tata chose not to integrate JLR. Instead, it let JLR operate as an independent company. Tata set targets and offered support in emerging markets but did not directly control JLR's operations. As the figure shows, this strategy of avoiding a potentially difficult cultural integration appears to have paid off.

Some analysts estimate that JLR now comprises 90 percent of Tata Motor's total valuation. In hindsight, Tata's decision not to integrate JLR worked out extremely well. But it's worth considering the risks, which include duplicative overhead expenses as well as competition and confusion in product and labor markets, when a new acquisition operates largely independently.

Tata Motors' stock performance, 2004–2018

means that their combined value is less than if the businesses were traded separately. Why would that be? In part, because capital allocation within a conglomerate is distorted by the pressure to treat all divisions equally. In the process, capital is distributed equally rather than allocated toward the best opportunities—weak divisions expand and promising divisions are starved. As a consequence, the divisions would be worth more apart than together.

Conglomerates aren't always problematic. In some emerging markets, conglomerates can be powerful because they overcome market imperfections in capital markets and labor markets by internalizing activity inside that conglomerate. But they aren't a panacea, and managers in conglomerates must be vigilant about the possibility of "socializing" capital.

Distributing Cash to Shareholders

Assuming a company doesn't have worthwhile projects to pursue, it should distribute cash to shareholders. If a firm decides to distribute cash, how should it do so? There are two primary options—dividends and stock buybacks. The more intuitive way to distribute cash is to pay a dividend. A company simply pays cash to its shareholders on a pro rata basis. Dividends can be part of a predictable flow or they can be larger, one-off events—so-called special dividends.

The second method of cash distribution—a share buyback—is less intuitive. A company buys back its own shares in the open market and then retires them. As a consequence, investors who choose not to sell their shares will own a slightly larger fraction of the company, and cash has been distributed. Share buybacks have become tremendously popular over the last decade. (See figure 6-2.)

So which is the better method of distributing cash—dividends or share buybacks? There is no right answer to this question, but it is useful to begin by debunking some misconceptions so you can develop some better intuitions on this decision. For example, some argue that stock prices rise after buybacks because the remaining shareholders own more of the company afterward. Others argue that dividends are bad for shareholders because their shares will be worth less. To debunk these ideas and clarify the nature of the decision, we will begin by showing that whether a company chooses to distribute cash *shouldn't matter*.

In terms of the raw mechanics, the choice between dividends and buybacks is irrelevant, but each method potentially sends a different signal to the market, and that can matter. First, let's prove that it *shouldn't matter* and that outcomes are equal. Let's look at the market-based balance sheet in figure 6-3.

The company in the figure has a large amount of cash and is considering distributing some via a dividend or buyback. Because this balance sheet is market-based, the equity values can easily be translated to share prices and the value of operating assets are market values. If the company distributes $70 of that cash as a dividend to shareholders, what will happen to that market value balance sheet? Given that there are a hundred shares outstanding, that's a $0.70 per share dividend. (See figure 6-4.)

The company's cash holdings drop $70 from $100 to $30, but the value of the operating assets remains the same.

FIGURE 6-2

US corporations' dividends versus buybacks, 2005–2016

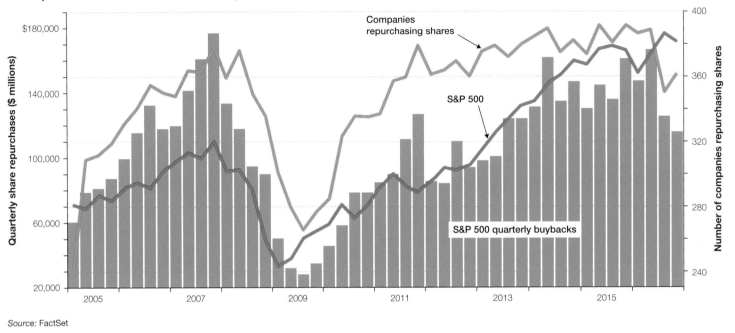

Source: FactSet

FIGURE 6-3

Preparing for a cash distribution

Assets		Liabilities and shareholders equity	
Cash	$100	Debt	$60
Operating assets	$100	Equity	$140 ← 100 shares at $1.40 per share

Because the debt remains the same, the equity value also has to drop $70 for the balance sheet to balance. The price per share would fall from $1.40 per share to $0.70 per share. As a shareholder, you might seem to be taking a hit. But when you factor in the $0.70 in cash you received, you're left with $1.40. Shareholders are economically in the same position as they were before. It's completely value-neutral. They could

FIGURE 6-4

Post-dividend, market-based balance sheet

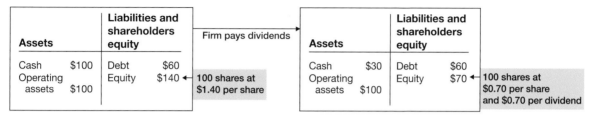

FIGURE 6-5

Post-buyback, market-based balance sheet

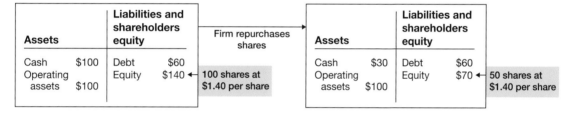

return to where they began by buying one share with that $0.70 in cash, and they would be left with $1.40 in shares, just as before.

Now, let's consider if the company distributes $70 of its cash by buying back $70 worth of shares. (See figure 6-5.)

Again, its cash drops to $30, and the operating assets and debt remain the same. The equity value drops to $70. The $70 used to buy shares retires fifty shares, given the stock price of $1.40. What is the new stock price? Total equity value is $70, and there are now fifty shares outstanding; that provides a $1.40 share price. So how are shareholders feeling? The shareholders who sold to the company are left with $1.40 in cash, and the shareholders who stayed have a share worth $1.40. Nothing has changed—it's value-neutral. (See figure 6-6.)

FIGURE 6-6

Cash distribution: dividends versus share repurchases

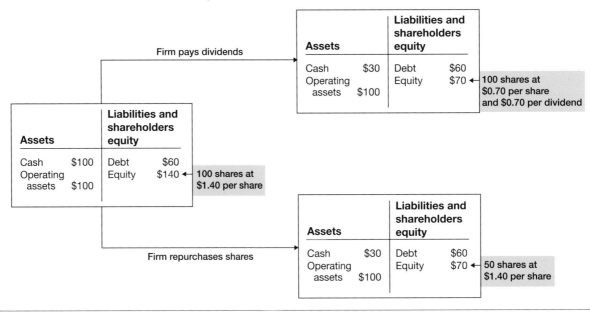

This exercise has an important core intuition. Value doesn't arise from taking cash from one pocket and placing it in the other. Value arises from pursuing positive NPV projects. If neither keeping nor distributing cash results in changed value, then why is there all the fuss? Why are people so worried about whether companies are holding on to cash or distributing it? And why are they so worried whether they pay a dividend or not? And why have more and more firms started to buy back shares?

The Decision to Distribute Cash

The value neutrality of keeping or distributing cash is true under idealized conditions, the so-called Modigliani and Miller conditions of no taxes, perfect information, and no transaction costs. Under these conditions, there are no value consequences to the mechanics of dividends or buybacks.

Real-world considerations have an impact on these decisions, however. First, taxes can change the consequences for value. For example, during a share buyback, investors have to sell their shares and incur a capital gain that may be taxed at a lower rate, while a dividend can be taxed at higher rates. Many people think that these tax consequences are one reason to prefer share buybacks over dividends.

The critical element in the real world is the asymmetric information and incentives discussed in chapter 3. How would you interpret a decision by Apple to undertake a share buyback? How would you react if it decided to pay a dividend?

If you think back to that asymmetric information problem, all actions are judged by the information they are thought to reveal. If the people with all the information about the company are buying back shares, they must think the firm is undervalued and are willing to put real money behind that sentiment. This decision is a very strong signal and helps explain why buybacks have become so popular and are often greeted with a price rise. Price reactions to share buybacks are driven by that signaling interpretation, not by the mechanics of dilution.

What about dividends? Dividend initiations can sometimes be met with the opposite reaction, even though dividends effectuate the same outcome as buybacks. Individuals with all the information about the company's prospects are saying that they can't find good investments and they don't think the company is undervalued. In effect, they don't have

anything better to do with your money, so they're giving it back to you. That's not exactly the most positive signal.

It is possible to interpret dividend increases positively. Since dividends are fairly sticky (once a company starts paying dividends, it's hard to stop), increasing dividends may mean the company has faith in the ongoing, increased profitability of the enterprise. Furthermore, if the company is going to maintain that dividend, it also binds management's hands to some degree, which some investors think reduces the principal-agent problem discussed in chapter 3.

Indeed, agency considerations are the other reason cash distribution decisions can have value consequences. Managers can use cash inside companies to pursue their own agendas, which may not coincide with shareholder interests. For example, as cash piles up, a CEO may be tempted by an acquisition that enhances their position in the CEO labor market but actually destroys value. So getting cash out of the corporation can have value consequences, not because of the mechanics of the distribution, but because it alleviates agency considerations.

Agency considerations can also provide a distinct interpretation of share buybacks. If the signaling argument were the whole story, we'd expect managers to time buybacks well and to be buying at low points in the market. As seen in figure 6–2, this doesn't appear to be happening in the aggregate, as the last market peak was also the peak for buybacks. So clearly some firms are doing buybacks well and some are doing it poorly.

Adopting an agency perspective can help explain this phenomenon. Share buybacks can also be used to achieve various operating metrics. Let's say a manager is a penny short on earnings per share (EPS) for a given quarter and knows that he'll be punished by the market for the error, possibly making him miss out on a bonus. How can he "manufacture" a penny of EPS? A share buyback reduces the number of shares outstanding and increases EPS. But that short-run illusion of higher EPS is likely not in the best interests of shareholders.

In short, the mechanics of cash distributions often lead people to fallacious arguments about value consequences associated with dilution or share counts. The raw mechanics of buybacks and dividends are all value-neutral. The reason these decisions attract so much attention is because they provide information and address the principal-agent problem discussed in chapter 3.

Myths and Realities in Financing Decisions

The notion of value neutrality can help us understand a variety of financial transactions—equity issuances, stock splits, leveraged recapitalizations, and venture financing—

Real-World Perspectives

Laurence Debroux, CFO of Heineken, commented:

Some people believe that if you distribute dividends or do share buybacks, that means that you don't have any good projects to invest in. It's more of a balance. You can be a growth company and distribute a good dividend at the same time. Ten years ago, some institutional shareholders were not interested in dividends. They didn't know what to do with it; it was complicated to collect. Some even sold the shares just before a dividend was distributed and bought back the shares afterward so they didn't have to deal with it.

and the illusions and mistakes they give rise to. This detour from capital allocation to financing transactions will help you cement many intuitions that we have developed.

Equity issuance

Many consider the value consequences of issuing equity problematic because of dilution. Specifically, equity issuance is thought to lead to stock price declines because investors end up with a smaller piece of the company.

FIGURE 6-7

Pre-transaction, market-based balance sheet

Assets		Liabilities and shareholders equity		
Cash	$100	Debt	$60	
Operating assets	$100	Equity	$140	← 100 shares at $1.40 per share

Let's return to the sample company and see how equity issuance works. Once again, we're looking at a market-based balance sheet. (See figure 6-7.)

If the company decides to issue $70 more in equity, what will happen to its market-based balance sheet and the stock price? (See figure 6-8.)

After the company issues $70 in equity, it will have $70 more in cash for a total of $170; its operating assets and debt level are unchanged, so the market value of equity is now $210. How much are the shares worth? To think this through, we need to know how many shares are outstanding after the issuance. Shares are selling at $1.40 each, so raising $70 would require the company to issue 50 shares ($70 divided by $1.40). That leaves 150 shares outstanding to split the $210 in equity. Shares must therefore be selling for $1.40 per share ($210 divided by 150), just as before.

Issuing equity has not diminished the price of the company's stock—it is exactly the same. In general, this is a manifestation of the lesson that value creation comes from the asset side of the balance sheet, not from financing. What about dilution? Shareholders may now have a smaller percentage share, but it is of a larger pie.

Even so, when companies issue stock, the stock price often does decline. Why do you think this happens? In chapter 3, we saw the nature of the information problem in capital markets. When companies are issuing shares, they are sellers of

FIGURE 6-8

Post-financing, market-based balance sheet

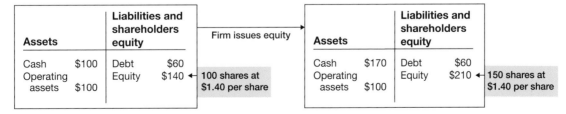

shares. This inevitably leads to questions about why they are choosing to raise funds by selling shares as opposed to using debt or internally generated profits. In short, equity issuance sends a negative signal.

Stock splits

A similar confusion can arise about stock splits. Let's say the company decides to split its stock two-for-one. In other words, for every share of stock that an investor currently holds, they will now hold two shares. This can also be termed a stock dividend—every holder of a share will receive one share. What will happen to the company's market-based balance sheet, and what will happen to the value of its shares? (See figure 6-9.)

There are no changes to the market-based balance sheet because there have been no changes in operations or to financing sources. What is each share worth? There's still $140 worth of equity, but now it's now split over 200 shares, so each share is worth $0.70 ($140 divided by 200). Investors haven't lost value. Each investor used to have one share worth $1.40. Now they have two shares worth $0.70 each, for a total of $1.40. No value has been created or destroyed by this stock split.

Some companies split their stock in order to make their stock price more enticing to smaller investors, but Warren Buffett has refused to ever split his stock. His company, Berkshire Hathaway, currently has A Class shares that trade at over $215,000 per share. His reasoning is that stock splits are meaningless and only encourage short-term interest in a stock through a seemingly cheaper price. In 1983, Buffett asked, "Could we really improve our shareholder group by trading some of present clear-thinking members for impressionable new ones who, preferring paper to value, feel wealthier with ten $10 bills than with one $100 bill?"[2] (In 1996, Buffett did introduce B Class shares that sold for one-thirtieth the price of

FIGURE 6-9

Post-split, market-based balance sheet

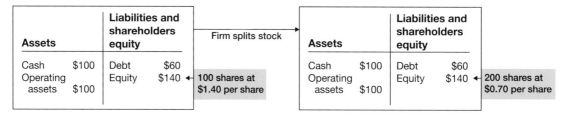

the A shares in order to allow more investors to buy his shares. These B shares have since undertaken stock splits.)

These kinds of actions can remove frictions in some circumstances. In 2011, Citigroup performed a reverse stock split: for every ten shares of stock held, investors received one share. Citigroup did this because its stock price had fallen to $4, and many institutional investors have guidelines that prevent them from purchasing stocks for less than $5. By performing the reverse stock split, Citigroup raised its price to $40 and was able to access an important group of investors for its shares. Stock splits do not create value *per se* but can have value consequences because of market imperfections, just as with stock issuance.

Leveraged recapitalization

A leveraged recapitalization sounds like a complicated and scary transaction, but it's just a combination of transactions we've already seen. In effect, it is a large dividend funded by the issuance of debt. Imagine that the private equity fund that owns a company wants to do a leveraged recapitalization. The company will borrow an additional $60 and combine it with $40 of its cash to pay out a special $100 cash dividend to its shareholders. What will happen to the market-based balance sheet, and what will the shares be worth? (See figure 6-10.)

First, debt will increase by $60, and cash will increase by $60 to $160. Then, cash will decrease by $100, because it is used to pay a dividend. Adding up the market value of the operating assets and remaining cash and subtracting debt, we're left with $40 of equity value. What does this mean for the shareholders? One hundred shares are now worth $0.40 per share ($40 divided by 100 shares), but shareholders have also received a dividend of $100, split up across those shares—or $1 each ($100 divided by one hundred shares). That adds up to the same $1.40 per share the fund had before.

FIGURE 6-10

Post-recapitalization, market-based balance sheet

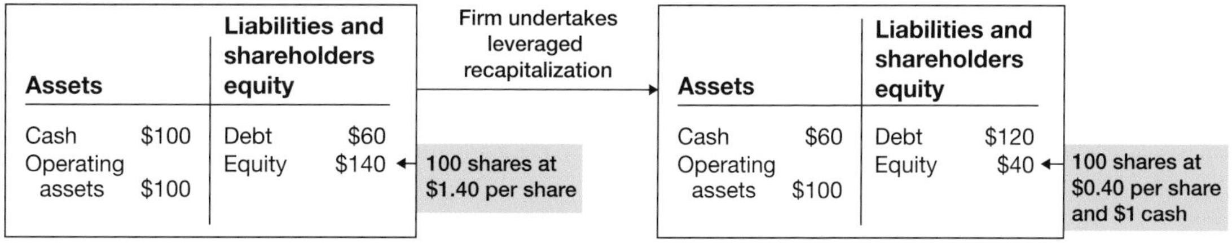

The mechanics of this transaction don't necessarily yield value consequences, but there can be value consequences because of other factors. Specifically, the equity is now substantially riskier, and that should be associated with higher expected returns (as we saw in chapter 4) and lower values.

Venture financing

As companies grow and require more funding, their founders find investors—called angel investors—to provide funding. This process often happens more than once, and the different rounds of funding are called Series A, Series B, and so on, and can also feature professional venture capital firms.

Let's imagine a brand-new enterprise. Before the first round of external financing, its balance sheet is a little ambiguous. The founders own the equity, and the founders' ideas are the assets of the company. The founders have allocated a hundred shares of company stock to themselves, but the company is still entirely private.

The company needs an additional $100 to invest in a positive NPV project and goes to a venture capitalist for that funding. The venture capitalist says, "I'll give you the $100 in funding you're requesting, but I want to own 20 percent of the company in return." By making that offer, the venture capitalist has implicitly valued the company.

If 20 percent of the company's equity is worth $100, then 100 percent of the company's equity must be worth $500. And if balance sheets have to balance, then $500 is the value of all the assets as well. Since the company will have $100 in cash immediately after the financing, this means the remaining asset—the business the founders have built so far—is worth $400. The $500 on the equity side is split between the founders (80 percent) and the venture capitalists (20 percent), so the founders' stake is worth $400 ($500 multiplied by 80 percent), and the venture capitalists' stake is worth $100 ($500 multiplied by 20 percent). Finally, 25 shares are issued to the venture capitalists to represent their share of the equity, for a total of 125 shares (the founders currently have 100 shares, and 100 shares are 80 percent of 125; likewise, 25 shares are 20 percent of 125). The value of each share is $4 ($500 of equity divided by 125 shares). This round of funding implicitly values the business before the funding (this is sometimes called the pre-money value) and by valuing the business after the funding (the post-money value). (See figure 6-11.)

Now, let's imagine that the company returns a few years later for a second round of financing (the B Series). The company doesn't have any more cash on hand (its cash bal-

FIGURE 6-11

Post–Series A, market-based balance sheet

Assets		Liabilities and shareholders equity		
Cash	$100	Equity (founders)	$400 }	125 shares at $4 per share
Enterprise value	$400	Equity (investors)	$100	

ance is $0), and it's asking for $1,000 in investment. The Series B investors ask for 50 percent of the company in return for the $1,000 investment. What does the balance sheet look like after this round of financing, and what are the founders' shares now worth?

The Series B investors are offering $1,000 for 50 percent of the company. After the investment, there will be $1,000 in cash and the existing business. If the $1,000 represents 50 percent of the company, then all of the equity is worth $2,000. This implies that the enterprise is now worth $1,000 ($2,000 total asset value − $1,000 cash).

The founders have 100 shares and the Series A investors have 25 shares. These 125 shares are worth $1,000, or $8 per share ($1,000 divided by 125). That means the value of the founders' shares is now $800 ($8 times 100), and the value of the Series A investors' shares is now $200 ($8 times 25).

Finally, 125 shares are issued to the Series B investors to represent their 50 percent ownership that is worth $1,000. (See figure 6-12.)

Have the founders seen their equity diluted? The founders have gone from owning 100 percent of the company and holding stock worth an unknown amount, to owning 80 percent of the company (after the first round of financing) and holding stock worth $4 per share ($400), to owning 40 percent of the company (after the second round of financing) and holding stock worth $8 per share ($800). With each round of financing, their equity is diluted, but their stakes grow in value because the pie is growing larger as well.

The process of share issuance is particularly fraught in the case of new ventures because those financings actually involve telling a founder what they are worth. But the mechanics of equity financings do not give rise to value consequences. Sim-

FIGURE 6-12

Post–Series B, market-based balance sheet

Assets		Liabilities and shareholders equity		
Cash	$1,000	Equity (founders)	$800 }	250 shares at $8 per share
Enterprise value	$1,000	Equity (A investors)	$200	
		Equity (B investors)	$1,000	

ilarly, distributions per se don't change value, but distributions that change the riskiness of shares, like leveraged recapitalization, can have an impact on value because they change risk, expected returns, and prices, as we saw in chapter 4.

Cash on Balance Sheets

What if corporations neither distribute nor invest? What if they just hoard cash? Over the last ten years, that situation has become more common and has exasperated many. Why hold on to cash? There are several possible reasons to hoard cash. First and foremost, there have been significant tax penalties to US companies for paying out cash if that cash is held abroad (these penalties were lessened by Congress at the end of 2017). Second, as we saw in chapter 1, cash balances can serve as insurance against rocky times. Finally, it's possible that they are just waiting to find the right investment.

Six Major Mistakes in Capital Allocation

Given the importance of capital allocation, it's useful to emphasize the precise places where things can go wrong. These are six of the biggest mistakes that happen during the capital allocation process.

- **Delaying decision making.** Not making capital allocation decisions results in rising cash levels on corporate balance sheets. These rising cash levels typically frustrate shareholders as they question why managers are unable to deploy capital. Moreover, cash on balance sheets can attract the attention of activist investors who can use that cash as financing to take that company private.

- **Trying to create value through share buybacks.** Managers sometimes justify buybacks by claiming that they create value for shareholders by buying shares cheaply. In fact, value can't be created through share buybacks. At best, share buybacks transfer value across shareholders, depending on the buyback prices for shares. Managers can only create value by investing in positive NPV projects.

- **Preferring acquisitions over organic investment because acquisitions are faster and safer.** Acquisitions appear to be faster and safer but can actually prove to be the opposite. Because of the informational problems between sellers and buyers, it can be risky to acquire companies, and the integration issues associated with acquisitions can offset any purported gains.

Costco's Distribution Choices

Since 2000, Costco (a membership-based wholesale retailer) has used a variety of cash distribution options (regular dividends, special dividends, and share repurchases). The graph shows Costco's stock performance compared to its usage of the different options.

Costco's cash distribution, 2000–2015

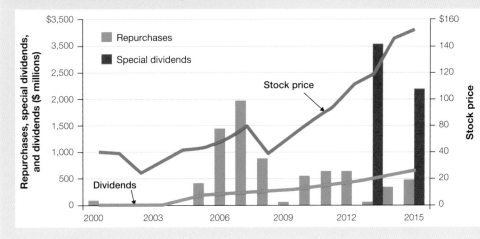

You can see how Costco has slowly grown its regular dividends while experimenting with other methods, such as heavy share repurchases from 2005 to 2008, and a heavy round of special onetime dividends in 2013 and 2015.

What do you think about the timing of Costco's decisions on buybacks and dividends?

It certainly looks as if Costco has repurchased wisely, given subsequent appreciation of the stock. Meanwhile, it has also used regular dividends and special dividends.

- **Preferring buybacks over dividends because buybacks are discretionary while dividends are not.** In fact, shareholders can become just as accustomed to a steady stream of buybacks as they do with dividends. Moreover, shareholders value a company's commitment to pay dividends, which can result in gains to shareholders. Finally, special dividends are a simple way to distribute cash that explicitly will not generate expectations for future dividends.

- **Preferring to reinvest cash to build a larger business.** Size, rather than value creation, can quickly become

IBM's Repurchases and EPS

In recent years, IBM has embraced share buybacks. Since 2005, it has distributed more than $125 billion through share buybacks and over $32 billion in dividends. This com-pares to $82 billion on R&D and $18 billion on capital expenditures.

In 2007, IBM announced a plan to increase its EPS to $10 per share by 2010, through a combi-nation of margins, acquisition, growth, and buybacks. In 2010, it increased that target to $20 per share by 2015, with at least a third of this increase coming from buybacks. (See the figure.)

IBM versus S&P 500, 2010–2018

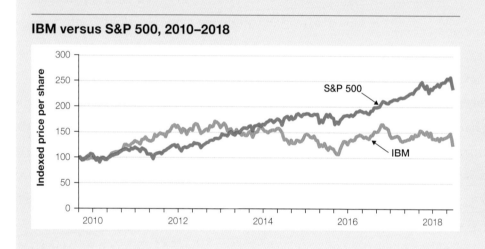

Looking at the graph, what do you think are the pros and cons of IBM's use of share buybacks over this period?

Given the subsequent stock perfor-mance and the rise of cloud com-puting, it's hard not to wonder if the company missed out on investment opportunities and if the buybacks were well-timed.

an objective of managers as it's more fun to run a larger business. Building empires can become a major objective for managers that can contradict their man-date to be good stewards of capitals.

- **Excessive distribution of cash to satisfy short-term shareholders.** Overlooking positive NPV projects is as problematic as pursuing size over value creation. Short-term earnings goals and pressure from share-holders who care only about these short-term earn-ings metrics can cause a manager to overlook good investments.

Biogen's Acquisition of Convergence Pharmaceuticals— Risks of Integration

In January 2015, Biogen announced the acquisition of Convergence Pharmaceuticals, a company working on developing drug therapies for neuropathic pain. Convergence was a small biotech company based in Cambridge, England. GlaxoSmithKline, a major player in the pharmaceutical industry, had deprioritized its therapies for pain management, spun off Convergence, and gave it some seed funding to continue its research. At the same time, Biogen began to prioritize therapies and drugs for nerve pain, and was looking for acquisition opportunities.

At a conference, one of Biogen's scientists learned about Convergence and its therapy for trigeminal neuralgia, a debilitating form of facial pain. At the time, Convergence was showing what is referred to as Phase II data—essentially, the company was close to achieving proof of concept.

For a small acquisition like this, Biogen started by examining the science, assessing the probability of the therapy going to market, and researching whether or not the therapy is protected by a patent. From there, the finance people got involved. Working with sales and marketing, they began to form the basis for a NPV model that took into account development costs. Then they looked at a range of outcomes and decided whether this was an attractive acquisition.

How would you incorporate the technological risk of a new pharmaceutical product into the valuation of an acquisition? How would the potential existence of synergies affect your opening and final bids?

You should model the technological risk by building various scenarios when developing your valuation. Based on the likelihood of these scenarios (e.g., anything from the technology being worthless to it taking off), you can create a weighted average of those scenarios to generate your final expected value for the acquisition.

You also want to think about the stand-alone value and the value you will be providing to that company. When bidding, the expected value, including the value-added, should be your final ultimate bid, while you may base your opening bid on the valuation from a stand-alone perspective.

Convergence is what Biogen's CFO Paul Clancy calls a one molecule product—that is, one therapy for one disease. Since the usage for the product is narrow, the risk is high. So Biogen sought to mitigate some of that risk. Because

Convergence was a small company that needed more funding, Biogen offered it cash up front to cover its funding costs and then a percentage of future profits. This way, both Biogen and Convergence had skin in the game.

With a contingent value right (CVR) instrument, the payoff to the seller is the function of a future event, such as drug performance or the performance of an acquisition. How does a CVR reallocate risks in the Biogen-Convergence deal and why would Clancy want to use one?

By using a CVR, Biogen has shifted some risk to the seller, relative to an outright acquisition. This transfer makes sense for several reasons. When faced with taking a CVR, only confident sellers would be willing to accept it, so it selects against those with weaker prospects. Additionally, Biogen has ensured it hasn't overpaid if the technology fails. Finally, the CVR gives the seller an incentive to work hard to ensure the success of the drug. The CVR addresses the deep asymmetric information problem in this setting—Convergence knows the value of the molecule that it's selling better than Biogen ever could.

After the acquisition was complete, Biogen began the integration phase. The question was: Should Convergence remain in England or be brought to the United States? At first, Biogen decided to keep Convergence where it was. If it turned out to be a marketable project, Biogen would reconsider. By keeping the Convergence team in England, Biogen thought that it could preserve the team's entrepreneurial spirit.

What would some of the challenges be if Biogen decided to fully integrate Convergence?

There are many challenges:

- The scientists who developed the treatment may not want to move to Boston, which could result in losing knowledge of how to continue development.

- Cultural clashes may impede integration if the team from Convergence is no longer fully stand-alone.

- Convergence's team members had incentives to work as a team and succeed. By integrating them fully, this team dynamic might be lost.

Ultimately, Biogen kept Convergence separate for two years before moving drug R&D and production to its other facilities, at which point it closed the original Convergence facility.

Heineken in Ethiopia—Risks of Expanding in Another Country

Like Biogen, Heineken is a large company that often expands through acquisitions, especially when it's trying to move into a new country. In 2012, Heineken purchased two companies in Ethiopia as part of its expansion into Africa. Heineken thought that Ethiopia, with its fast-developing economy, young population, and relatively low beer consumption, was worth investing in.

In addition to all of the normal concerns when acquiring a company, what are the financial concerns of acquiring a company in another country?

There are several potential risks, including:

- The risk of being exposed to a foreign currency. Since revenue is denominated in the currency of the other country, changes in the value of its currency could have an impact on total cash flows once those flows are converted to the home currency.

- The risks associated with trade agreements or taxation.

- The risks that revenue projections will be lower than expected because of differing cultural tastes.

- The political risk of the country—a possibility that a future government could seize state-owned breweries.

Whenever a company has operations in a new country, logistics can be particularly problematic. Large companies like Heineken have specialists in logistics and negotiations who can deliver the best cost estimates. But logistics costs can wreak havoc on financial forecasts. For example, there are discharge costs to remove goods from ships; if you're unable to load the goods onto trucks in a timely manner, suppliers will charge a fee for every day you're late. These extra costs can skew forecasts.

In an emerging market like Africa, there are often surprise costs, such as logistics costs. How might you incorporate them into your initial NPV for the acquisition?

As with the risk of bringing a new drug to market, you can use scenarios to analyze the likelihood of pessimistic outcomes. To do those scenarios correctly, you need to research the company and country you are thinking of investing in. The weighted average of those scenarios, with their associated probabilities, is the best valuation you can arrive at amid this kind of uncertainty.

What challenges do you think a foreign acquisition creates for integration?

The chance of cultural differences can be higher, in the work practices of not only the business but also the country. Synergies may be harder to realize than expected. For example,

Real-World Perspectives

Heineken's CFO Laurence Debroux commented:

There is nothing worse than putting two organizations next to each other and saying, "We're going to take the best of both worlds, and we're going to take our time and choose our ERP system, and we're going to see what we do with the IT." People will be totally demotivated and not know where they are. It is actually better for someone to know that their boss has not been appointed as a future boss of the organization than to be in the middle of nowhere and not know what's going to happen to the organization. They can then make a clear choice—"Do I stay, do I leave? If I stay, am I motivated enough? Do I work with the person that I'm told is going to be driving the show tomorrow?" You need clarity, and the sooner you have clarity, the better it is for the business and the people.

you can't integrate an IT call center if there is a language barrier. Additionally, there are the hazards of integrating a company thousands of miles away. Local management may not have an incentive to work with you and may resist your changes. Incorporating all of these potential issues into a scenario analysis is critical to making the right decision.

Biogen's Share Repurchases

Leading up to 2015, Biogen had achieved top-line growth of between 20 percent and 40 percent. Driven by the success of Tecfidera, a treatment for multiple sclerosis, Biogen had nearly doubled its business. Since the company was building up cash, and its financial outlook was robust, investors were especially keen to understand what the company planned to do with its excess cash.

In 2015, CFO Paul Clancy met with the board and got approval for a $5 billion share-repurchase program, which the company planned to implement over many years. When the board approved the program, the company's stock price was high, hovering between the mid- and high $300s, so the company decided to wait to implement the program.

A few months later, as Tecfidera's growth began to moderate, its stock price dropped into the mid-$200s. In Clancy's calculations, the market was wrong and was undervaluing the company by about 20 percent. The company had also been, according to Clancy, "working on [its] pipeline pretty intently through tuck-in acquisitions and a number of organic programs that . . . could come to fruition over the next couple of years."

What advantages and disadvantages does Clancy have over analysts and investors in Biogen when he performs a valuation of his own company?

Unlike outside analysts, Clancy likely knows much more about the future prospects of the company and its drugs. The disadvantage is that he may not have an outside perspective and his views may be colored by being an insider. Given the stock price drop, Clancy and his team at Biogen decided to go ahead and expedite its share-repurchase program.

What are the advantages to undertaking share buybacks over a short time? (Hint: think about signaling.)

The benefits are that a company would send a strong signal that it believes that its stock price is undervalued. Performing share repurchases regularly suggests a policy of repurchasing, while buying back many shares at once signals a belief in the undervaluation of stock. Figure 6-13 shows Biogen's share buyback program, including the amounts and the company's stock performance since January 2015. Until July 2017, Biogen stock hovered just below $300 per share before jumping to around $350 with the announcement of a new Alzheimer's disease therapy.

FIGURE 6-13

Biogen's share buyback program versus stock performance, 2012–2018

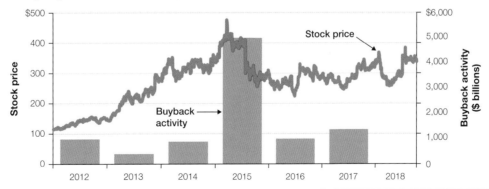

Do you think Biogen's stock repurchase has been successful? Why or why not?

Altogether, Biogen bought back $5.46 billion, at a weighted average of $303.66. By late 2018, the Biogen stock price was $325.

A Shareholder Revolt against Apple

Activist investors are increasingly pressuring managers to justify their capital allocation decisions. In 2012, just as Apple was succeeding in the product markets, shareholders revolted. At the time, Apple had amassed more than $130 billion in cash. The market value of Apple's stock was $560 billion, which meant that the company was valued at $430 billion (its market value minus its excess cash). Investors, led by David Einhorn and Carl Icahn, decided to revolt.

In Einhorn and Icahn's view, Apple was acting like a bank, and its cash was stockpiled at zero percent interest. They called upon Apple to distribute some of its cash. Apple resisted these calls on two grounds. First, the world economy wasn't stable, so the stockpiled cash could be necessary at a future date to ward off trouble. Second, it could use the cash for future investment opportunities.

Apple's explanations were fine in theory. The problem was that the amount of cash far exceeded plausible values associated with those explanations. If the business fell apart, for example, it could continue for many years with much less cash. The same goes for its investments. Even if Apple wanted to acquire a company—which had never been a part of its growth history—$130 billion was enough to buy Hewlett-Packard three times over. In fact, its most recent acquisition at the time was Beats, for just $3 billion.

There was another big reason Apple was resistant to dividends and buybacks. Since most of its cash was in Ireland, bringing back the cash to the United States might trigger tax consequences that Apple didn't want. To get around the issue, Einhorn proposed what he called an iPref. Einhorn noted that Apple was currently trading at $450 per share and was producing $45 in EPS for a P/E multiple of 10X. Einhorn proposed to take $10 of the $45 in EPS and give it to the shareholders in the form of iPref dividends. More specifically, each shareholder would receive five iPrefs for each common share owned, and each of those iPrefs would receive $2 in dividends per year. Effectively, Einhorn was dividing the $45 of EPS into $35 of earnings associated with their common shares and $10 of earnings associated with their iPref shares.

Why go to this trouble? According to Einhorn, this move would unlock large amounts of value. The new common shares would be valued at the same P/E ratio of 10X, as the original common shares were, and would be worth $350. And the new iPref would be valued as a very safe bond because of the cash in Ireland, so investors would be happy with a 4 percent return. The willingness to live with a 4 percent return implies that the five iPrefs would collectively be valued at $250 ($250 × 4% = $10 dividends). That is, the iPref would be valued at a multiple of 25X, or a 4 percent return. So a share previously worth $450 would be split, and the combined value would rise to $600 ($250 + $350).

How could Einhorn create $150 per share by this financial engineering? What's wrong with this plan? What happened to the idea of value neutrality?

Einhorn was suggesting that by splitting $45 of earnings into $35 for the common shares and $10 for the iPref, value would jump. How did he accomplish that? The key is thinking he could safely assume those multiples of 25X for the iPref and 10X for the new common shares.

Which of those two assumptions—25X for the iPref or 10X for the common—is suspect? Initially, the 25X assumption might seem suspect, but that's reasonable given how low yields were on regular bonds and how safe the iPref would be. The suspect assumption is keeping the P/E multiple on the common stock the same as it was before, at 10X. That's

effectively saying the $45 earnings stream on the old common shares should be valued the same as the $35 earning stream on the new common shares.

But are those two earning streams the same? Because of the iPref in Apple's capital structure, the new common stock is quite a bit riskier. In effect, Einhorn is saying you don't care about risk. You'll pay the same amount for the common stock before, 10X, as you will after there's an additional claim ahead of it. That's effectively saying you won't charge any additional return for bearing that additional risk. That is likely a dubious assumption. The common stock would trade at a lower earnings multiple because of the higher expected return associated with bearing more risk (see figure 4-11).

Imagine that you are Apple. Einhorn has created a revolt over the iPrefs, and your shareholders are demanding that you do something. Do you agree to the iPref idea, even though you know it won't do what Einhorn is promising? Do you try to point out to your shareholders that his math is dubious? Do you give a dividend? Buy back shares?

Even though Einhorn's logic was a little dubious, Apple effectively buckled and launched one of the largest share buyback programs ever and increased its dividend severalfold over time. It committed to distributing over $100 billion by the end of 2015. At the same time, Apple agreed to distribute cash, it borrowed about $20 billion. Why borrow money when you're sitting on large sums of cash? One reason is it wanted to avoid taxes on the cash it was bringing back from Ireland. That pattern continues. In 2018, Apple had around $115 billion of debt, had distributed $290 billion largely through buybacks, and held around $280 billion of cash. It funded much of its returns to shareholders by borrowing.

Over time, and particularly at the announcements of these distributions of cash, Apple stock rose quite a bit and ultimately split. Einhorn's logic was wrong, and he likely knew it. But he succeeded in shining a light on the problem of cash at Apple. And Apple management effectively said, "Fine, we'll distribute these cash flows and go down the distribution branch of the capital allocation tree."

Quiz

Please note that some questions may have more than one answer.

1. **On February 14, 2017, Humana, Inc., announced a $2 billion share-repurchase program, with $1.5 billion accelerated to the first quarter of 2017. Immediately, the stock price increased from $205 per share to $207 per share. Which of the following is a reason stock prices go up after the announcement of a stock buyback?**

A. Signaling

B. Antidilution

C. Value creation

D. Taxes

2. **In September 2016, Bayer announced the acquisition of Monsanto for $66 billion. Which of the following is a concern for Bayer after completing the acquisition of Monsanto? (Choose all that apply.)**

A. Due diligence

B. Realization of synergies

C. Cultural integration

D. Accurate terminal growth rates

3. **Your company has $1 million in free cash flows and is trying to determine how to allocate that capital among organic growth, dividends, and share buybacks. The company has the opportunity to engage in organic growth, which requires an investment of $1 million and has an NPV of $2.3 million. Alternatively, it can offer a $1 dividend to each of its one million shareholders. Or it could buy back 100,000 shares at $10 each. What should your company do?**

A. Use the $1 million for the organic growth project.

B. Distribute $1 million in dividends.

C. Distribute $1 million through a share buyback program.

D. Offer a $0.50 dividend and use the remaining $500,000 to purchase 50,000 shares.

4. From a finance perspective, what concern might be raised about conglomerates?

A. They gain valuable diversification benefits that create value for their shareholders.

B. They are able to horizontally integrate for pricing control.

C. Breadth of experience in multiple industries allows for better valuations.

D. Shareholders can diversify on their own and do not need the company to do it for them.

5. In October 2016, Microsoft announced a $40 billion share buyback program. Which of the following is a reason shareholders might prefer share buybacks to dividends? (Choose all that apply.)

A. Share repurchases can be taxed at a favorable rate compared to dividends (using the capital gains tax rate instead of the income tax rate).

B. Share repurchases signal that the company thinks its stock is undervalued.

C. Dividends dilute the value of existing shares.

D. Dividends destroy value by reducing the amount of cash held by the company.

6. Which of the following valuation techniques reduces the risk of overpaying for an acquisition?

A. Signaling

B. Cultural integration

C. Maximizing synergy valuation

D. Scenario analysis

7. In 2016, Canadian companies issued more equity than ever before. Why does issuing equity often cause a company's stock price to decrease?

A. Dilution

B. Signaling

C. Issuing equity always destroys value.

D. Investors prefer that companies use the money raised by issuing equity in order to perform share buybacks.

8. Why might an unscrupulous CEO perform a share buyback? (Choose all that apply.)

A. To increase EPS to meet a target

B. To send a false signal that the CEO believes their stock is undervalued

C. Dividends are taxed differently than share buybacks.

D. Unlike dividends, which are regulated by the Securities and Exchange Commission, share buybacks are regulated by the Department of Labor.

9. **Which of the following creates the most value?**
   A. Positive NPV projects
   B. Dividend distribution
   C. Stock buybacks
   D. None of the above

10. **Which of the following is a reason for an acquisition to fail? (Choose all that apply.)**
   A. Synergies not realized
   B. Overpayment for the acquired company
   C. Cultural clashes
   D. Different costs of capital

Chapter Summary

Capital allocation is increasingly a manager's central preoccupation. The value creation and destruction possible from poor allocation decisions—for example, ill-conceived mergers and ill-timed buybacks—can dwarf the possibilities of other managerial decisions. The opportunities and pitfalls of the capital allocation decision tree are summarized in figure 6-14.

The central impetus should be, as always, to pursue value-creation opportunities, and buying back shares cheaply is not value creation but simply value redistribution. If you have those opportunities to create value, the critical decision is whether to pursue them organically or inorganically. This fork in the road is a particular minefield—typical logics such as "M&A is faster" and "think of the synergies!"—often get things completely wrong.

The other fork in the road for how to distribute cash is similarly fraught with mistakes. A key lesson is that cash within and outside the corporation should be worth the same—value is created on the asset side of the balance sheet, not through financing decisions. These decisions really matter only in the context of market imperfections, such as taxes and information asymmetries. Within this fork, thinking through the signaling, agency costs, and tax consequences of these decisions is critical. Varying distribution strategies and using special dividends is particularly powerful.

FIGURE 6-14

Capital allocation decision-making chart summary

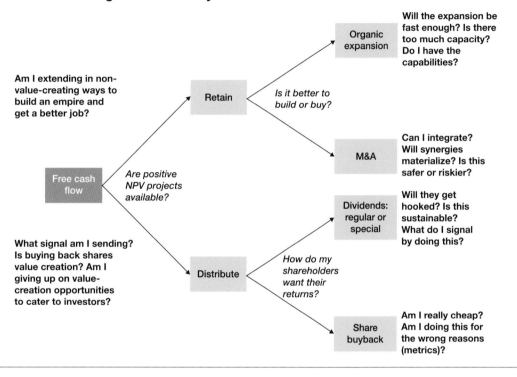

Conclusion

Congratulations! I hope you've found the process of working your way through this book demanding, rigorous, and fun. I hope you've become more comfortable with a variety of financial tools, such as discounted cash flows, ratio analysis, and multiples, and understand the overarching, big ideas of finance. Here's a recounting of some of those big ideas and suggestions for continuing your journey in the world of finance.

- Capital markets and finance are all about information and incentives, not money. Finance, at its heart, is trying to solve the deepest problem in modern capitalism—the principal-agent problem, or the separation of ownership and control.

- Capital allocation is the most important financial problem facing a CFO and CEO. The question of when to distribute or reinvest cash, whether to grow organically or inorganically, and whether to distribute via repurchases or dividends can occasion tremendous value creation or destruction.

- All value comes from the future, and today's values reflect expectations of that future value creation. Value creation can only arise from earning returns above and beyond the cost of capital for long periods and reinvesting cash flows at those higher returns.

- Return on equity (ROE) is a critical measure of performance, and these returns are driven by profitability, productivity, and leverage. Analyzing financial performance requires a comparative and relative framework; no number is meaningful without reference to another and without considering industry and temporal dynamics.

- The idea of profitability is incomplete and problematic because it detracts from the idea of cash. Economic returns are better measured by cash; there are many ways to measure cash—EBITDA, operating cash flow, and, most usefully, free cash flow.

- Valuation is an art, not a science; it is an art informed by science, but the most critical elements of it are subjective, and the process is prone to error. Be mindful of the hidden biases inherent in the process, especially the allure of synergies and the incentives of advisers.

- Returns should correspond to risks, and risks need to be considered in the context of diversified portfolios. Excess returns are hard to earn, and it's difficult to ascertain whether you've ever earned them.

- Managers are the stewards of capital for their capital providers. Delaying the return of capital must be associated with commensurate rewards to compensate for the delay and the risks borne by owners.

- Returning cash to shareholders and various other financing decisions alone won't create or destroy value. The significance of these decisions arises from the informational problems between managers and capital markets and other imperfections.

Next Steps

I hope you consider this book a beginning rather than an ending. With the tools and the skills learned here, you're on your way to a lifetime of understanding finance. The recipe for value creation should serve you well as you consider the next steps:

- First, invest your precious time well. Pick a set of companies that you'd like to research, track their financial results, and listen to their conference calls. Consume the financial press. Sit down with financial managers in your companies and engage them with probing questions.

- Second, keep growing. Let these intuitions form the basis for further financial knowledge. Teach others what you've learned. Try to go through the exercise in chapter 1 with a loved one. Push your finance friends to see if they really understand the language they're using.

- Finally, keep at it. Learning finance is a lifelong journey, and the rewards get bigger and bigger as you invest more and more.

Answers

Chapter 1

1. **C. Leverage multiplies losses, too, as it increases a company's risk.** Leverage multiplies both gains and losses, adding to overall risk. On the positive side, this multiplication can increase profits; in times of negative profitability, however, leverage increases the magnitude of losses.

2. **B. Companies in stable, predictable industries with reliable cash flows.** Because leverage increases risks, the companies most likely to have high amounts of leverage are those whose business models expose them to the least amount of risk. Companies in new industries are typically risky, so financial risk would compound that business risk.

3. **D. Preferred stock dividends must be in even-numbered percentages (2 percent, 4 percent, etc.).** Preferred stock is a form of equity and thus represents ownership in the business. However, it is "preferred" in the case of bankruptcy, where it receives payment before common stockholders, and in the case of dividends, in which preferred shareholders must receive a dividend before common stockholders are eligible.

4. **A. Gilead Sciences Inc.'s patent for the highly profitable hepatitis C treatment it developed in-house.** A patent is a form of intellectual property and typically does not show up on a balance sheet as an asset unless and until the company that developed it is purchased by another company. In that case, it may show up as part of the goodwill asset. Cash accounts, such as Facebook holds, are cash assets; buildings are property, plant, and equipment assets; and payments owed to a company are accounts receivable assets.

5. **A. Subway, a fast-food restaurant company.** Inventory turnover measures the number of times per year a company sells out its inventory. Companies that sell food—such as a grocery store or a fast-food restaurant company—typically sell out inventory faster and will have a higher inventory turnover. Since the grocery store also sells nonfood items (such as light bulbs and paper towels), the fast-food restaurant company likely has the highest inventory turnover. Bookstores can keep their items on the shelf for a long time with little concern, and airlines do not have physical inventory.

6. **B. Low receivables collection period.** Retail companies typically have a low receivables collection period, since many of their customers pay immediately for the goods they purchase. The receivables collection period can be a good way to tell if a business typically sells to other businesses (with a long receivables collection period) or to customers (with a short receivables collection period). ROE, inventory turnover, and debt levels will be influenced largely by the type of item being sold, and none of these are uniform across all retailers.

7. **D. United States Steel Corporation, a steel manufacturer.** For a company to owe BHP Billiton money, it would need to regularly purchase goods that a mining company would produce—raw ores for processing. BHP Billiton may owe money to Bank of America, Mining Recruitment Agency, or Sysco (i.e., they may be part of BHP Billiton's accounts payable), but of the four options listed, only United States Steel Corporation, which buys raw ores to turn them into steel, would be likely to owe BHP Billiton money (and be part of its accounts receivable).

8. **B. Its suppliers.** The current ratio measures how easily a company can pay its short-term liabilities with short-term assets. In other words, it measures how well the company can pay its bills. While all four of the listed parties would be interested in a company's current ratio, suppliers would have the greatest interest—they are the ones owed those bills.

9. **B. False.** While a high ROE is desirable, it is not always a good thing—the elements that make up that ROE can help to determine whether that ROE is sustainable or built on a foundation that will destroy the company. The Timberland case is an example of

a high ROE that was created by leverage, rather than profitability.

10. **A. Debt carries an explicit interest rate.** Debt is unusual as a liability because it carries an explicit interest rate. Unlike equity, plain debt provides no ownership claim to the company, and equity is typically the residual claimant. Debt can be owed to anyone who loans money to a company, such as a bank, not only suppliers.

Chapter 2

1. **B. Increasing sales.** The funding gap is calculated as days inventory + receivables collection period – payable period. You can decrease the funding gap by decreasing the days inventory or the receivables collection period, or by increasing the payable period. Increasing sales would not change the funding gap as measured in days, though it might increase the total amount you would need to finance because you would need more working capital overall.

2. **A. What constitutes economic returns (net profit or free cash flows); B. How to value assets (historical cost or future cash flows); and D. How to value equity (book value or market value).** Finance and accounting disagree about economic returns (net profit or free cash flows), the value of assets (historic cost or future cash flows), and the valuation of equity (book values or market values). Both agree that inventory should be recorded on the balance sheet.

3. **B. $400 million** and **C. $500 million.** Companies should invest in projects only where the present value is greater than the cost of investment in the project—in other words, they should invest in projects only where the net present value is greater than zero. In this case, only the $400 million and $500 million present values are greater than the $350 million cost of investment.

4. **B. $230,000.** To determine the present value of an investment, add up all the discounted cash flows associated with that investment. In this case, adding each of the cash flows yields $480,000 ($90,000 + $80,000 + $70,000 + $60,000 + $180,000). The net present value of an investment is its present value minus its cost. In this case, that equals $230,000 ($480,000 – $250,000).

5. **C. Because depreciation isn't a cash charge.** Depreciation does not correspond to a cash outlay but does

decrease net profit. So, economic returns that emphasize cash must add back depreciation and amortization.

6. **A. The present value of all future free cash flows from Facebook's business, after netting out cash and debt, implies a Facebook stock value of $150.** For any investment for which the net present value is greater than zero, anyone able to invest should do so. For a stock in the market, this demand should increase its price until the net present value is exactly zero. For the net present value to be exactly zero, the price for the stock must equal the present value of expected cash flows from that stock. In the case of Facebook stock, if it is traded at $150, that means that investors believe the present value of all future free cash flows to equity holders of that stock will be $150 as well.

7. **B. 52 days.** The funding gap is calculated as days inventory + receivables collection period – payables period. For United States Steel, that yields a funding gap of 52 days (68 days + 33 days – 49 days).

8. **C. 2 percent.** If you pay your supplier earlier, your funding gap will increase, and you will need to finance that increase with a loan from your bank. Currently, you are financing that period through not receiving the discount—which carries a rate of 2 percent. Therefore, a supplier offering you a 2 percent discount if you pay twenty days earlier is implicitly offering you a 2 percent interest rate on a twenty-day loan.

9. **B. No, the present value is still $50 million.** In finance, sunk costs don't matter, so the original cost of investment and the projected free cash flows are no longer relevant. All that matters is the current situation. In this case, the cost of investment is now zero (it has already been paid), and the present value of the investment is $50 million. That means the net present value of keeping the plant open is $50 million—which is positive—and the firm should choose to keep it open rather than shutting it down.

10. **B. It is for all capital providers and is tax adjusted.** Free cash flows are the cash flows available for all capital providers—both debt and equity. They are calculated using the following equation:

$$\text{Free cash flow} = \text{EBIAT} + \text{depreciation \& amortization} \pm \text{change in net working capital} - \text{capital expenditures}$$

Chapter 3

1. **A. Long General Motors, short Ford.** When constructing a hedge, you should find two companies that are similar, then buy (long) the one you think will outperform and sell (short) the one you think will not do as well. In this case, that means you should long (buy) General Motors and short (sell) Ford.

2. **B. It decreases the amount of risk in your portfolio, relative to the amount of return.** Diversification is the process of using an increased number of stocks in your portfolio to decrease the overall risk. Because different companies perform in disparate ways, they are not perfectly correlated. So diversification can provide benefits to investors by reducing the variability of returns without reducing risk-adjusted returns.

3. **D. Investors can't be certain if the company failed to meet its estimates because of coincidence or bad luck, or if the missed estimate is a signal that management is obscuring deeper problems.** Stocks can be punished for missing earnings estimates because investors are uncertain about the source of the missed earnings.

Because of the information asymmetry between investors and managers, investors often assume the worst possible explanation for earnings surprises. For example, in November 2016, Pfizer reported earnings of 61 cents per share, missing the consensus expectation of 62 cents per share. Despite only falling a single cent short, Pfizer's stock dropped around 3.5 percent on the announcement.

4. **A. Bayer, a multinational chemical and pharmaceutical company.** When constructing a hedge, you usually want to find a roughly comparable company. In this case, you should match Dow Chemical with Bayer, another chemical company. Diversification will reduce your overall risk, but it does not isolate the risk of Dow Chemical precisely and hedge that risk.

5. **B. Analysts are afraid to recommend "sell" for a company's stock, because that company may not do business with their employer in the future.** The company may retaliate by taking its business elsewhere, and this business is the principle source of revenue for the analyst's employer. Investors investing in companies that do well and pension funds investing in high-quality companies are examples of *good* incentives,

and CEOs typically *reduce* risks, perhaps excessively, when a large amount of their personal wealth is tied up in stock options.

6. **C. A sell-side firm.** Most equity research analysts are employed by a sell-side firm. Sell-side firms, like investment banks, employ equity research analysts to provide ideas and information to their institutional investor clients on the buy side, which can lead those investors to direct more of their business through the investment bank that employs the analyst they like.

7. **A. Analysts will work hard to provide accurate valuations for companies; B. High-ranking analysts may "herd" by choosing valuations similar to other analysts to protect their position in the rankings; and D. Low-ranked analysts may make outlandish and contrary predictions, hoping that a lucky break will propel them to the top of the rankings.** Because analysts are compensated based on rankings, they will work to ensure their rankings are high. This may provide good incentives, such as working hard to provide accurate valuations, and bad incentives, such as herding to protect their position or making bold, outlandish predictions to rise quickly through the ranks. Herding

behavior among analysts has been found to exacerbate the information asymmetry problem by reducing the quality of analyst reports, creating more earnings surprises and, consequently, more volatility in the market.

8. **C. The sell side.** Initial public offerings are a sale of stock. As such, they are managed by sell-side firms. Facebook's IPO—with a peak market capitalization of $104 billion—was one of the largest in internet history and was underwritten by three investment banks: Morgan Stanley, JP Morgan, and Goldman Sachs.

9. **B. Buys companies, improves them, and then sells them to another private investor or the public markets.** The private equity industry has grown rapidly in the last few decades. A report from McKinsey & Co. indicated that private equity assets under management had risen to $5 trillion by 2017.[1]

10. **D. The principal-agent problem.** In this case, the real estate agents—the agents—are not working as hard or as well on behalf of the owners—the principals—as they do when they are working on behalf of themselves. A 1992 article in the *Journal of the American Real Estate and Urban Economics Association* by

Michael Arnold[2] analyzed three methods of realtor compensation structures (fixed-percentage commission, flat fee, and consignment) and found that impatient sellers are best served by a fixed-percentage commission (in which the realtor receives a percentage of the final price as a commission), while patient sellers are best served by a consignment (in which the seller receives a predetermined amount and the realtor receives any payment above that amount).

Chapter 4

1. **A. Returns to capital that exceed costs of capital** and **B. Reinvesting profits to grow.** Value creation comes from three sources: returns to capital that exceed the costs of capital, reinvested profits for growth, and doing both for long periods of time. Earnings per share is an accounting measure that does not capture value creation, and gross profits—sales minus cost of goods sold—tell us nothing about whether operating expenses then offset those gross profits.

2. **B. A measure of how much a stock price moves with the broader market.** In an environment where diversification is costless and most investors hold the entire market, the relevant measure of risk for a company is its correlation with the market portfolio—this is beta. For example, if Apple has a beta of 1.28, this means that, on average, when the market goes up by 10 percent, Apple stock goes up by 12.8 percent; if the market goes down 10 percent, Apple stock goes down by 12.8 percent.

3. **C. Division C.** Using a beta that's inaccurately high will cause the cost of equity to be inaccurately high, which causes the cost of capital to be too high. This will result in the present values for projects being too low, and the company will shy away from these projects. Conversely, a beta that's too low will cause the cost of equity to be too low, the cost of capital to be too low, and present values to be too high, causing the company to overinvest. In this case, using the average beta of 1.0 is too low for division C, so the company will overinvest in that division.

4. **A. Your lender can tell you what your current borrowing costs are.** The lender identifies the cost of debt from a combination of the risk-free rate and a credit spread based on the riskiness of a company (it does not do this by multiplying the company's current ratio by its credit

rating). Calculating the cost of debt by subtracting the cost of equity from the WACC is backward—you determine the WACC from costs, not vice versa.

5. **B. Less than 1.** When returns to capital are lower than costs of capital, market-to-book ratios are less than 1. In this case, free cash flows going into the future will be discounted each year at a greater rate (the cost of capital) than they are growing (the return to capital). In such a situation, the owners of the company should consider shutting down operations, as the company is destroying value by continued operation.

6. **B. False.** Up to a certain point, company value can be increased by adding leverage through tax benefits created by interest payments on debt (in countries that allow interest payments to serve as tax deductions). At some point, the company will reach its optimal capital structure; adding further leverage will increase the costs of financial distress faster than the benefits gained from the tax code.

7. **B. Take the risk-free rate and add the product of your equity beta and the market risk premium.**

Following the capital asset pricing model, the cost of equity is the risk-free rate, plus beta times the market risk premium. In 1990, William Sharpe, Harry Markowitz, and Merton Miller jointly received a Nobel Prize recognizing their contributions to the development of the CAPM during the 1960s.

8. **A. Higher costs of equity.** Following the capital asset pricing model, the cost of equity is the risk-free rate, plus beta times the market risk premium. Higher betas, therefore, produce higher costs of equity. Since the cost of equity represents the return that shareholders expect from companies, this implies that shareholders expect higher returns from high-beta industries than low-beta industries.

9. **D. Because they create value by having returns greater than the cost of capital.** Positive NPV projects have returns greater than the cost of capital, and as we saw in chapter 2, NPV is a method of determining which projects create value. NPV considers the discounted free cash flows of a project, and those cash flows are discounted at the cost of capital. When all free cash flows are summed up in this manner, they

will only net to a positive number if the returns of the project are greater than its costs of capital.

10. **A. Reinvest as many of its profits as possible.** Value creation comes from three sources: returns to capital greater than the cost of capital, reinvestment in growth, and time. In this situation, since the company already has returns to capital greater than its costs of capital, it should reinvest as much as possible to maximize value creation. We'll look at the alternative to reinvestment—distributions to shareholders—in greater length in chapter 6.

Chapter 5

1. **C. $112.5 billion.** When conducting scenario analysis, the objective is to determine expected values. Expected values are a weighted average based on the likelihood of each scenario occurring. In this case, take the weighted average of $50 billion (times 25 percent), plus $100 billion (times 50 percent), plus $200 billion (times 25 percent), which equals the expected value of $112.5 billion. This expected value should be the highest bid because it is the amount you expect the company to be worth. If you bid solely based on the best-case scenario, you would have to reach that best case just to have an NPV of zero.

2. **C. $500 million.** If you value the company at $500 million and estimate $50 million in synergies, and you wish to keep all the synergies to yourself, you should not pay more than $500 million for the company. If you bid more than $500 million—such as $550 million—you would be giving all the synergies to the shareholders of the lumber company.

3. **A. The market believes that Yum! Brands has more growth opportunities than Wendy's or McDonald's.** A price/earnings (P/E) ratio is a multiple that can be traced back to a growing perpetuity formula. In the denominator of that formula is the discount rate minus the growth rate. Therefore, companies with higher P/E ratios need to have either a lower discount rate or a higher growth rate. While we can't be certain of the exact values for these companies, only Yum!, with more growth opportunities, provides a possible explanation for why its P/E ratio is higher than either Wendy's or McDonald's.

4. **C. Value destruction, transfer of wealth from acquirer to target.** Your company lost value while your target gained value, which indicates a transfer of value from acquirer to target. Target shareholders gained $25 million in value, while your shareholders lost value, so this wasn't a case of splitting synergies; it was a transfer of your value to the target. Also, since the value you lost was greater than the value the target gained, that indicates value destruction. Imagine now that the two companies are one entity, and that entity has both gained $25 million and lost $50 million—the net loss of $25 million is value destruction.

5. **C. Current assets to current liabilities.** P/E, enterprise value/EBITDA, and market capitalization/EBITDA are all valuation multiples. These values—price, enterprise value, or market capitalization—are all expressions of value, so these multiples are valuation multiples. The current ratio—current assets to current liabilities—does not indicate value. While it is a useful ratio, especially for suppliers, it doesn't provide any information about the valuation of a company.

6. **C. A discount rate of 9 percent and 3 percent growth.** An enterprise value to free cash flow ratio can be thought of as a growing perpetuity formula in which the numerator is 1 (because the multiple will be multiplied by free cash flows to determine total valuation) and the denominator is the discount rate minus the growth rate. If the enterprise value to free cash flow ratio is 16.1, then $(r - g)$ in the growing perpetuity formula (the denominator) for Goodyear must be equal to 1/16.1. That works out to roughly 6 percent, so the discount rate minus the growth rate must equal 6 percent. In this case, only one option (9 percent and 3 percent) works as an explanation.

7. **D. $10,000.** Using a growing perpetuity formula, you can calculate the value of this educational opportunity as $1,000/(13% - 3%), or $10,000. This value should then be the maximum you are willing to pay.

8. **D. The project with an IRR of 25 percent is probably preferable, but you should conduct a DCF analysis.** The first rule with IRR is you should never invest in a project with an IRR lower than the WACC. Since both projects have IRRs higher than the WACC, you need a way to compare them. However, because IRR is not a good measure of value creation, it is not possible to tell based solely on the IRR which project will create

more value. The project with an IRR of 25 percent is likely to produce more value, but an NPV analysis will provide the right answer.

9. **A. Too high a growth rate in the terminal value; B. Basing his growth rate on the industry; and C. Basing a purchase price on the company's value, not the equity value.** A terminal value with a growth rate significantly higher than the overall economy implies that the company will eventually take over the world—with an overall economic growth rate between 2 percent and 4 percent, the 6 percent chosen is too high. Additionally, your assistant is suggesting a bid that includes synergies, which transfers all the value from the acquisition to the target, not to your company. Finally, he is recommending a price that doesn't consider the $50 million in debt and $10 million in cash, which will make the equity valuation lower than that $100 million valuation of the company. He did do one thing right—choosing a growth rate in the near term based on the industry is a good practice, since companies within the same industry likely have similar growth rates.

10. **A. A project with an NPV of $100 million.** Projects with positive NPV are value creating, because they

consider all the value above the costs of the project and the costs of capital. The payback period and IRR are problematic and cannot determine with certainty if a project is value creating, so we don't want to use those. A PV is an accurate measure of the value of the project, but does not tell you anything about value creation because it does not factor in the cost of investment (for example, if this project cost $250 million, it would be value destroying).

Chapter 6

1. **A. Signaling.** Stock buybacks do not create value, but they may send a signal to the market that corporate management believes its stock price is undervalued; accordingly, this can cause the stock price to rise. This explanation comes back to information asymmetry. If the people with the relevant information think that their stock price is an attractive investment, other investors may want to follow.

2. **B. Realization of synergies** and **C. Cultural integration.** After the acquisition, due diligence and accurate terminal growth rates become less important because the valuation and bid are complete; the values placed

on them have already been paid. Cultural integration and the realization of synergies remain important concerns that Bayer should pay attention to. If it does not give them appropriate attention, then the value gained from the acquisition will likely not be as much as the valuation used to determine the $66 billion purchase price.

3. **A. Use the $1 million for the organic growth project.** Companies should always invest in positive NPV projects when available, as these create value for the company, while distributing cash in the form of dividends and buybacks does not.

4. **D. Shareholders can diversify on their own and do not need the company to do it for them.** The finance principle is that managers shouldn't do for shareholders what shareholders can do for themselves. In some countries, however, conglomerates may be able to overcome some frictions in labor, product, or capital markets and therefore create value.

5. **A. Share repurchases can be taxed at a favorable rate compared to dividends (using the capital gains tax rate instead of the income tax rate)** and **B. Share re-** **purchases signal that the company thinks its stock is undervalued.** Shareholders may prefer share buybacks because they are taxed at the preferential capital gains tax rate instead of the income tax rate at which dividends are taxed and because they send a signal that corporate management thinks its shares are undervalued. Dividends do not dilute the value of existing shares nor do they destroy value—they are value-neutral. That different groups of shareholders might prefer different capital allocation decisions is called the "clientele effect," where companies will establish policies around what their shareholders' preferences are.

6. **D. Scenario analysis.** Overpaying is a concern before the bidding process and the acquisition, and scenario analysis allows the company to determine a more accurate value before they begin bidding. Cultural integration occurs after the valuation process, and maximizing synergy valuation during the valuation will likely *result* in overpayment, rather than reducing the risk of it.

7. **B. Signaling.** Issuing equity is a value-neutral activity; however, it can often cause the stock price to decrease. This is because of signaling, as investors wonder why

the company isn't confident enough to invest in the project using debt or internal financing. Shareholders might ask, If the company thought that the investment would create value, why wouldn't it want to keep that value for its existing capital providers? Because of information asymmetry, shareholders might conclude that the company is bringing in new investors because it lacks confidence in its ability to create value.

8. **A. To increase EPS to meet a target** and **B. To send a false signal that the CEO believes her stock is undervalued.** A share buyback decreases the number of shares outstanding, which can increase EPS (because it decreases the denominator). An unscrupulous CEO might do this to meet a target (perhaps for a bonus package). Also, since investors see share buybacks as a signal from management that the share is undervalued, an unscrupulous manager

could use this assumption to manipulate the stock price, counting on the signaling effect to increase stock values.

9. **A. Positive NPV projects.** Dividend distributions and stock buybacks are value-neutral—only positive NPV projects create value. While stock prices may rise through stock buybacks because of signaling, this is not creating value; it is merely providing more information to shareholders that the value of the company may be higher than they thought.

10. **A. Synergies not realized; B. Overpayment for the acquired company;** and **C. Cultural clashes.** An acquisition can fail for all these reasons. Different costs of capital should be considered during the valuation process, but should not determine the success or failure of the acquisition.

Glossary

accounts payable A liability account used to show the obligation to pay suppliers that have provided goods or services on credit terms.

accounts receivable An asset account used to show the claim to receive cash at some future date for goods or services that have been supplied to a customer on credit terms.

accrual accounting An accounting method most companies follow; required under US Generally Accepted Accounting Principles (GAAP) and International Financial Reporting Standards (IFRS). The method follows the revenue recognition principle, which says that revenue should be recognized in the period in which it is earned, not necessarily when the cash is received, and the matching principle, which says that expenses should be recognized in the period in which the related revenue is recognized rather than when the related cash is paid.

acquisition The process of purchasing a company or asset by an existing company.

active mutual funds Mutual funds for which managers make active choices regarding which stocks or assets to invest in.

activist investing An investment strategy that requires the acquisition of a significant portion of a public company's stock in order to enact significant changes in strategy.

alpha The excess return of an investment above the suitable risk-adjusted benchmark.

amortization An accounting method that spreads the cost of an intangible asset across its life. Amortization can also refer to repayment of loan principal over time.

ask The price a seller is willing to sell for.

asset turnover The measure of productivity in the DuPont framework. Calculated by dividing the total revenue for a period by the average total assets.

assets Resources owned or controlled by a business and expected to provide some future economic benefit to the business. Examples include cash, inventory, and equipment.

asymmetric information A situation where not all parties involved in a transaction have the same information. In capital markets, this can be associated with the informational advantage of companies, of sellers, or of agents relative to principals.

balance sheet A financial report that shows the financial position of a company at a specific point in time; it serves as a snapshot of the resources that a company owns or controls and how it financed those resources.

bankruptcy The process by which companies resolve their inability to pay back their debts.

beta A measure of risk for an asset in the context of a diversified portfolio. Emphasizes the correlation of the asset's return with the wider market of investable assets.

bid The maximum price at which a buyer is willing to buy.

board of directors A group established to represent and protect the interests of shareholders or a broader group of stakeholders. Directors are normally elected, but can be appointed in certain situations. The board has the most senior level of authority for the company and sets corporate governance policies, monitors the performance of the company, and has hiring authority over the senior executive team.

book value The accounting value of an asset. Often varies from the market value of the asset because of the conservatism principle and historic cost accounting.

brokers Agents that handle the transactions of buying and selling shares of public corporations on behalf of clients.

buy side The class of institutional investors that purchase shares of a company. They typically are pools of capital, such as mutual funds, that serve to buy and hold shares on behalf of a larger group.

buyout *See* acquisition.

capital allocation The process by which free cash flows are allocated to either investing in the business with new projects or M&A or are distributed to shareholders by a dividend or share repurchase.

capital asset pricing model (CAPM) A framework for pricing risk in the context of a diversified portfolio.

capital expenditures The money that companies spend to buy fixed assets or assets for long-term use.

capital intensity A relative measure of capital required to generate future cash flows. A higher intensity implies greater amounts of required capital.

capital markets Marketplaces where financial claims, such as equity and debt, are bought and sold. In essence, capital markets match suppliers of capital (investors) with users of capital (businesses).

capital structure The proportion of debt relative to equity used to finance a company.

capitalization The total value of a company's equity and debt, typically given in market prices.

carried interest An incentive contract for private equity and hedge fund managers that pays them based on their returns.

cash An asset account that includes currency, checking accounts and, often cash equivalents (deposits or other liquid investments typically redeemable within ninety days).

cash conversion cycle A measure of the length of time a business takes to pay for inventory from its suppliers to when it collects cash from its customers. Calculated as the days inventory, plus the receivables collection period, minus the days payable.

cash distribution Cash allocated to shareholders through either dividends or share buybacks.

cash flow A measure of the cash a business generates; may refer to EBITDA, operating cash flow, or free cash flow.

cash flow from financing activities The portion of the statement of cash flows for a business that includes all sources and uses of financing. Includes securing or paying off debt principal (loans, bonds, promissory notes) and offering or buying back equity.

cash flow from investing activities The portion of the statement of cash flows for a business that covers all investing activities (i.e., acquisitions and divestitures). Includes investments made in tangible assets like property, plant, and equipment but can also include investing in other companies.

cash flow from operating activities The portion of the statement of cash flows for a business that accounts for all cash generated and used in operations. Sources are all cash generated by sales of products or services, and uses are all cash used in the process of making and delivering the product or service.

chief financial officer (CFO) The senior executive responsible for all financial transactions and management of the company. Reports to the chief executive officer (CEO) and is ultimately accountable to the board of directors.

common stock The most typical stock or share type representing an ownership interest in the business. Although there can be different classes of common shares, owners of these shares usually have certain rights, including the right to share proportionately in the profits of the business and the right to elect directors and vote on proposals that the directors make to the shareholders.

company A legal entity created typically for the purpose of engaging in any type of business with the goal of delivering a product or service for profit. The legal structure for ownership and liability varies by jurisdiction, but most are classified as some form of sole proprietorship, partnership, or corporation.

conflict of interest A situation in which an individual's professional and public interests oppose each other.

conglomerate A company composed of several unrelated businesses, operating somewhat independently, but under a common holding company.

contingent value right (CVR) instrument The rights given to shareholders of an acquired company to buy more shares of the acquired company or to receive cash.

control premium The additional value above the current share price associated with the benefits of controlling an entire company.

correlation A measure of the degree to which two variables move in correspondence with each other.

cost accounting A method that tries to capture a company's cost of production.

cost of capital The cost to a business for deploying capital as charged by the capital providers.

cost of debt The cost to a business for raising debt, usually measured as a percentage rate for borrowing; can also be measured in annual dollar costs.

cost of equity The cost to a business for raising equity. Unlike the cost of debt, this cost is not explicit but is mea-

sured as an expected rate of return (%) to investors; can also be measured in annual dollar costs.

cost of financial distress The costs a company bears by being in financial distress (e.g., the loss of talent or suppliers demanding immediate payment instead of paying in thirty or sixty days).

cost of goods sold (COGS) The expense corresponding to the cost of the inventory that is sold to customers; may also be called cost of sales.

cost structure An analysis of the component costs of a product or service, including fixed costs and variable costs.

credit spread The interest rate difference or premium a company must pay above the risk-free interest rate to account for the risk of its business.

current assets Cash and other assets that are expected to be converted into cash within a year (or within one operating cycle, if the company's operating cycle is longer than one year).

current liabilities The liability account that contains obligations that will be settled or paid in cash within a year (or within one operating cycle, if the company's operating cycle is longer than one year).

current ratio A measurement of a business's ability to pay its short-term obligations. Calculated by dividing current assets by current liabilities.

days inventory A component of the cash conversion cycle that measures the average number of days the inventory is held before it is sold. Calculated by dividing average inventory by the cost of goods sold (COGS) per day. Alternatively calculated by dividing 365 by the inventory turnover.

debt A financial obligation to a lender that has a fixed rate of return. The principal amount loaned is paid back to the lender either on demand or on a planned payment schedule. If a company encounters financial difficulty or dissolves, the debt holders have priority for repayment over stockholders and can take control of the assets.

defined benefit An employer-sponsored retirement plan in which employee retirement benefits are defined by certain factors (e.g., length of employment or salary history). The company manages a pension portfolio and bears the risk of the investment strategy as it is responsible for the ultimate payment to beneficiaries.

defined contribution An employer-sponsored retirement plan in which both employer and employee contribute to employee retirement benefits; the employee bears the risk of the investment strategy.

depreciation An accounting method that spreads the cost of a tangible asset (e.g., a piece of equipment) across its life.

discount rate A percentage rate a company employs to calculate the present value for a stream of future cash flows. The discount rate should account for factors that impact the time value of money, which typically include inflation and a risk premium.

discounting A process applied to a series of cash flows over time; discounting brings the value of the future stream of cash to the present value. The discount rate (percentage) accounts for the relevant opportunity costs for the capital providers.

diversification The allocation of wealth across different companies and across different assets, rather than in concentrated investment positions.

dividend Cash paid to shareholders on a per share basis to distribute a portion of the free cash generated by the business.

due diligence The process of examining a project, before completing any agreements, to fully understand all aspects of the project, including values, risks, and expected outcomes.

DuPont framework An analysis that breaks down a return on equity (ROE) into three components: profitability, productivity, and leverage.

earnings before interest and taxes (EBIT) Calculated by adding interest and taxes to net profit. Also known as operating profit.

earnings before interest, taxes, depreciation, and amortization (EBITDA) A proxy to determine the cash a business generates by excluding noncash costs and financing costs. Typically calculated by adding depreciation and amortization back to EBIT.

earnings per share (EPS) The ratio of net profit to the number of shares outstanding.

EBITDA margin A measure of profitability that uses EBITDA rather than profit as the numerator (EBITDA ÷ revenue) in order to shift emphasis to cash.

efficient market theory An investment theory that emphasizes that share prices reflect all available information and that consistently outperforming the market benchmark is not possible. More specifically, different forms of this theory emphasize distinctive informational conditions of markets.

endowment funds Institutional funds with the dual purpose of long-term growth and generation of income to provide for the mission of the institution. Common endowment funds include those managed by universities, hospitals, and nonprofit organizations.

enterprise value The total value of a company that can be calculated as the present value of all future cash flows generated by the company. It can also be calculated as market capitalization of equity plus debt minus excess cash.

equity analyst An individual, typically employed by an investment bank, who provides research services on public companies to their institutional investor clients. The analyst assesses the value of a stock and will recommend that the client buy, sell, or hold that stock.

equity issuance When a company sells shares of ownership to raise cash.

expected return The rate of return an investor expects from an investment based on the risks assumed.

expected values The sum of probability-weighted outcomes for multiple potential scenarios of a project or acquisition.

firm value *See* enterprise value.

forecasting Using available data and assumptions to develop a set of future incomes, expenses, and cash flows.

free cash flows (FCF) Cash flows that are available to distribute to investors or to reinvest in the business after the business has covered all its requirements. FCF does not consider the impact of how a business is financed. Calculated by: Free cash flow = (1 − tax rate) × EBIT + depreciation and amortization − capital expenditures − change in net working capital.

goodwill The value of an intangible asset that is the result of buying another company. Reflects the portion of the purchase cost in excess of the value of the net tangible assets of the acquired business.

gross margin A measure of profitability that demonstrates what percentage of revenue is left after subtracting the cost of goods sold from revenues. Calculated by dividing the gross profit by the total revenue for the period. Also known as gross profit margin.

growing perpetuity Similar to a perpetuity (a stream of cash flows expected to last forever) but growing at a prescribed rate.

hedge funds Investment funds typically open only to sophisticated investors. Their relatively light regulations compared to those of mutual funds allow them to employ leverage and take on concentrated and short positions.

hedging An investment strategy that uses offsetting positions to reduce the risk of adverse price movements.

incentives The perceived rewards that motivate individuals in their roles.

income statement Financial report that shows the summary of the earnings of a business (revenues minus expenses) over a designated period of time. Shows activity during the period for all nominal accounts.

industry A part of the economy in which a group of companies provides similar products or services.

initial public offering (IPO) The process of converting a privately held company to a public company by issuing and selling shares on a stock exchange.

inorganic growth Growth achieved through the acquisition of other companies or portions of those companies.

institutional investors Entities that pool capital from various constituents and invest on their behalf (e.g., mutual funds, hedge funds).

intangible asset An asset that is not physical (e.g., brands, patents, and copyrights).

integration The process of merging the operations of two companies to form a single entity.

interest coverage ratio Used to assess a company's financial durability by examining whether it is profitable enough to pay its interest expenses: EBIT ÷ interest expense or EBITDA ÷ interest expense. The higher the ratio, the better the company's ability to pay its interest expenses.

interest rate The return paid by a borrower and received by a lender. Sometimes used interchangeably with discount rate for analyzing the time value of money.

internal rate of return (IRR) Utilizing the formula for net present value (NPV), the discount rate that brings the NPV to zero. Thus, if an IRR is above a company's minimum rate of return, then a project is deemed to be worthwhile.

inventory An asset account that contains materials manufactured or purchased for the purpose of being sold to customers. In its final form, inventory is the product that is being sold; when it is sold, the cost of the inventory that was sold is recognized as an expense, as cost of goods sold.

A manufacturing company may have inventory in various stages of completion, such as raw materials inventory, work-in-process inventory, and finished-goods inventory.

inventory turnover A ratio used to measure how efficiently a business is managing its inventory levels. Calculated by dividing the cost of goods sold for the period by the average inventory for the period. It represents how many times the inventory was sold during the period. Inventory turnover = COGS ÷ average period inventory.

investment banks Financial institutions that help companies raise capital, either as debt or equity offerings, and advise companies undergoing mergers and acquisitions.

investor Any person or entity that invests their own capital in the capital markets across a range of available financial products.

just-in-time An inventory method that minimizes the time that raw materials, work-in-process, and finished goods inventories are stocked. In other words, inventory turnover is maximized.

leverage The use of debt as a funding source. A company that is highly leveraged has a large amount of debt financing compared to other funding sources.

leveraged buyout (LBO) A transaction that employs a large amount of debt to purchase a company from its cur-rent owners, often taking a public company private. This allows the purchasers to gain control of a large company for a relatively small equity investment.

leveraged recapitalizations A financing strategy that increases the amount of debt employed that is accompanied with a payout to equity holders.

liability An obligation that a company has incurred to pay another entity, including banks, vendors, the government, or employees, or the obligation to provide goods or services in the future.

liquidity How quickly and easily assets can be converted to cash. For example, accounts receivable are more liquid than inventory because the inventory must be sold to become a receivable and then the receivable must be collected to become cash. Hence, the receivable is one step closer to being converted to cash than the inventory and is, therefore, more liquid.

market efficiency The concept that a market is efficient, implying that all available information about a stock is built into its price. *See* efficient market theory.

market imperfections How reality deviates from an ideal marketplace because of, for example, asymmetric information, transaction costs, or taxes.

market index A measurement of an aggregation of various stocks. For example, the S&P 500 Index measures the price movements of five hundred of the largest public companies traded in the United States.

market risk premium The excess returns investors expect to earn for bearing the risk of holding risky market assets.

market-to-book ratio A ratio of the market value to the book value.

market value The value a company or asset would obtain if sold on the open market. Typically, it varies from the book value due to historic cost accounting.

marketable securities Any security that can be converted to cash relatively easily. Maturity dates are normally one year or less and might include certificates of deposit, treasury bills, or other money market securities.

maturity date When the principal of a bond is due and the bond is extinguished.

merger When two companies agree to combine into one new entity.

multiples A valuation method that compares the values of comparable companies to operating metrics and applies that ratio to the operating metric of the entity being valued.

mutual funds Funds that pool the capital of many individual investors into one fund with a mission to follow a specified investment strategy, ranging from investing in narrow industry segments to mimicking the broad mar-

ket as an index fund. The fund is priced at net asset value (NAV); investors purchase or sell shares of the mutual fund based on this price.

net debt A leverage metric that incorporates cash held by companies and considers cash as negative debt.

net present value (NPV) The result of subtracting the initial investment in a project from the present value of future cash flows. A positive NPV project is considered to be a valid potential investment.

net profit A company's total earnings (or profit). Although net profit can be a negative number, this does not always indicate that a company is in poor financial health. Calculated by subtracting all expenses (cash and noncash) from revenue. Also known as net income.

notes payable A liability account for debts that are due in the near future.

operating income *See* earnings before interest and taxes (EBIT) and operating profit.

opportunity cost The foregone returns from an opportunity not pursued.

organic growth Growth achieved by investing in projects within the company to generate positive free cash flows.

other assets An asset account that contains any assets that do not fit into a defined category (such as inventory or accounts receivable). Other current assets are assets that do not include cash, securities, receivables, inventory, and prepaid assets, and can be convertible into cash within one business cycle, which is usually one year. Other non-current assets include items that are not included in long-term assets (such as property, plant, and equipment).

passive mutual funds Mutual funds that invest in indices such as the S&P 500 and don't allow for discretionary choices by their managers.

payables period A component of the cash conversion cycle that measures the average number of days a company waits to pay its suppliers for items purchased on credit.

payback period The length of time required for a series of positive cash flows to recoup the investment made in a project, asset, or company. It is typically calculated without consideration of the time value of money.

pension funds Funds that invest the accumulated money an organization sets aside for the future payout of retirement benefits to its employees. Pension funds invest in the capital markets with the goals of growth for their funds as well as current and future cash flows for their beneficiaries.

perfect information A situation in which every market player has access to the same information.

perpetuity An unchanging stream of cash flows that is expected to last forever.

preferred stock A special class of stock that differs from common stock because of preferential dividend rights, voting rights, or liquidation rights.

present value The discounting of a stream of future cash flows at a prescribed discount rate, resulting in the current value of these cash flows.

price-to-earnings ratio The ratio of the price of a share for a company to the earnings per share.

principal-agent problem A problem occurring when tasks are delegated by a principal to an agent in a setting characterized by conflicting objectives and imperfect information.

principle of conservatism A principle recognizing that some estimates are involved in accounting and that accounting should reflect the more cautious estimated valuation rather than the more optimistic one. For assets, it means recording the lower valuation, while for liabilities, it means recording the higher possible valuation. For revenues and gains, it means recording them when they are reasonably certain, but for expenses and losses, it means recording them when they are reasonably possible.

private equity A source of capital that provides equity or debt financing to private companies outside the public capital markets. Included are private equity firms, venture capitalists, and angel investors. Investment strategies can encompass new startups, growth capital, the turnaround of distressed companies, or funding management or leveraged buyouts.

productivity A number of measures for output per unit of input for any type of business activity. Example measures include revenue per employee hour, or revenue over assets.

profitability A number of measures that divide a net amount (after deducting some or all costs) by revenue. Examples include gross profit, operating profit, and net profit.

profit margin The ratio of gross operating or net profit to revenue for a company.

property, plant, and equipment (PP&E) An asset account that contains physical assets of a company that are used either directly or indirectly in the normal course of generating the product or service of the company, including land, machinery, buildings, office equipment, vehicles, and other physical assets with significant cost. Gross PP&E is typically the amount originally invested; net PP&E reflects accumulated depreciation of these assets.

quick ratio A measure of a business's ability to pay its short-term obligations that is a more stringent test than the current ratio. Calculated by subtracting inventory from current assets, then dividing the result by current liabilities.

ratio A method of comparing two related items by dividing one by the other. For example, total debt ÷ total assets calculates the amount of assets financed by debt.

receivables collection period A component of the cash conversion cycle that measures, in days, how quickly a company collects payments from customers who pay on credit.

recession A prolonged decline in economic activity.

return Money made or lost on an investment.

return on assets (ROA) An indicator of how effectively a company is generating profit based on its asset base. Calculated as net profit ÷ total assets.

return on capital (ROC) The return received by capital (debt and equity) providers divided by the capital provided. Calculated by dividing EBIT by the value of debt and equity. Also known as return on capital employed (ROCE) or return on invested capital (ROIC).

return on equity (ROE) The return that an owner receives on the equity invested in the business. Calculated by dividing net profit by average total owners' equity.

revenue The gross receipts from normal business activities.

risk A broad term for the variability of outcomes that most individuals will prefer to avoid given their risk aversion.

risk-free rate The interest rate for a borrower when there is no possibility of a default. The interest rate for US government debt is the most common standard.

rounds of funding The sequential issuance of stock by a startup in exchange for funding. Also known as venture capital funding rounds.

scenario analysis A method of projecting possible future outcomes and associating them with specific probabilities.

security A financial instrument that represents a claim on corporate assets.

sell side The opposite of the buy side; includes all parties involved in creating and selling equity and debt financial instruments. Investment bankers, traders, and some analysts are all considered part of the sell side.

shareholders' equity The residual claim belonging to the shareholders of the business. After adding up all the resources of the business (assets) and subtracting all the claims that third parties (such as lenders and suppliers) have against those assets, the residual (what is left over) is shareholders' equity. It includes two elements: money contributed to (invested in) a business in exchange for some degree of ownership, and earnings that the business generates and retains over time. Also commonly known as common stock, owners' equity, stockholders' equity, net worth, or equity.

Sharpe ratio A measurement of return per unit of risk where risk is often defined in terms of the standard deviation of returns.

short selling The process of borrowing shares, selling those shares, rebuying them at a lower price, and then returning those shares, thereby profiting from the price decline. This strategy is designed to capitalize on the potential downward movement of stocks or for hedging purposes.

signalling To indirectly provide information to investors or the marketplace via a financial transaction such as a dividend or buyback.

sovereign wealth funds A state-owned fund that invests on behalf of its citizens, often funded from natural resource royalties such as oil revenue. The goal of these funds is to seek long-term growth and to fund future payouts to the citizenry.

spot market A marketplace or exchange where a financial instrument or commodity is purchased for immediate delivery. The opposite of the futures market in which the purchaser agrees to pay a price for the item at a future date.

statement of cash flows A financial report that shows the net change in cash during the year and includes three sections: cash flows from operating activities, cash flows from investing activities, and cash flows from financing activities.

stock buyback A company's purchase, at management's discretion, of its own shares as part of a capital allocation strategy. Also known as stock repurchase.

stock options The right, but not the obligation, to either buy or sell a share at a predetermined price by a certain date.

stock split The division of existing shares into new shares, with the effect of splitting the value of each existing share into a different number of shares.

sunk costs Any cost incurred by a business in the past that should not be considered for decision making.

synergies The value created by merging two companies in excess of the sum of their individual market values.

systematic risk The risk of a financial security that cannot be eliminated by diversification.

terminal value A valuation method employed to capture the value of all future cash flows at some future date without forecasting those cash flows forever.

time horizon The length of time over which an investment is made or held before it is liquidated.

time value of money The concept that a unit of currency received today is worth more than the same unit of currency received at some future point. Arises because of the opportunity cost of not having the currency immediately.

traders Individuals who purchase or sell stocks on their own behalf rather than as an agent for their clients, as would be the case for a broker. In the process, they provide liquidity to a market and attempt to earn returns over relatively short horizons based on these transactions.

valuation The process of determining the value of a company, project, or asset.

value neutrality The proposition that market values do not change because of certain changes such as financing transactions.

venture capital A source of investment capital focused on startup and small businesses. These are typically high-risk investments that are believed to have high future growth potential. The company is a private entity not listed on any public exchange.

volatility A measure of the degree to which a variable deviates from its own average through time.

weighted average cost of capital (WACC) The cost of capital (%) for a company that considers the cost of debt and equity, the relevant capital structure, and the associated tax benefit of issuing debt.

working capital The amount of capital required to fund basic operations of a company, often calculated as the difference between current assets and current liabilities, or inventories + accounts receivables − accounts payable.

yield curve A line that represents the interest rate or yield of the same quality bond across maturity dates.

Notes

Chapter 1

1. Bill Lewis et al., "US Productivity Growth, 1995–2000," McKinsey Global Institute report, October 2001, https://www .mckinsey.com/featured-insights/americas/us-productivity-growth -1995-2000.

Chapter 2

1. Barry M. Staw and Ha Hoang, "Sunk Costs in the NBA: Why Draft Order Affects Playing Time and Survival in Professional Basketball," *Administrative Science Quarterly* 40, no. 3 (September 1995): 474–494.

Chapter 3

1. William Alden, "PepsiCo Tells Activist Investor Its Answer Is Still No," *New York Times DealBook* (blog), February 27, 2014, https:// dealbook.nytimes.com/2014/02/27/pepsico-tells-activist-investor-its -answer-is-still-no/.

Chapter 5

1. Michael J. de la Merced, "Southeastern Asset Management to Fight Dell's Takeover," *New York Times DealBook* (blog), February 8, 2013, https://dealbook.nytimes.com/2013/02/08/southeastern-asset -management-to-fight-dells-takeover/.

2. Dan Primack, "Icahn: I've Lost to Michael Dell," *Fortune*, September 9, 2013, http://fortune.com/2013/09/09/icahn-ive-lost-to -michael-dell/.

3. *In re:* Appraisal of Dell Inc. (Del. Ch., May 31, 2016), C.A. No. 9322-VCL, https://courts.delaware.gov/Opinions/Download.aspx ?id=241590.

4. Sydra Farooqui, "Leon Cooperman on Dell, Taxes, Equity Prices, More" (video), Valuewalk.com, March 6, 2013, https://www .valuewalk.com/2013/03/leon-cooperman-on-dell-taxes-equity-prices -more-video/.

5. Steven Davidoff Solomon, "Ruling on Dell Buyout May Not Be the Precedent That Some Fear," *New York Times DealBook* (blog), June 7, 2016, https://www.nytimes.com/2016/06/08/business /dealbook/ruling-on-dell-buyout-may-not-be-precedent-some-fear .html.

6. *In re:* Appraisal of Dell Inc.

Chapter 6

1. "AOL-Time Warner—How Not to Do a Deal," *Wall Street Journal Deal Journal* (blog), May 29, 2009, https://blogs.wsj.com/deals /2009/05/29/looking-at-boston-consultings-deal-rules-through-an-aol -time-warner-prism/.

2. Philip Elmer-Dewitt, "Is Apple Ripe for a Stock Split?" *Fortune*, February 9, 2011, http://fortune.com/2011/02/09/is-apple-ripe -for-a-stock-split/; Mark Gavagan, *Gems from Warren Buffett—Wit*

and Wisdom from 34 Years of Letters to Shareholders (Mendham, NJ: Cole House LLC, 2014).

Answers, Chapter 3

1. McKinsey & Company, "The Rise and Rise of Private Markets," McKinsey Global Private Markets Review, 2018, https://www.mckinsey.com/~/media/mckinsey/industries/private%20equity%20and%20principal%20investors/our%20insights/the%20rise%20and%20rise%20of%20private%20equity/the-rise-and-rise-of-private-markets-mckinsey-global-private-markets-review-2018.ashx.

2. Michael A. Arnold, "The Principal-Agent Relationship in Real Estate Brokerage Services," *Journal of the American Real Estate and Urban Economics Association* 20, no. 1 (March 1992): 89–106.

Index

Acknowledgments

This book wouldn't have been possible without the feedback of the many Harvard MBA and executive education students who have inspired me with their curiosity and perseverance. Through hours of teaching group meetings and hallway conversations about the best way to teach finance, my colleagues in the Finance Unit have contributed greatly to this book. My director of research at Harvard Business School, Cynthia Montgomery, and the dean of HBS, Nitin Nohria, have been particularly encouraging and generous.

The teaching approach embodied in the book was born out of the efforts to create the Harvard Business School Online course, *Leading with Finance*. Bharat Anand and Patrick Mullane were instrumental in encouraging me to undertake that effort and in making the course a reality. Brian Misamore was a fantastic partner in creating that course from whole cloth, and Peter Kuliesis helped in many thoughtful ways. I'm particularly grateful to all the students who inspired me to translate the approach from the course into a book.

The idea for the book came from the generous mind of Tim Sullivan; his encouragement was pivotal in making this book happen. Kevin Evers was a terrific partner at Harvard Business Review Press. He guided me through the process and contributed greatly to shaping the manuscript. Anne Starr was the perfect production editor—organized, tough, and ultimately forgiving. Brian Misamore and Leanne Fan provided excellent research assistance as we completed the manuscript, and Lucas Ramirez provided very helpful feedback. Darlene Le expertly managed to keep me focused on the tasks at hand.

Teena Shetty and Mia, Ila, and Parvati Desai continue to provide the ultimate inspiration—they've taught me so much about the way the world should work. This book wouldn't have been possible without their patience, support, and encouragement.

About the Author

MIHIR A. DESAI is the Mizuho Financial Group Professor at Harvard Business School and a professor at Harvard Law School. Desai teaches finance, entrepreneurship, and tax law and recently developed *Leading with Finance* on the Harvard Business School Online platform. His scholarship centers on tax policy and corporate finance. His most recent book was *The Wisdom of Finance: Discovering Humanity in the World of Risk and Return*.